y of

England in the 1970s

Ian Palmer

First edition published 2021

Gift Book For Dad
Rugeley
Staffordshire

ISBN 978-1-840-41025-9

The information in this book has been compiled from numerous sources over many years. The author and publisher cannot be held responsible for any errors or inaccuracies.

One or two fictional snippets may have been added for devilment.

Once upon a time, a happy time,
long before Covid-19 ...

Winter 1969 - 1970

Did you think I would leave you crying?

38-year-old Bert Foord presents the weather forecast on BBC One ... Dense fog gives way to brisk winds ... "You've painted up your lips and rolled and curled your tinted hair. Ruby are you contemplating going out somewhere?" - ***Ruby Don't Take Your Love To Town*** by Kenny Rogers and the First Edition climbs to number two in the pop chart ... "Something in the way she moves, attracts me like no other lover" - The double A-sided single ***Something / Come Together*** by The Beatles moves down to number eight ... Children are excited - Christmas is coming! ... Schoolboys crave a die-cast model of the *Batmobile* (manufactured by - *Corgi Toys*) for 13s/6d ... The Smith family from Chigwell hire a new-fangled colour TV set from *Radio Rentals* ... "We are the Diddymen, itsy-bitsy Diddymen" - *Ken Dodd and the Diddymen* is hugely popular with younger viewers ... Teenagers listen to music on portable HMV record players ... Hallmark Records release *The Best of Top of the Pops "69"* - a budget priced cover-version pop compilation LP with pretty girls on the sleeve ... ***Wonderful World Beautiful People***

("... you and your girl, things could be pretty") by Jimmy Cliff is number six in the pop chart ... ***The Liquidator*** by The Harry J Allstars is number nine ... In an act of frustration, 23-year-old footballer 'super' Georgie Best knocks the ball from the hands of referee Jack Taylor after a League Cup semi-final defeat to Manchester City. Best will now face FA disciplinary action for his petulance ... 25-year-old footballer Franny Lee of Manchester City misses a penalty, and 34-year-old Jack Charlton of Leeds Utd heads a goal from his brother's corner kick, as Sir Alf Ramsey's England team (Bonetti, Reaney, E Hughes, Mullery, J Charlton, Moore, F Lee, Bell, Astle, R Charlton, Ball and substitute Peters) beats Portugal 1-0 on a rain sodden Wembley pitch ... 31-year-old Wimbledon tennis champion Ann Jones is voted BBC's 'Sports Personality of the Year' ... 33-year-old Gordon Honeycombe reads the news for ITN ... The Troubles prevail in Northern Ireland ... Sectarian violence is commonplace as skirmishes continue between Loyalists, Nationalists and the Royal Ulster Constabulary ... The Provisional Irish Republican Army (a splinter group from the IRA) is formed ... Back in England - people spend an evening at the cinema ... 30-year-old George Lazenby is the new James Bond (aka 007) in *On Her Majesty's Secret Service*. 31-year-old Diana Rigg captures Bond's heart and becomes his screen wife - but with tragic consequences. 45-year-old Telly Savalas plays master criminal, Ernst Stavro Blofeld. 61-year-old Bernard Lee is M. 55-year-old Desmond Llewelyn is Q. 42-year-old Lois Maxwell is Miss Moneypenny ... 35-year-old

Alan Bates and 31-year-old Oliver Reed wrestle naked in front of the fire in *Women In Love* ... 62-year-old John Wayne stars in *True Grit* ... The abolition of the death penalty is made permanent by 57-year-old Home Secretary Jim Callaghan ... ***Love's Been Good To Me*** by 54-year-old Frank Sinatra from New Jersey is number eight on the hit parade ... ***Without Love (There Is Nothing)*** by 29-year-old Tom Jones from Pontypridd is number ten ... A fire at the *Rose and Crown* in Saffron Walden kills eleven people ... An eighteen mile stretch of dual carriageway opens between Horwich and Preston in Lancashire ... 'Well off' young men drive their cars fast on the country's ever expanding network of motorways ... A new 'H' reg Ford *Escort Mexico RS* has a top speed of 103 mph and can reach 60 mph in 11.5 seconds ... The new *Mini 1275GT* has a redesigned front end and 'go-fast' stripes - its top speed is 91 mph and 0-60 mph comes in 14.5 seconds ... 'Here we go! Morning ray-de-oh!' - 26-year-old Tony Blackburn presents the breakfast show on Radio One ... "Two little boys had two little toys. Each had a wooden horse" - ***Two Little Boys*** by 39-year-old Rolf Harris from Australia is number one in the weekly pop chart ... "The world is just a great big onion" - ***The Onion Song*** by 30-year-old Marvin Gaye and 24-year-old Tammi Terrell is number nine ... 53-year-old prime-minister, Harold Wilson, and 49-year-old Chancellor of the Exchequer, Roy Jenkins, are relieved to see significant improvement in the economy ... The balance of payments has moved to a surplus of £100 million - it's the first time in ten years that the value of exports has been greater than the value of imports ... More than 300,000 men are employed in the coal industry - many working long, hard shifts in dangerous conditions. 156 million tonnes of coal have been produced in 1969 - that's 54 million tonnes less than ten years ago ... Families gather around the television set ... Morecambe & Wise feature in their first ever Christmas Day TV 'special' - Frankie Vaughan, Nina, Sacha Distel and 42-year-old Fenella Fielding are the guest stars ... 20-year-old model Twiggy appears on ITV's *This Is Your Life* ... "All my sorrow, sad tomorrow. Take me back to my old home" - ***Reflections Of My Life*** by The Marmalade climbs to number three in the pop chart ... 23-year-old 'super' Georgie Best plays football for Manchester Utd on Boxing Day (in front of 52,732 spectators at Old Trafford) in a 0-0 draw against Wolverhampton Wanderers in Division One ... 18-year-old Kevin Keegan plays football for Scunthorpe Utd (in front of 7,796 spectators at London Road) in a 2-2 draw against Peterborough Utd in Division Four ... Schoolboys update their football 'League Ladders' each week ... Just one point separates Harry Catterick's Everton (with West, Labone, Kendall, Ball, Morrissey and Royle) from Don Revie's hard-tackling Leeds Utd (with Sprake, Charlton, Bremner, Giles, Lorimer and Clarke) at the top of Division One ... 18-year-old Steve Perryman scores his first league goal for mid-table Tottenham Hotspur in a 2-0 victory over Crystal Palace ... 11-year-old Simon Mayo from Southgate in Middlesex plays football with his friends in the park ... ***Yester-Me, Yester-***

You, Yesterday by 19-year-old Stevie Wonder is number two in the pop chart ... "Take a pinch of white man, wrap it up in black skin, add a touch of blue blood, and a little bitty bit of red Indian boy" - ***Melting Pot*** by Blue Mink is number three ... 32-year-old footballer Bobby Charlton is on the score-sheet as Manchester Utd beat Liverpool 1-4 at Anfield ... Bill Shankly sells 31-year-old striker Roger Hunt to Bolton Wanderers for £30,000 ... "I wish to complain about this parrot what I purchased not half an hour ago from this very boutique" - 30-year-old John Cleese and 26-year-old Michael Palin perform the 'dead parrot sketch' on *Monty Python's Flying Circus* ... "This is the planet Earth. Our planet. It is a small planet, wrapped in clouds" - The *Clangers* is new on TV for children ... Families listen to music on Ferguson *Solid State* radiograms ... "We can't go on together, with..." ***Suspicious Minds*** by 34-year-old Elvis Presley climbs to number two in the pop chart ... "I've got to leave old Durham Town, and that leaving's gonna get me down" - ***Durham Town (The Leavin')*** by 33-year-old Roger Whittaker is number twelve ... The Kinks play gigs in Canada ... The Rolling Stones play to three hundred-thousand people in California, with Hells Angels providing security around the stage ... 18-year-old Meredith Hunter is stabbed and killed ... Back in England - The Who play gigs at Liverpool (Empire), London (Coliseum) and Newcastle-upon-Tyne (City Hall) ... Construction work is nearing completion on the new Strensham to Tewkesbury section of the M5 motorway ... Men of all ages drink and smoke together in pubs ... Adverts say, 'Castella. The man-sized cigar for the man who likes his pint' ... New year arrives, and a new decade: the 1970s ... The weather is cold and frosty ... Families gather around coal-effect, two-bar electric fires ... "My love, the days are colder. So let me take you by your hand, and lead you through a snow white land" - ***Winter World Of Love*** by 33-year-old Engelbert Humperdinck is number eight on the hit parade ... ***Tracy*** ("... you're gonna be, happy with me. I'll build a world around you") by The Cuff Links is number nine ... 51-year-old Arsenal manager, Bertie Mee, signs 19-year-old striker Peter Marinello from Hibernian for £100,000 ... 34-year-old Derby County manager, Brian Clough, signs 27-year-old defender Terry Hennessey from Nottingham Forest for £110,000 ... 23-year-old Manchester Utd star 'super' Georgie Best is fined £100, and suspended for four weeks, by an FA Disciplinary Committee ... 26-year-old rock star Mick Jagger is fined for possession of cannabis ... 23-year-old Keith Moon accidently drives his Bentley over his chauffeur Neil Boland, and kills him ... 11-year-old Simon Le Bon from Bushey in Hertfordshire dreams of one day becoming a famous pop star ... The first jumbo jet (a Boeing *747*) lands at Heathrow airport, carrying 324 passengers from New York ... 47-year-old Eamonn Andrews surprises 43-year-old Jimmy Savile on ITV's *This is Your Life* ... ***Two Little Boys*** by Rolf Harris remains at number one in the pop chart for six weeks ... ***Let It All Hang Out*** by 25-year-old Jonathan King stalls at number thirty-one ... 53-year-old leader of the Tory opposition, Edward Heath, and his shadow

Chancellor, Iain Macleod, begin devising economic strategies based on a free-market economy, where 'consumer choice' is key ... A plain coloured *Bri Nylon* shirt costs 32s/11d ... A striped *Bri Nylon* shirt costs 35s/11d ... A pack of twenty Player's *No. 6* cigarettes costs four shillings ... A pack of twenty menthol-fresh Consulate cigarettes costs 5s/5d ... 26-year-old boxer Smokin' Joe Frazier becomes the undisputed heavy-weight champion of the world - by beating Jimmy Ellis by a Technical Knock Out at Madison Square Garden in New York ... Back in England - 29-year-old footballer Jimmy 'Greavsie' Greaves scores for Bill Nicholson's Tottenham Hotspur in a 2-1 victory over Brian Clough's Derby County ... 21-year-old goalkeeper Ray Clemence makes his league debut for Bill Shankly's Liverpool in a 1-0 defeat against Nottingham Forest ... 21-year-old Prince Charles joins the Royal Navy ... "Oh..." ***Love Grows (Where My Rosemary Goes)*** ("... and nobody knows like me") by Edison Lighthouse climbs to number one in the pop chart - and stays there for five weeks! ... "So kiss me and smile for me. Tell me that you'll wait for me. Hold me like you'll never let me go. 'Cause I'm..." ***Leavin' On A Jet Plane*** ("... don't know when I'll be back again") by Peter, Paul and Mary is number two ... *Skippy* - 'The Bush Kangaroo' is new on ITV ... 23-year-old footballer 'super' Georgie Best returns from suspension and scores six goals, as Wilf McGuinness' Manchester Utd thrash Northampton Town 8-2 in the fifth round of the FA Cup ... 20-year-old Joe Royle scores twice, and 23-year-old Howard Kendall scores once, as Harry Catterick's high-flying Everton defeat Bobby Robson's Ipswich Town 3-0 at Goodison Park in Division One ... Aston Villa (currently struggling at the bottom of Division Two) sack their manager, Tommy Docherty, and appoint 38-year-old Vic Crowe as a replacement ... "Oh baby, give me one more chance" - ***I Want You Back*** by The Jackson Five reaches number two in the pop chart ... "If you want it, here it is..." ***Come And Get It*** ("... But you'd better hurry 'cause it's goin' fast") by Badfinger reaches number four ... 24-year-old midfielder Alan Ball scores twice, and 23-year-old striker Peter 'Ossie' Osgood makes his international debut, as Sir Alf Ramsey's England team (G Banks, T Wright, Cooper, Moore, Labone, E Hughes, F Lee, Ball, Osgood, G Hurst, Peters) beats Belgium 1-3 in Anderlecht ... 35-year-old Johnny Haynes plays his final match for Fulham before retiring ... 'Billy's Boots' - schoolboy Billy Dane wears Dead-Shot Keen's old football boots in a fantastic new sports comic for boys called *Scorcher* ... 'Not that it matters, but most of it is true' - 44-year-old Paul Newman and 33-year-old Robert Redford star in *Butch Cassidy and the Sundance Kid* at cinemas ... "Raindrops keep falling on my head, and just like the guy whose feet are too big for his bed, nothing seems to fit" - 37-year-old Sacha Distel sings ***Raindrops Keep Falling On My Head*** - and the song climbs to number ten in the pop chart ... "Come on, come on..." ***Let's Work Together*** by Canned Heat is number two ... The Hillman *Avenger* motorcar, with its distinctive 'hockey-stick' shaped rear lights, is launched. The *de Luxe* model is £766, the

Super is £811 and the *Grand Luxe* is £903. Top speed of the *Avenger* (with 1500cc engine) is 91 mph ... The latest Alfa Romeo *Spider* now has a square tail instead of a rounded tail ... ***Na Na Hey Hey Kiss Him Goodbye*** by Steam is number nine in the pop chart ... "Sing a song of..." ***Temma Harbour*** ("... climb a coconut tree. Catch a fish and light a fire, drink some wine with me") by 19-year-old Mary Hopkin is number six ... 25-year-old Cyd Hayman stars alongside Robert Hardy in *Manhunt* on ITV ... 50-year-old Jon Pertwee is the new *Dr. Who* on BBC - taking over from 49-year-old Patrick Troughton ... Actor Jimmy Hanley dies of cancer aged 51 at Fetcham in Surrey ... The sun shines in late February ... People feel good about the future and book their summer holidays ... *SkyTours* offer low priced package holidays abroad ... Eight days in Majorca costs around £29 ... Fifteen days in Corfu is £70 ... New housing estates with modern semi-detached, three-bedroomed homes are springing up all around the country. Many of the new houses come with gas central heating already installed! ... The average price of a house in the UK is £4,300 ... With the economy currently in a healthy state, 53-year-old Labour prime-minister Harold Wilson considers calling a general election - but doesn't do so yet ... "Instant Karma's gonna get you. Gonna knock you right on the head" - ***Instant Karma!*** by Lennon/Ono with the Plastic Ono Band peaks at number five in the pop chart ... ***All I Have To Do Is Dream*** by 27-year-old Bobbie Gentry and 33-year-old Glen Campbell reaches number three.

Spring 1970

When I get to heaven, tie me to a tree

46-year-old Jack Scott presents the weather forecast on BBC One ... Unexpected snowstorms arrive. Depths of up to twelve inches are reported in the Midlands - and traffic grinds to a halt ... People stay indoors, watching television ... A new series of *Steptoe and Son* begins (with 44-year-old Harry H. Corbett and 57-year-old Wilfrid Brambell) and now it's in colour! ... *The Adventures of Parsley* (a spin-off from popular children's programme *The Herbs*) is on TV for the first time ... The *Apollo 13* spacecraft develops a serious technical hitch on its journey to the Moon and astronauts Jim Lovell, John Swigert and Fred Haise radio through to Mission Control with the message, "Houston, we have a problem" ... Back in England - the weather clears and 34-year-old jockey Lester Piggott rides *Nijinsky* to victory in the Two-Thousand Guineas at Doncaster ... Don Revie's hard-tackling Leeds Utd football team beats Standard Liege 2-0 (on aggregate, over two matches) in the quarter-final of the European Cup and will now face Celtic in the semi-finals ... Revie fields an under-strength Leeds team in a First

Division match against Brian Clough's Derby County - and loses 4-1 ... "Wheels are made for rollin'. Mules are made to pack. I've never seen a sight that didn't look better looking back. I was born under a..." ***Wand'rin Star*** by 46-year-old Lee Marvin is number one in the pop chart ... ***Gimme Dat Ding*** by Pipkins is number four ... 33-year-old Gordon Honeycombe reads the news for ITN ... Production workers at car windscreen manufacturer Pilkington Glass go on strike ... British Leyland staff are on a go-slow. The corporation's chairman, Lord Stokes, says, "We don't control our factories, the work people do. People these days just walk out because a place is too hot, or too cold" ... 'D-Day. One Year From Now' - a short TV information film explains the new decimal currency system which will begin next year ... 23-year-old star footballer 'super' Georgie Best opens a fashionable new clothes boutique in Manchester called *George Best Rogue* ... "I still get..." ***That Same Old Feeling*** ("... tearing at this heart of mine") by Pickettywitch is number five in the pop chart ... "Like a..." ***Bridge Over Troubled Water*** ("... I will lay me down") by Simon and Garfunkle is new at number one ... 35-year-old writer David Nobbs pens humorous scripts and one-line gags for Les Dawson and other comedians ... 'The Carry On team in Starkest Africa' - *Carry On up the Jungle* is now showing at cinemas, with 53-year-old Frankie Howerd as Professor Tinkle, 56-year-old Sid 'cor blimey' James as Bill Boosey and 26-year-old Valerie Leon (36-26-36) as leader of the (all-women) Lubby-Dubby tribe ... "Wise men say, 'Only fools rush in.' But I..." ***Can't Help Falling In Love With You*** by 42-year-old Andy Williams is number three on the weekly hit parade ... The legal voting age in Britain is lowered from 21 to 18 ... Younger people vote for the first time at a by-election in Bridgwater, where Tom King is elected for the Conservatives ... The bodies of 11-year-old Susan Blatchford and 12-year-old Gary Hanlon are found in woodland at Lippitts Hill in Epping Forest. Police search for the murderer, but despite numerous public appeals, the perpetrator cannot be found ... Cambridge win the Boat Race for a third consecutive year ... *L'Escargot* wins the Cheltenham Gold Cup at odds of thirty-three to one ... 18-year-old Dana wins the Eurovision song contest for Ireland singing ***All Kinds Of Everything*** ("... remind me of you") - and the record reaches number one in the pop chart ... ***Knock, Knock Who's There?*** by 20-year-old Mary Hopkin is number two ... 37-year-old Ray 'Dracula' Reardon wins the Player's *No.6* World Snooker Championship, beating 46-year-old John Pulman by 37 frames to 33 in the final ... 23-year-old winger Glyn Pardoe scores the winning goal as Joe Mercer's Manchester City achieve a 2-1 victory over Alan Ashman's West Bromwich Albion in the League Cup final at Wembley ... 30-year-old Jimmy 'Greavsie' Greaves plays his final game for Tottenham Hotspur before transferring to West Ham Utd in an exchange deal for 26-year-old Martin Peters ... Peters scores on his debut for Spurs in a 1-2 defeat against Coventry City at White Hart Lane ... Greavsie scores twice on his debut for 'The Hammers' in a 1-5 victory over

Manchester City (on a quagmire pitch) at Maine Road ... 23-year-old 'super' Georgie Best is sent off for Northern Ireland, in a match against Scotland, after throwing mud at referee, Eric Jennings ... 41-year-old racing driver Graham Hill makes his return to Formula One, in the South African Grand Prix, after breaking both legs five months ago ... Don Revie's hard-tackling Leeds Utd lose a two-legged European Cup semi final against Celtic ... The first leg is a 0-1 defeat in front of 46,381 spectators at Elland Road ... The second leg is 2-1 defeat in front of 136,505 spectators at Hampden Park ... "Oh, mother tell your children not to do what I have done. Spend your lives in sin and misery in the..." ***House Of The Rising Sun*** by Frijid Pink is number four on the hit parade ... ***Who Do You Love*** by Juicy Lucy is number fourteen ... Arsenal beat Anderlecht 3-0 on a muddy Highbury pitch to turn around a 1-3 deficit from the first leg - and win the Inter Cities Fairs Cup 4-3 on aggregate ... Manchester City beat Gornik Zabrze 2-1 in the European Cup Winners Cup final in Vienna - with goals from Neil Young and Franny Lee ... Back in England - 32-year-old Bobby Charlton and 23-year-old 'super' Georgie Best score the goals as Manchester Utd draw 2-2 with Sheffield Wednesday in front of 36,649 at Old Trafford ... Harry Catterick's Everton beat West Bromwich Albion 2-0 in front of 58,523 at Goodison Park - to clinch the First Division title, with two games of the season still remaining. Gordon West, Tommy Wright, Keith Newton, Howard Kendall, Brian Labone, Tommy Jackson, Colin Harvey, Jimmy Husband, Alan Whittle, John Hurst, John

Morrissey, Sandy Brown, Alan Ball, and 21-year-old top scorer Joe Royle, have all been outstanding for 'The Toffees' ... Don Revie's hard-tackling Leeds Utd (with Sprake, Reaney, Cooper, Bremner, Charlton, Hunter, Madeley, Lorimer, Jones, Clarke, Giles, Gray, Yorath, Hibbitt and Bates) are runners-up ... Dave Sexton's Chelsea (with Bonetti, Webb, McCreadie, Hinton, Dempsey, Harris, Osgood, Hollins, Hutchinson, Hudson, Cooke, Baldwin and Houseman) are third ... 21-year-old Mick Channon has scored fifteen goals (in thirty-seven matches) for Ted Bates' Southampton - and 'The Saints' avoid relegation at the expense of Sunderland and Sheffield Wednesday ... "Prepare yourself. You know it's a must. Gotta have a friend in Jesus" - ***Spirit In The Sky*** by 27-year-old Norman Greenbaum reaches number one in the pop chart ... "They call me..." ***The Seeker*** ("... I've been searchin' low and high") by The Who is number twenty-four ... Chelsea's Ron 'Chopper' Harris nobbles Leeds Utd's Eddie Gray early on in the FA Cup final (on a heavily sanded Wembley pitch) and the match finishes 2-2 after extra-time. (6-year-old Ged O'Brien from Reading attends the match with his dad). A ticket for the standing enclosure at the Empire Stadium costs 12s/6d. A seat in the South Terrace is twenty-five shillings ... Chelsea win the replay 2-1 at Old Trafford, with 23-year-old Peter 'Ossie' Osgood scoring a diving header ... Vic Crowe's Aston Villa and Alan Ball Sr.'s Preston North End are relegated to the Third Division for the first time in their histories ... ***Farewell Is A Lonely Sound*** by 34-year-old Jimmy Ruffin is number eight in the pop chart ... "To be..." ***Young, Gifted And Black*** by Bob Andy and Marcia Griffiths is number five ... Radio One's weekday schedule is: Tony Blackburn (7 a.m. to 9 a.m.), Pete Murray (9 a.m. to 10 a.m.), Jimmy Young (10 a.m. to 12 noon), Johnnie Walker (12 noon to 2 p.m.) and Terry Wogan (2 p.m. to 4.15 p.m.) ... Speculation in the media is rife: The Beatles are about to split up!? ... The group's latest LP, *Let It Be*, is number one in the album chart ... *McCartney*, the debut solo LP from 27-year-old Paul McCartney is number two ... ***ABC*** ("... it's easy as 1, 2, 3") by The Jackson Five is number eight in the singles chart ... ***Do The Funky Chicken*** by Rufus Thomas is number eighteen ... 'Dice was his vice. Men hers' - 33-year-old Warren Beatty stars alongside 38-year-old Elizabeth Taylor in *The Only Game in Town* at cinemas ... Children watch *Play School, Jackanory* and *Marine Boy* on BBC One television at tea-time ... The four-wheel drive *Range Rover* 'off road' motorcar is launched. This wonderful new luxury car has a V8 engine and returns around 15 mpg ... The Triumph *Stag* sports car is also new - a stylish convertible with a top speed of 115 mph, and capable of 0-60 mph in 11.6 seconds ... Adverts warn of the dangers of smoking in bed ... A pack of twenty Benson & Hedges *Gold Bond* cigarettes costs 4s/6d ... Young people, in denim jackets and flared jeans, hang around on high streets ... A *Wimpy* hamburger costs two shillings ... A King Size *Wimpy* is 3s/9d ... The average weekly wage in the UK is £31/4s ... Great excitement is building in the country ... There's huge expectation for England's world-champion footballers to do well in the upcoming FIFA World Cup tournament in Mexico ... “We’ll fight until the whistle blows, for the folks...” ***Back Home*** by the England World Cup Squad climbs to the top of the hit parade - and stays there for three weeks ... ***Daughter Of Darkness*** by 29-year-old Tom Jones is number five ... 54-year-old Labour prime-minister Harold Wilson calls a general election for the eighteenth of June and campaigning begins ... Anti-immigration parties are expecting to win plenty of votes ... John O’Brien succeeds Arthur K. Chesterton as chairman of the National Front ... 11-year-old schoolboy Steven Patrick Morrissey from Manchester sits in his bedroom writing clever lyrics ... “And when you stop and think about it, you won’t believe it’s true; that all the love you’ve been giving, has all been meant for you” - ***Question*** by The Moody Blues is number two in the pop chart ... ***Cottonfields*** by The Beach Boys is number five ... 71-year-old businessman Sir Jack Cohen retires from his position as chairman of *Tesco* ... 23-year-old footballer Keith Weller transfers from Benny Fenton’s Second Division Millwall to Dave Sexton’s First Division Chelsea for £100,000 ... 50-year-old wartime football legend Tommy Lawton is out of work and claiming unemployment benefit.

Summer 1970

Have a drink, have a drive

The sun shines ... Boys climb trees ... Children take their buckets and spades to the seaside ... Families enjoy picnics on the beach ... Everything is 'groovy' ... 58-year-old Jimmy Chipperield opens a new safari park at Woburn Abbey, and families travel from all around to see the monkeys ... Lester Piggott rides *Nijinsky* to victory in the Epsom Derby ... ***Yellow River*** ("... yellow river, is in my mind and in my eyes") by Christie is new at number one in the pop chart ... ***Goodbye Sam Hello Samantha*** ("... Goodbye Lou. Hello Louise") by 29-year-old Cliff Richard is number six ... 24-year-old footballer 'super' Georgie Best moves into a 'futuristic' £30,000 house at Bramhall in Cheshire ... 'Space! The final frontier' - *Star Trek* (with 39-year-old William Shatner as Captain Kirk and 39-year-old Leonard Nimoy as Spock) is on BBC One on Monday evenings ... 46-year-old Robin Day presents *Panorama* straight afterwards ... Millions of viewers tune-in for *It's A Knockout* on Wednesday evenings. (In one exciting contest, a team from Margate plays its joker in the 'Tea for Two' event, and goes on to beat a team from Ramsgate by eleven points to ten) ... ***In The Summertime*** by Mungo Jerry (with 24-year-old lead singer, Ray Dorset) climbs to number one in the pop chart - and stays at the top for seven weeks! ... ***Groovin' With Mr. Bloe*** by Mr. Bloe is number two ... ***Honey Come Back*** by 34-year-old Glen Campbell is number four ... 'For safety learn the new wiring colours' - there's a change to the wire colours in 3-pin electrical plugs. 'Live' is now brown. (Previously it was red). 'Neutral' is now blue. (Previously it was black). 'Earth' is now green and yellow. (Previously it was green) ... The Reliant Motor Company launches the *Bond Bug*. The sporty three-wheeler comes in bright orange, has a top speed of 76 mph and costs £629 ... ***Everything Is Beautiful*** ("... in its own way. Like a starry summer night or a snow covered winter's day") by 31-year-old Ray Stevens is number six in the pop chart ... ***Sally*** ("... Sally, pride of our alley") by 37-year-old Gerry Monroe is number four ... Hundreds of workers at Lucas in Birmingham go on strike, demanding higher pay ... Thousands of workers at British Leyland are laid-off ... 'When it comes down to it, aren't Labour's ideals yours as well?' - campaigning is underway for the general election ... 'For a better tomorrow, Vote Conservative' ... "And I mean that most sincerely, folks" - 50-year-old Hughie Green presents a new series of *Opportunity Knocks* on ITV ... Kids wear denim jackets and jeans ... ***Alright Now*** ("... baby, it's alright now") by Free climbs to number two in the singles chart ... Teenage rock band, Stray, release their eponymous debut album with ***All In Your Mind*** the opening track on side one, and ***Only What You Make It*** the opening track on side two ... 41-year-old Leonard Parkin reads the news for ITN ... Politics and sport are at odds ... A planned tour of England by the South African cricket team is cancelled. England's captain Ray Illingworth scores 94 runs in a hastily arranged match against a Rest of the World XI at Lord's ... There's a flurry of activity on football's transfer market ... Chelsea players, 24-year-old midfielder Alan Birchenhall and 28-year-old striker Bobby Tambling, leave Stamford Bridge and transfer to Bert Head's Crystal Palace for £140,000 ... 23-year-old striker Bobby Gould leaves Arsenal and joins Wolverhampton Wanderers for £55,000 ... 19-year-old goalkeeper Phil Parkes leaves Walsall and joins Queens Park Rangers for £15,000 ... ***Back Home*** ("... they'll be watching and waiting and cheering every move") by the England World Cup Squad crackles out of transistor radios all across the country ... 29-year-old England captain Bobby Moore is arrested on suspicion of stealing a bracelet in Colombia, and detained by police for four days ... Prime-minister Harold Wilson intervenes, and Moore is set free and allowed to join his team-mates in Mexico ... Alf Ramsey's reigning world champions are poised and ready ... The FIFA World Cup tournament gets underway ... Referees use red and yellow cards for the first time ... *Adidas* introduce the iconic *Telstar* football ... England qualify for the knock-out stages by beating Romania (1-0) and Czechoslovakia (1-0) but losing to Brazil (0-1) - in a match where 32-year-old England goalkeeper, Gordon Banks, pulls off an incredible save from a header by 29-year-old superstar, Pele. On the fourteenth of June at the Estadio Leon, 28-year-old Alan Mullery and 26-year-old Martin Peters score the goals to put England 2-0 up against West Germany in the quarter finals. Then disaster strikes. Late goals from Beckenbauer, Seeler and Muller secure a 3-2 victory for the Germans (after extra time) and England are out. Gordon Banks, Peter 'the cat' Bonetti, Keith Newton, Terry Cooper, Brian Labone, Bobby Moore, Alan Ball, Franny Lee, Bobby Charlton, Colin Bell, Geoff Hurst, Martin Peters and Alan Mullery all return home disappointed ... Back in England - the sun is shining ... 24-year-old footballer 'super' Georgie Best takes a spin in his *E-Type* Jaguar with model girlfriend Siv Hederby at his side ... "When the weather's fine, you got women, you got women on your mind. Have a drink, have a drive. Go out and see what you can find" - ***In The Summertime*** by Mungo Jerry remains at number one in the pop chart ... "She walked up to me and she asked me to dance. I asked her name, and in a dark brown voice she said 'Lola'. L-O-L-A Lola, lo-lo-lo-lo..." ***Lola*** by The Kinks is number two ... The day of the general election arrives and 28 million people cast their votes ... 53-year-old Conservative Edward Heath is the surprise victor and takes over from Harold Wilson at Number 10. (Conservatives: 330 seats, Labour: 288 seats, Liberals: 6 seats) ... 44-year-old Margaret Thatcher is appointed Minister for Education and Science in the new government ... 56-year-old Chancellor of the Exchequer, Iain Macleod, dies after just one month in office and is replaced by Anthony

Barber ... 39-year-old Conservative Norman Tebbit is the new MP for Epping ... "Rainbow, look me up, look me down. Rainbow, you were fun to have around" - ***Rainbow*** by The Marmalade is number three in the pop chart ... ***Signed, Sealed, Delivered, I'm Yours*** by 20-year-old Stevie Wonder is number fifteen ... 32-year-old Caroline Thorpe (wife of Liberal party leader Jeremy Thorpe) dies in a car crash ... Jack Walker, landlord of 'The Rovers Return' in ITV's ever popular soap-opera *Coronation Street*, dies of a heart attack, and his widow Annie is now in sole charge of the pub ... 24-year-old Douglas Fielding plays PC Alec Quilley in BBC's long-running police drama *Z Cars* ... Dock workers go on strike for higher pay - raising fears of possible food shortages in shops ... Young boys push toy cars across the carpet at home, or send them speeding down slopes of plastic track on the stairs ... *Matchbox* bring out *Superfast* die-cast model cars with new improved wheels ... The *Matchbox* model of a BP Service Station and Forecourt is extremely popular ... 'J' reg cars go on sale ... The new V6 Ford *Capri 3000GT* has a top speed of 122 mph and can reach 60 mph in 8.4 seconds ... Princess Anne is presented with a Reliant *Scimitar GTE* for her 20th birthday ... A new elevated section of M6 motorway opens between Walsall and Great Barr in the Midlands ... Four-star leaded petrol has risen in price to 6s/6d a gallon ... A leaflet called, 'Your Guide To Decimal Money' is widely available ... ***In The Summertime*** by Mungo Jerry remains at number one in the pop chart ... ***Black Night*** by Deep Purple climbs to number two ... "Like, crazy man! That's far out" - Jimi Hendrix, The Who and The Doors play the Isle of White festival, where 600,000 people attend (over five days). 27-year-old festival compare, Rikki Farr, addresses the crowd and tells them to, "Go to hell!" when some people break through the security barriers - in an attempt to gain free entry ... Elsewhere in the country, industrial unrest prevails and new prime-minister Edward Heath is under intense pressure ... Dock workers continue their strike ... Troops are put on standby and a State of Emergency is declared ... Production workers at Pilkington Glass in St. Helens have been on strike for two months ... Car production at British Leyland, Rover and Jaguar has slowed because of a shortage of windscreens ... "That's the wonder..." ***The Wonder Of You*** by 35-year-old Elvis Presley climbs to number one in the pop chart - and stays there for six weeks! ... "I'm a Neanderthal man. You're a Neanderthal girl. Let's make Neanderthal love in this Neanderthal world" - ***Neanderthal Man*** by Hotlegs reaches number two ... *Ace of Wands* is a new TV program for teenagers ... Millions watch as Elsie Tanner (played by 46-year-old Pat Phoenix) marries Alan Howard (played by 44-year-old Alan Browning) in ITV's *Coronation Street* ... 46-year-old Kenneth Kendall reads the news on BBC One ... The dock strike comes to an end after two weeks of disruption when union leaders accept a 7% pay rise ... Repeats of last year's series of *Dad's Army* are transmitted on BBC One on Saturday evenings ... 37-year-old Freddie Goodwin is the new football manager at Second Division Birmingham City ... 37-year-old John Bond is new at Fourth Division Bournemouth ... 24-year-old 'super' Georgie Best scores a goal as Manchester Utd lose 4-1 to Brian Clough's Derby County in the final of the Watney Invitation Cup at the Baseball Ground ... 25-year-old Everton captain, Alan Ball, wears trendy white football boots as 'The Toffees' beat Dave Sexton's Chelsea 2-1 in the Charity Shield at Stamford Bridge ... 23-year-old John Radford bags a hat-trick as Bertie Mee's Arsenal thrash Manchester Utd 4-0 at Highbury in Division One ... ***The Wonder Of You*** by Elvis Presley remains at number one in the pop chart ... ***Mama Told Me (Not To Come)*** ("... That ain't the way to have fun, son") by Three Dog Night is number three ... After weeks of speculation, 27-year-old Paul McCartney confirms that he has left The Beatles - and the 'Fab Four' are no more ... All around the world, pop music fans are devastated.

Autumn 1970

We are stardust, we are golden

54-year-old Edward Heath's Conservative government introduces the Industrial Relations Bill - triggering a wider rift with the unions ... Workers at Pilkington Glass in St. Helens continue their strike ... With no windscreens being produced, thousands of men at British Leyland's Cowley and Longbridge factories are idle ... 29-year-old John Lennon and 37-year-old Yoko Ono record songs at Abbey Road Studios in London for their new album: *Lennon/ Plastic Ono Band* ... "Now if there's a smile on my face, it's only there trying to fool the public" - ***Tears Of A Clown*** by Smokey Robinson and the Miracles is new at number one in the singles chart ... Families stay in and watch TV together ... *Magpie* (with 28-year-old Pete Brady, 26-year-old Tony Bastable and 31-year-old Susan Stranks) is a popular ITV tea-time show on Tuesdays and Thursdays ... *Please Sir!* (with 29-year-old John Alderton and 56-year-old Deryck Guyler) is popular on Sunday evenings ... A new series of *Dad's Army* (with 55-year-old Arthur Lowe as Captain Mainwaring, 58-year-old John Le Mesurier as

Sergeant Wilson, 50-year-old Clive Dunn as Lance-Corporal Jones, 74-year-old Arnold Ridley as Private Godfrey, 73-year-old John Laurie as Private Fraser, 41-year-old James Beck as Private Walker and 24-year-old Ian Lavender as Private 'stupid boy' Pike) begins on BBC One on Friday evenings ... Children are back at school after the summer holidays ... Boys play conkers on the playground ... 11-year-old Robert Mortimer from Middlesbrough plays kiss-chase with the girls ... Footballers Ray Kennedy, George Graham and George Armstrong score the goals for Arsenal as Bertie Mee's team thrashes West Bromwich Albion 6-2 at Highbury in Division One ... 20-year-old centre-forward Malcolm MacDonald bags a hat-trick for Luton Town in a 1-5 away win against Sheffield Wednesday in Division Two ... ***Give Me Just A Little More Time*** ("... and our love will surely grow") by Chairman of the Board climbs to number three in the pop chart ... "And if you're wondering what this song is leading to, I want to..." ***Make It With You*** by Bread is number five ... 42-year-old Alastair Burnet reads the news for ITN ... A *BOAC* passenger plane is hijacked en-route to Heathrow and forced to land at Dawson's Field in Jordan ... Back in England - 43-year-old Don Revie's hard-tackling Leeds Utd are the early league leaders in Division One ... 23-year-old Peter Lorimer scores twice as Leeds beat newly promoted Huddersfield Town 2-0 at Elland Road ... 32-year-old Bobby Charlton of Manchester Utd makes his 500th league appearance for the club as Utd lose 0-1 at home to Crystal Palace ... 27-year-old Ernie Hunt of Coventry City scores an amazing goal, from a free-kick twenty yards out, when his team mate Willie Carr flicks the ball into the air (using both of his heels) and Hunt volleys into the net. The 'Sky Blues' defeat Everton 3-1 and climb to fourteenth in the table ... Gerry Summers' Oxford Utd move to the top of Divison Two with a 0-2 victory over Bolton Wanderers. (31-year-old Big Ron Atkinson is on the score-sheet for Oxford) ... ***Something*** ("... in the way he moves attracts me like no other lover") by 33-year-old Shirley Bassey reaches number four in the pop chart ... ***It's So Easy*** by 42-year-old Andy Williams is number thirteen ... 34-year-old jockey Lester Piggott rides *Nijinsky* to victory in the St. Ledger at Doncaster - and *Nijinsky* is the first racehorse to win 'the triple crown' since *Bahram* in 1935 ... Jimi Hendrix dies aged 27 at Notting Hill in London ... The Kinks pull out of a new pop festival at Pilton in Somerset, and 34-year-old festival organiser Michael Eavis books Tyrannosaurus Rex (with 22-year-old lead singer Marc Bolan) instead ... "Ooh, baby, baby it's a... ***Wild World*** by 22-year-old Jimmy Cliff climbs to number eight in the pop chart ... "Here's one I made earlier" - 33-year-old Valerie Singleton, 36-year-old John Noakes and 31-year-old Peter Purves present *Blue Peter* on BBC One ... A new series of *The Flaxton Boys* (a gripping drama for children, set in Yorkshire in the year 1870) is on ITV ... 56-year-old Robert Dougall presents the first *Nine O'Clock News* program ... Concorde (the supersonic passenger plane) reaches a speed of 1,135 mph during a test flight from Scotland to Cornwall ... ***You Can Get It If You Really***

Want by 29-year-old Desmond Dekker and the Aces is number two ... "Whoa-oh, whoa-whoa, whoa-whoa-whoa. Whoa-oh, whoa-whoa, whoa-whoa-whoa Come sing me loud. Come sing me..." ***Montego Bay*** by 24-year-old Bobby Bloom is number three ... 24-year-old Manchester Utd footballer 'super' Georgie Best glides past Chelsea's hardman defender Ron 'Chopper' Harris and rounds goalkeeper Peter Bonnetti to score the winning goal for Utd in a 2-1 victory in the fourth round of the League Cup ... 45-year-old Richard Baker reads the news on BBC One ... For the third year running - the clocks do not get 'put back', as the government continues to assess the benefits of moving to a 'British Standard Time' ... Children wear orange reflective armbands on their way into school - as the mornings stay darker for longer ... 'Doing Their Bit for Laughter! In a Tale of Love, Lust and of course a Perfect Pair'" - *Carry On Loving* is now showing at cinemas with Kenneth Williams, Sid 'cor blimey' James and 28-year-old Imogen Hassall (aka the Countess of Cleavage) as Jenny Grubb ... Stephanie Rahn is the first topless page three girl in *The Sun* ... Women's Liberation activists throw flour at Bob Hope during the annual Miss World contest - pretty little 22-year-old Jennifer Hosten (36-24-38) is the eventual winner ... "Beryl, we live in a permissive society / Not on this street we don't / Everybody's at it / Not with me they're not / All girls are supposed to be crying out for it / Not this one Geoffrey, I'm the silent majority" - 20-year-old Paula Wilcox is Beryl, and 23-year-old Richard Beckinsale is Geoffrey in ITV's new sit-com *The Lovers* ... 39-year-old blonde sex-siren

Diana Dors (37-25-36) stars in *Queenie's Castle* ... "Now that you're gone, all that's left is a..." ***Band Of Gold*** by Freda Payne is top of the hit parade for five weeks! ... "Finished with my woman 'cause she couldn't help me with my mind. People think I'm insane because I am frowning all the time" - ***Paranoid*** by Black Sabbath climbs to number four ... BP discovers a large oil field in the North Sea ... The fabulous new Ford *Cortina MkIII* goes on sale with a range of models comprising of *L, XL, GT and GXL* ... British Leyland makes improvements to the *Maxi* - the gear change is now much smoother ... Production staff return to work at Leyland's Cowley and Longbridge factories ... The 'jam sandwich' police car is new as motorway patrol vehicles get a coat of white paint and a broad horizontal orange/red luminous stripe ... A new forty mile stretch of M6 motorway between Lancaster and Penrith (crossing the summit at Shap) is now open to motorists ... "Goodies! Goody, goody, yum, yum" - 27-year-old Graeme Garden, 29-year-old Bill Oddie and 30-year-old Tim Brooke-Taylor debut as *The Goodies* on BBC Two ... England's fast bowler Fred Trueman makes a guest appearance in *Dad's Army* - playing in a cricket match between the Home Guard platoon and the ARP wardens. The episode ends with 71-year-old Private Godfrey (played by 74-year-old Arnold Ridley) hitting the winning runs for Captain Mainwaring's Home Guard team ... "Papa was a great old man. I can see him with a shovel in his hands, see" - ***Patches*** by Clarence Carter climbs to number two in the pop chart ... "We are stardust, we are golden, and we've got to get ourselves back to the garden" - ***Woodstock*** by Matthews' Southern Comfort is number one ... 38-year-old Ray Illingworth leads England's cricketers down-under on a seven match Ashes series against Australia. 30-year-old Geoffrey Boycott and 31-year-old Brian Luckhurst stride out together to open the batting for England at Brisbane in the first Test. Boycott scores 37 runs. Luckhurst makes 74 (before being run out) and the match ends in a draw ... Back in England - Technicians at ITV go on strike - refusing to work with new-fangled 'colour' equipment ... 26-year-old maverick footballer Rodney Marsh scores a hat-trick as Queens Park Rangers defeat Birmingham City 5-2 in front of 13,074 spectators at Loftus Road. (27-year-old Terry Venables is also on the score-sheet for QPR) ... 24-year-old Bobby Gould scores a hat-trick as Wolverhampton Wanderers beat Manchester Utd 3-2 in front of 38,692 spectators at the Molineux ... 21-year-old John Toshack leaves Cardiff City and joins Liverpool for £110,000 - Toshack makes his debut in a 0-0 draw against Noel Cantwell's Coventry City in front of 50,503 spectators at Anfield ... 17-year-old winger Leighton James makes his debut for bottom-of-the-table Burnley in a 2-1 victory over Nottingham Forest in front of 13,036 spectators at Turf Moor ... "Oh, me and my life..." ***Me And My Life*** by The Tremeloes is number four in the pop chart ... ***Ain't No Mountain High Enough*** ("... Ain't no valley low enough. Ain't no river wild enough, to keep me from you") by 26-year-old Diana Ross is number six ... 21-year-old goalkeeper Peter Shilton makes his debut for Sir Alf Ramsey's

England football team (Shilton, Hughes, Cooper, Mullery, Sadler, Moore, F Lee, Ball, G Hurst, A Clarke, Peters) in a 3-1 victory over East Germany at Wembley. Franny Lee, Martin Peters and Allan 'sniffer' Clarke score the goals for England ... A loaf of bread costs one shilling ... Adverts say, '*Wonderloaf* is wonderful every day of the week'.

Winter 1970 - 1971

Wear a tall hat like a druid in the old days

It's a white Christmas for most of the UK ... *Blue Peter* presenters 36-year-old John Noakes, 31-year-old Peter Purves and 33-year-old Valerie Singleton urge people to send in old spoons and forks to raise money to provide suitable holiday homes for disabled children ... "I don't believe in Beatles. I just believe in me" - ***God*** is one of the songs to feature on *John Lennon/Plastic Ono Band* - the first solo album from 30-year-old John Lennon ... "'Cause I'm a voodoo chile. Lord knows I'm a..." ***Voodoo Chile*** by the late Jimi Hendrix is top of the hit parade ... *Breakaway* is a new type of chocolate bar ... 11-year-old schoolboy Simon Cowell from Elstree in Hertfordshire annoys his teachers with glib answers ... "Bah, humbug" - 34-year-old Albert Finney stars as *Scrooge* in a musical version of Charles Dickens' *A Christmas Carol* at cinemas. 56-year-old Alec Guinness is Jacob Marley and 56-year-old Kenneth More is the Ghost of Christmas Present ... 37-year-old Frank Bough presents *Grandstand* on BBC One ... 33-year-old Brentford goalkeeper Chic Brodie is badly injured after colliding with a dog on the pitch in a match away against Colchester Utd ... Reports in newspapers suggest that football has become 'dirty' ... Three players are booked in a First Division match between Everton and hard-tackling Leeds Utd ... Five players are booked in a Second Division match between Middlesbrough and Hull City ... Four players are booked, and a fifth is sent-off, in a Second Division match between Orient and Blackburn Rovers ... 11-year-old Uriah Rennie from Sheffield in Yorkshire plays out with his friends ... ***Cracklin' Rosie*** ("... get on board. We're gonna ride till there ain't no more to go. Takin' it slow") by 30-year-old Neil Diamond is number three in the pop chart ... ***My Prayer*** by 37-year-old Gerry Monroe is number nine ... Conservative prime-minister Edward Heath continues to push his Industrial Relations Bill through parliament - it will restrict trade unions from calling instant walk-out strikes ... British Leyland announce that five-thousand jobs are to be axed from its Austin-Morris manufacturing division ... NCB coal production is at its lowest level since 1926. Just 147 million tonnes have been mined in 1970 and the number of mine workers has fallen below 300,000 ... Wilf McGuinness' Manchester Utd lose 4-1 at home to Joe Mercer's Manchester City - and 'super' Georgie Best is booked for a dangerous tackle on Glyn Pardoe ... A week later, Utd lose again (this time 3-1 at home to Bertie Mee's Arsenal) and slip down to eighteenth position in Division One ... The winter mornings remain dark each day until around 9 a.m. - as the experiment continues to assess if a new 'British Standard Time' should be established ... 'Always Use The Green Cross Code' - the Green Cross Man warns children to be safe when crossing the road ... "Cherokee people, Cherokee tribe. So proud to live, so proud to die" - ***Indian Reservation*** by 27-year-old Don Fardon from Coventry peaks at number three in the pop chart ... "This feeling inside me could never deny me, the right to be wrong if I choose. And this pleasure I get from say, winning a bet, is to lose" - ***Nothing Rhymed*** by 24-year-old Gilbert O'Sullivan from Waterford in Ireland reaches number eight ... "Rupert, Rupert the bear. Everyone knows his name" - *The Adventures of Rupert Bear* is on TV ... 28-year-old actress Julie Goodyear plays Bet Lynch (a new barmaid in 'The Rovers Return') on *Coronation Street* ... 45-year-old comedian Benny Hill stars in *The Benny Hill Show* - the program is broadcast in black and white due to the ITV technicians' strike ... The hugely popular 36-year-old boxer Henry Cooper (aka Our 'Enry) is BBC's 'Sports Personality of the Year' - for the second time in his career ... Excitement builds for Christmas ... 'It's Here!' - 40-year-old Rolf Harris promotes the amazing *Stylophone* - a Pocket Electronic Organ ... A GAF *Talking-Viewmaster* (batteries not included) is also popular ... Children go crazy for the new Raleigh *Chopper* bicycle which costs £34/19s ... The latest 'World Cup' edition of the table-top football game from *Subbuteo* is popular with young boys - and their dads! ... Hallmark Records release *The Best of Top of the Pops '70'* - a budget priced cover-version pop compilation LP with pretty girls pictured on the sleeve ... "You went away and left me, long time ago" - ***I Hear You Knocking*** by 26-year-old Dave Edmunds from Cardiff climbs to number one in the pop chart - and stays there for six weeks! ... "You and I must make a pact, we must bring salvation back. Where there is love..." ***I'll Be There*** ("... I'll be there") by The Jackson Five is number four ... People write out Christmas cards and send them in the post to their friends and family ... All Christmas mail is postmarked with 'Remember to use the Postal Code' ... 27-year-old Cilla Black introduces *Christmas Night With The Stars* on BBC One ... Programs on ITV are broadcast in black and white due to on-going industrial action by technicians ... Public Information programs explain the new decimal currency system - which is to be introduced soon ... The Gay Liberation Front marches through London ... "Wear a tall hat like a druid in the old days. Wear a tall hat and a tattooed gown. Ride a white swan like the people of the Beltane. Wear your hair long babe, you can't go wrong" - ***Ride A White Swan*** by T-Rex is number six in the pop chart ... ***Home Lovin' Man*** by 43-year-old Andy Williams is number seven ... Don Revie's hard-tackling Leeds Utd football team (with Gary Sprake, Billy Bremner and 24-year-old Peter Lorimer) and Bertie Mee's Arsenal (with Bob Wilson, Frank McLintock and 23-year-old John Radford) battle it out for top spot in Division One ... Manchester Utd sack 33-year-old Wilf McGuinness after a poor run of results in Division One, and a League Cup semi-final defeat to Third Division Aston Villa. 61-year-old Sir Matt Busby returns to Old Trafford as Utd manager ... Ten football league matches are postponed on Boxing Day because of snow ... Ray Illingworth's England cricket team draws the second Test down-under in Perth, Australia. Brian Luckhurst scores 131 runs and Geoffrey Boycott scorers 70 and 50 ... 'Would You Believe I'm A Virgin Witch?' - a Bumper 100-page edition of *Mayfair* magazine is on sale ... 18-year-old Jenny Agutter stars in *The Railway Children* at cinemas (along with 16-year-old Gary Warren, 20-year-old Sally Thomsett and 41-year-old Bernard Cribbins) ... "Scooby! Dooby! DOO!!" - *Scooby Doo Where Are You?* is on TV ... The snow thaws ... Children play out ... The future seems bright ... Cadbury's launches the *Curlywurly* chocolate bar ... Conservative prime-minister Edward Heath is in an optimistic mood as the new year begins ... The weather is dry and mild, turning wet and windy at the end of January ... Millions of TV viewers tune into BBC's long-running police drama *Z Cars* on Monday and Tuesday evenings ... Regulars of 'The Rovers Return' pub in ITV's ever popular soap-opera *Coronation Street* are shocked to learn that they're drinking watered down gin ... Manchester Utd footballer 'super' Georgie Best is in trouble after failing to turn up for a match against Chelsea. Utd Manager Sir Matt Busby bans the 24-year-old from the club for fourteen days. Best is also summonsed to appear before an FA Disciplinary Committee - where he receives a record fine of £250 and a six week suspended ban ... 30-year-old Jimmy 'Greavsie' Greaves spends an evening drinking in a Blackpool nightclub (until the early hours). The following day, Greavsie plays for West Ham Utd in a 4-0 defeat against 'The Seasiders' ... ***Grandad*** ("... grandad, you're lovely. That's what we all think of you") by 51-year-old Clive Dunn is number one in the pop chart ... "There's nothin' I can do if it don't get through, just..." ***Blame It On The Pony Express*** by Johnny Johnson and the Bandwagon is number seven ... Millions of people complete a pools coupon each week (and say a prayer) in the hope of winning a fortune ... Father James Curtin from Walsall wins over £100,000 on *Vernons* ... The new decimal currency system gets underway on Monday the fifteenth of February, with the introduction of three bronze coloured coins - the ½p (with the Royal Crown on the front), the 1p (with portcullis and chains) and the 2p (with the 'three feather' emblem of the Prince of Wales). The silver coloured 5p, 10p and 50p coins have been in circulation for a few years - serving respectively as one shilling, two shilling and ten shilling coins. Under the new system - one old penny is equal to ½ new pence and one shilling is equal to 5 new pence ... Travelling Sales Representatives, driving white Hillman *Hunter* estate cars, stop for lunch at *Little Chef* cafés ... A plate of sausages, eggs and French fried potatoes costs 5s/6d (that's 27½ new pence) ... A side order of buttered bread is 7d (3 new pence) ... A cup of tea is 9d (4 new pence) ... A cup of coffee is 1s/3d (6 new pence) ... Fashions are changing ... Young people apply brightly coloured make-up to their eyelids and spray glitter on their faces ... ***Ride A White Swan*** by T-Rex (with 23-year-old Marc Bolan) climbs back up the pop chart to number two (after previously peaking at number six) ... School children are mesmerised as

Mr. Benn (of number fifty-two Festive Road) makes his debut on television ... Fred the *Homepride* flour character is a popular new kitchen accessory ... *Apollo 14* (with astronauts: Alan Shepard, Stuart Roosa and Edgar D. Mitchell) lands on the Moon and sends back colour photographs ... 'Kill the Bill' - the TUC holds a demonstration against Edward Heath's Industrial Relations Bill - one million people march through London ... Thousands of British Leyland car workers stage a 24-hour walk-out ... Postal workers go on strike after their demand for a 15% pay increase is rejected ... Richard Branson's mail-order music business grinds to a halt because of the strike - and so, the 20-year-old entrepreneur sets up a retail operation instead ... *Virgin Records* (a small shop) opens on Oxford Street in London ... "Doesn't matter what you do, girl. Ooh girl, want you" - ***No Matter What*** by Badfinger climbs to number five in the pop chart ... ***Baby I Won't Let You Down*** ("... when you call, I'll be 'round") by Pickettywitch stalls at number twenty-seven ... A bomb explodes at Hadley Green near Barnet - outside the home of government minister Robert Carr. A group called The Angry Brigade claims responsibility ... Scotland Yard sets up a specialist Bomb Squad division ... The Troubles escalate in Northern Ireland - a British soldier is killed in Ulster for the first time in fifty years ... "I don't feel safe in this world no more, I don't want to die in a nuclear war, I want to sail away to a distant shore, and make like an..." ***Apeman*** by The Kinks is new at number five in the pop chart ... 28-year-old Desmond Lynam presents *Sport on 2* on BBC Radio Two on Saturday afternoons ... England's cricketers are in action in Australia ... 30-year-old batsman Geoffrey Boycott scores a century in each of the Test Matches at Sydney and Adelaide. Brian Luckhurst, John Edrich and Basil D'Oliveira also make centuries during the seven match series. 21-year-old fast-bowler Bob Willis makes his debut for England - and takes the wickets of Marsh, Chappell and Lillee in the final Test at Sydney. Ray Illingworth's team is triumphant - England regain the Ashes from Bill Lawry's Aussies - winning the series 2-0. G Boycott, B W Luckhurst, A P E Knott (wk), J H Edrich, M C Cowdrey, K W R Fletcher, B L D'Oliveira, R Illingworth (cpt), J H Hampshire, J A Snow, D L Underwood, K Shuttleworth, P Lever and R G D Willis are all buoyed by this historic Ashes victory - the first since 1956! ... Rock music fans queue outside record shops ... Black Sabbath release their *Paranoid* album ... Stray release their *Suicide* album ... "Now behave yourself" - 37-year-old Michael Caine stars as Jack Carter in *Get Carter* at cinemas ... "Are you dancin'? / Are you askin'? / I'm askin' / I'm dancin'" - *The Liver Birds* is a new sit-com on BBC One, starring 29-year-old Polly James as Beryl and 29-year-old Nerys Hughes as Sandra ... "Get on board. Get on board. Come and join the Double Deckers. Take a ticket for a journey, on our double decker London bus" - children watch TV on Fridays at teatime to see Doughnut, Scooper, Brains, Billie, Sticks, Spring and Tiger in *Here Come The Double Deckers!* ... ITV programs are broadcast in colour once more, as the technician's strike comes to an end ... 57-year-old Sid 'cor blimey' James, 42-year-old Diana Coupland and 20-year-old Sally Geeson star in new sit-com *Bless This House* ... The first edition of *Look-In* ('a great new TV magazine for boys and girls') is published for 5 new pence ... "Oh, oh, oh, oh..." ***When I'm Dead And Gone*** ("... I wanna leave some happy woman living on") by McGuinness Flint spends four weeks at number three on the hit parade ... ***Amazing Grace*** by 31-year-old Judy Collins reaches number five ... Derby County football manager Brian Clough signs 22-year-old defender Colin Todd from Sunderland for £175,000 ... Norman Hunter and Johnny Giles score late goals for Don Revie's hard-tackling Leeds Utd, but the 'all-whites' crash out of the FA Cup in a shock 3-2 defeat against Fourth Division Colchester Utd ... 25-year-old Martin Chivers scores twice as Bill Nicholson's First Division Tottenham Hotspur beat Vic Crowe's Third Division Aston Villa 2-0 in the League Cup final at Wembley ... 20-year-old Charlie George is on the score-sheet as Arsenal beat 38-year-old Bobby Robson's Ipswich Town 3-2 at Highbury ... Big band leader Harry Roy (aka the King of 'Hot-Cha') dies in London aged 71 ... "My sweet Lord. Oh, my Lord. My sweet Lord..." ***My Sweet Lord*** by 27-year-old George Harrison spends five weeks at the top of the pop chart ... 30-year-old footballer Jimmy 'Greavsie' Greaves is on the score-sheet for West Ham Utd in a 0-1 victory over Coventry City in Division One ... 16-year-old apprentice footballer Trevor Francis scores all four goals as Second Division Birmingham City thrash Bolton Wanderers 4-0 at St. Andrew's. In the next game, young Francis scores twice as 'The Blues' beat Swindon Town 1-2 at the County Ground ... 'A Great Guy with his Chopper!' - *Carry On Henry* is now showing at cinemas with Sid 'cor blimey' James as King Henry VIII, 45-year-old Kenneth Williams as Thomas Cromwell and 33-year-old Barbara Windsor (36-23-34) as Bettina - a buxom serving wench ... "There's a little bear like you've never seen before, who's a lot of fun. Children everywhere grow to love him more and more, he's the number one" - ***Rupert*** by Jackie Lee is number fourteen in the pop chart ... "Don't ya hear the wind a-blowing..." ***Stoned Love*** ("... Oh, yeah") by The Supremes is number three ... 35-year-old writer David Nobbs pens humorous scripts and one-line gags for a new TV show called *The Two Ronnies* ... BBC One TV programs on a Saturday evening include: *Dr. Who* - with 51-year-old Jon Pertwee as the Doctor; *Here's Lucy* - with Lucille Ball; *It's Cliff Richard* - hosted by 30-year-old popstar Cliff; and *Dixon of Dock Green* - with 75-year-old Jack Warner in the title role ... Families enjoy an evening in, playing records on the teak-effect *PYE* stereogram ... "You looked so pretty as you were riding along. You looked so pretty as you were singing this song" - ***The Pushbike Song*** by The Mixtures is number two on the hit parade ... ***It's Impossible*** by 58-year-old Perry Como is number four ... Kids hang about near the new shopping precinct ... Fish and chips wrapped in newspaper costs 25 new pence ... A Cadbury's *Curlywurly* chocolate bar costs 3 new pence.

Spring 1971

I beg your pardon, I never promised you a rose garden

Postal workers return to work after being on strike for seven weeks ... Thousands of British Leyland car production workers are sent home due to a shortage of component parts ... Production of Ford's new *Cortina MKIII* motorcar is slowed by a strike at the Dagenham factory ... Unemployment in the country reaches 815,000 and Edward Heath's new Conservative government is under pressure to take immediate action to improve the economy ... 50-year-old Chancellor of the Exchequer Anthony Barber delivers his first Budget ... It's announced that a new value added tax (VAT) will come into effect in 1973 ... Trade and Industry secretary John Davis unveils government plans to build a new international airport at Maplin Sands in Essex ... "Baby, baby..." ***Baby Jump*** ("... into my dreams") by Mungo Jerry (with 24-year-old lead singer Ray Dorset) is new at number one ... ***Sweet Caroline*** ("... de-de-der. Good times never seemed so good") by 30-year-old Neil Diamond is number eight ... 24-year-old cricketer David Lloyd (an opening batsman for Lancashire) scores 54 runs as his team defeats

Gloucestershire by an innings and 24 runs in the opening match of the County Championship ... 'The Fight of the Century' takes place at Madison Square Garden in New York, where 27-year-old heavy-weight boxer Smokin' Joe Frazier beats 29-year-old Muhammad Ali in fifteen rounds ... Back in England - 21-year-old Joe Bugner beats 36-year-old Henry Cooper (aka Our 'Enry) by ¼ point at Wembley ... 24-year-old footballer 'super' Georgie Best scores twice as Manchester Utd beat Stoke City 1-2 at the Victoria Ground - Utd climb up to ninth position in Division One ... 31-year-old Jimmy 'Greavsie' Greaves scores twice as West Ham Utd draw 2-2 against Ipswich Town - 'The Hammers' stay just above the relegation zone ... 19-year-old Kevin Keegan scores a goal as Scunthorpe Utd beat Southport 2-0 at the Old Show Ground - 'The Iron' climb up to fourteenth in Division Four ... Boys and girls sit together in youth club halls, listening to pop records on the ITT *KP-820* stereo record player ... Glam rock is exciting and new ... "Well she's faster than most and she lives on the coast, a-ha-ha" - ***Hot Love*** by T-Rex (with 23-year-old Marc Bolan) climbs to number one in the chart - and stays there for six weeks! ... ***Bridget The Midget (The Queen Of The Blues)*** by 32-year-old Ray Stevens is number two ... TV viewers are shocked when Valerie Barlow (wife of Ken and mother of 5-year-old twins Peter and Susan) dies from an electric shock caused by a faulty power socket at number 14 *Coronation Street* ... 36-year-old Wendy Craig stars in a new sit-com called *And Mother Makes Three* ... "It's just..." ***Another Day*** by 28-year-old Paul McCartney is number two in the pop chart ... "I beg your pardon. I never promised you a..." ***Rose Garden*** by 23-year-old Lynn Anderson is number three ... 34-year-old Glenda Jackson wins an Oscar for her role in *Women in Love* ... Racehorse *L'Escargot* (ridden by 29-year-old Tommy Carberry) wins the Cheltenham Gold Cup for the second year running ... *Specify* (ridden by 33-year-old Johnny Cook) wins the Grand National ... Bertie Mee's Arsenal and Don Revie's hard-tackling Leeds Utd are neck and neck at the top of Division One ... 19-year-old Ray Kennedy scores twice for Arsenal as 'The Gunners' defeat Chelsea 2-0 in front of 62,087 spectators at Highbury ... 24-year-old Alan 'sniffer' Clarke scores all four goals for Leeds as 'The Whites' thrash Burnley 4-0 in front of 31,192 at Elland Road ... "It's good-night from me / And it's good-night from him" - *The Two Ronnies* debuts on TV, with 41-year-old Ronnie Barker and 40-year-old Ronnie Corbett ... "Hannibal Heyes and Kid Curry, the two most successful outlaws in the history of the West. And in all the trains and banks they robbed, they never shot anyone" - the American 'Western' series *Alias Smith and Jones* begins on BBC Two, with 31-year-old Pete Duel and 28-year-old Ben Murphy ... "They don't like it up 'em!" - a film version of *Dad's Army* is now showing at cinemas, starring 55-year-old Arthur Lowe as Captain Mainwaring, 58-year-old John Le Mesurier as Sergeant Wilson, 51-year-old Clive Dunn as Lance-Corporal Jones, 75-year-old Arnold Ridley as Private Godfrey and 25-year-old Ian Lavender as Private 'stupid boy' Pike ... ***Hot Love*** by T-Rex remains at number one in the pop chart ... Adolescent boys and girls pin glossy posters of 23-year-old Marc Bolan to their bedroom walls ... 43-year-old Sam Leitch presents the weekly Football Preview every Saturday on *Grandstand* on BBC One ... Leeds Utd fans invade the pitch at Elland Road when Jeff Astle's goal for West Bromwich Albion is allowed to stand, even though the off-side flag was raised. Leeds lose the match 1-2 and slip down to second place in Division One, behind Arsenal ... *Match of the Day* shows slow motion action replays for the first time ... "I'm just your..." ***Jack In The Box*** ("... you know when ever love knocks, I'm gonna bounce up and down on. my spring") by 24-year-old Clodagh Rodgers finishes fourth in the Eurovision Song Contest (held in Dublin) - and climbs to number four in the UK pop chart ... ***If Not For You*** ("... my sky would fall, rain would gather too") by 22-year-old Olivia Newton-John is number seven ... The football season draws to a close ... Johnny Carey's Blackburn Rovers and Jimmy Meadows' Bolton Wanderers are relegated to the Third Division for the first time in their histories ... 21-year-old centre-forward Malcolm MacDonald scores a hat-trick as Luton Town beat Cardiff City 3-0 at Kenilworth Road in Division Two ... The names 'Best, Charlton, Law' feature together on the same score-sheet as Sir Matt Busby's Manchester Utd beat Joe Mercer's Manchester City 4-3 on the final day of the season - to finish in eighth position in Division One ... Bertie Mee's Arsenal pip Don Revie's hard-tackling Leeds Utd to the title, with a 0-1 victory over Tottenham Hotspur at White Hart Lane. Arsenal players

Bob Wilson, Pat Rice, Bob McNab, Frank McLintock (captain), Peter Storey, John Roberts, Peter Simpson, Jon Sammels, Eddie Kelly, John Radford, George Armstrong, Charlie George, George Graham and 19-year-old, top scorer, Ray Kennedy have all been outstanding ... 'The Gunners' also clinch the FA Cup - and achieve a wonderful 'double' - when 20-year-old Charlie George scores the winning goal in extra-time to snatch a 2-1 victory over Bill Shankly's Liverpool. A ticket for the standing enclosure at the Empire Stadium in Wembley costs £1.00 ... Dave Sexton's Chelsea draw 1-1 against Real Madrid in the UEFA Cup Winners Cup final in Greece. Chelsea go on to win the replay 2-1 - with John Dempsey and Peter 'Ossie' Osgood scoring the goals ... ***Indiana Wants Me*** ("... Lord, I can't go back there") by R Dean Taylor is number three in the pop chart ... "I said Jake, now won't you wait? What's got into you?" - ***My Brother Jake*** by Free climbs nine places to number eleven ... 54-year-old prime-minister Edward Heath travels to Paris for a summit meeting with 59-year-old French President Georges Pompidou over Britain's entry into the European Economic Community. The meeting is a success - France agrees to lend its support to Britain joining the Common Market ... 27-year-old rock star Mick Jagger marries 26-year-old model Bianca De Macias in Saint-Tropez ... ***Hot Love*** by T-Rex continues to occupy top spot in the weekly pop chart ... ***Strange Kind Of Woman*** by Deep Purple is number eight ... 36-year-old writer David Nobbs pens humorous scripts and one-line gags for comedian Les Dawson ... 20-year-old Richard Branson (boss of *Virgin Records*) is arrested for purchase-tax fraud and ordered to pay costs of £60,000 ... 57-year-old Bill Shankly (manager of Liverpool Football Club) signs a promising young midfielder called Kevin Keegan from Scunthorpe Utd for £35,000 ... "I am double-U O-O-O, and I'm still up here again!" - ***Double Barrel*** by Dave and Ansil Collins is the new number one record ... "Gotta pay your dues if you wanna sing the blues, and you know..." ***It Don't Come Easy*** by 30-year-old Ringo Starr is number four ... Production of the Triumph *Herald* motorcar comes to an end after twelve years ... The all new Triumph *Toledo* is launched ... 11-year-old schoolboy Jeremy Clarkson from Doncaster flicks through the pages of a car magazine in his bedroom ... 31-year-old racing driver Jackie Stewart wins the Monaco Grand Prix in a blue Tyrrell-Ford (number 11). 42-year-old Graham Hill finishes in ninth position. 37-year-old John Surtees is tenth ... 41-year-old pop star Dickie Valentine dies in a car crash (travelling in a Hillman *Avenger*) at Crickhowell in Wales ... The new British Leyland *Morris Marina* goes on sale. The *1.3 De Luxe Coupe* costs £923, has a top speed of 82 mph and accelerates from 0-60 mph in 17.5 seconds ... The *1.8 TC* costs £1,177 has a top speed of 100 mph and can reach 60 mph in 12.5 seconds ... 44-year-old Jimmy Savile says, "Clunk, click, every trip."

Summer 1971

Woke up this morning and my mamma was gone

The sun shines ... "Blackpool Tower isn't as big as I thought it would be either!" - saucy postcards continue to sell well at seaside resorts ... Groovy kids wear flared jeans and platform shoes, and sit together in the park drinking alcohol ... 'Pull a bird tonight. Woodpecker for the wild life' - *Woodpecker* cider is available from the 'off-license' ... "Oh my darling, knock three times on the ceiling if you want me. Twice on the pipe, if the answer is no" - ***Knock Three Times*** by Dawn spends five weeks at number one in the pop chart ... ***Let Your Yeah Be Yeah*** by The Pioneers reaches number five ... Dennis Filkins wins the annual *News of the World* darts tournament at the Ship Inn in Weymouth - beating Derek White, by two legs to nil, in the final ... 10-year-old schoolboy Phil Taylor from Burslem in Staffordshire enjoys a game of 'arrows' with his mates ... Schoolboys kick orange *Wembley Trophy* footballs in the park ... 10-year-old Gary Lineker from Leicester scores a hat-trick, then goes home for a packet of crisps ... ***Don't Let It Die*** by 47-year-old Hurricane Smith climbs to number two in the pop chart ...

Banner Man by Blue Mink reaches number three ... 36-year-old jockey Geoff Lewis from Wales rides *Mill Reef* to victory in the Epsom Derby ... Kenneth Kendall from Cornwall reads the news on BBC One ... Production at British Leyland car factories remains slow - with many workers idle due to a lack of component parts ... Conservative MPs are split on the issue of Europe ... A number of Tory back-benchers inform 54-year-old prime-minister Edward Heath that they will not support his plan to take Britain into the Common Market ... 'The Milk Snatcher' - thousands of protestors take to the streets as 45-year-old Education Secretary Margaret Thatcher ends the provision of free milk for children in primary schools ... "Take an eye for an eye and a life for a life. And somebody must die for the death of my wife. Yes..." ***I Did What I Did For Maria*** by Tony Christie peaks at number two in the pop chart ... People enjoy a night in, watching television on rented *PYE CT-71* (22-inch) sets ... *The Black and White Minstrel Show* is broadcast on BBC One on Saturday evenings - followed by *A Man Called Ironside*, starring 54-year-old Raymond Burr ... 36-year-old Michael Parkinson hosts *Parkinson*, a brand new, late night chat show. 27-year-old tennis player Arthur Ashe, 36-year-old jazz singer Marian Montgomery and 59-year-old actor Terry-Thomas are the first guests to be interviewed ... 40-year-old comedian Les Dawson appears in a new series of *Sez Les* on ITV ... 17-year-old Rosemary Letts murders 8-year-old Charmaine West in Gloucester ... 29-year-old Fred West (recently released from prison) murders his former wife Rena Costello and buries her body in a field near Kempley in Gloucestershire ... "Scared old slaver knows he's doin' alright, hear him whip the women just around midnight..." ***Brown Sugar*** ("... how come you taste so good?") by The Rolling Stones peaks at number two on the hit parade ... ***Me And You And A Dog Named Boo*** by Lobo makes it to number four ... Don Revie's hard-tackling Leeds Utd win the Inter Cities Fairs Cup by beating Juventus (with 24-year-old midfielder Fabio Capello in their team) on the away goals rule ... 23-year-old winger Ray Graydon transfers from Third Division Bristol Rovers to Third Division Aston Villa for £50,000 ... 21-year-old striker Malcolm MacDonald transfers from Second Division Luton Town to First Division Newcastle Utd for £180,000 ... ***Good Old Arsenal*** by The Arsenal First Team Squad reaches number sixteen in the pop chart ... ***He's Gonna Step On You Again*** by 25-year-old John Kongos is number four ... Cricketers John Edrich and Brian Luckhurst stride out together to open the batting for England at Edgbaston in the first Test against Pakistan. Edrich is out for a duck. Luckhurst makes 35. 25-year-old wicketkeeper Alan Knott (batting at number seven) scores a century, and the match ends in a draw. 30-year-old Geoffrey Boycott scores 121 not out in the second Test at Lord's, and England win the series 1-0 ... The sun shines ... Girls wear hotpants ... "Welcome to *Top of the Pops*. Lots of nice young ladies about with us this evening" - 44-year-old disc jockey Jimmy Savile introduces *Top of the Pops* from a crowded TV studio ... "Where's your mamma gone? Where's your mamma gone? Far, far away. Far, far away" - ***Chirpy Chirpy Cheep Cheep*** by Middle of the Road (with 26-year-old vocalist Sally Carr) moves up sixteen places to number one - and stays at the top for five weeks! ... ***Leap Up And Down (Wave Your Knickers In The Air)*** by St. Cecilia is number twelve ... 59-year-old Jimmy Chipperfield opens a new safari park at Knowsley on Merseyside, and families travel from all around to see the monkeys ... 45-year-old Queen Elizabeth II opens the Kingsway tunnel under the River Mersey between Liverpool and Wallasey ... ***Co-Co*** by The Sweet (with 25-year-old vocalist Brian Connolly) climbs to number two in the pop chart ... ***Tom-Tom Turnaround*** by New World is number six ... 'K' reg cars go on sale on the first of August ... There's a waiting time of up to four-months due to a shortage of cars at Morris and Austin dealers ... Ford promote the new *Cortina MkIII* with an advertising strap-line that claims the new model, 'takes motoring to a new peak' ... Sales of foreign cars are increasing ... The new Datsun *100A Cherry* has a top speed of 87 mph and can reach 60 mph in 14.6 seconds ... The latest BMW *2002tii* has a top speed of 115 mph and can reach 60 mph in 9.8 seconds ... Four star leaded petrol is 34 new pence a gallon ... 32-year-old racing driver Jackie Stewart wins the British Grand Prix at Silverstone in a blue Tyrrell-Ford (number 12) and goes on to be crowned Formula One world champion for a second time ... ***We Won't Get Fooled Again*** by The Who (with 27-year old Roger Daltrey, 26-year-old Pete Townshend, 26-year-old John Entwistle and 24-year-old Keith Moon) climbs to number nine in the pop chart ... ***Street Fighting Man*** by The Rolling Stones (with 28-year-old Mick Jagger, 27-year-old Keith Richards, 30-year-old Charlie Watts, and with the late Brian Jones on sitar) peaks at number twenty-one ... 43-year-old Frank O'Farrell leaves Leicester City to take over from Sir Matt Busby as manager of Manchester Utd ... 31-year-old Denis Law scores for Utd in a 2-2 draw against Derby County on the opening day of the season ... 20-year-old Kevin Keegan scores on his debut for Bill Shankly's Liverpool in a 3-1 win against Nottingham Forest ... A week later, 21-year-old Malcolm MacDonald scores a hat-trick as Newcastle Utd beat Liverpool 3-2 at St. James' Park ... A light-blue, three-wheeled *Invacar* is parked at the side of the football pitch at Highfield Road as Coventry City draw 2-2 with Derby County ... Uncouth show jumper 32-year-old Harvey Smith causes an outrage at Hickstead by making a 'V' sign at Douglas Bunn - one of the judges ... "W'alright everybody!" - ***Get Down And Get With It*** by Slade (with 25-year-old Noddy Holder) is number sixteen in the pop chart ... "This is! A heavy, heavy monster sound" - ***Monkey Spanner*** by Dave and Ansil Collins is number seven ... *Apollo 15* (with astronauts: David Scott, Alfred Worden and James Irwin) lands on the Moon and stays for three days ... Back in England - 25-year-old Manchester Utd footballer 'super' Georgie Best is sent off for swearing at the referee in a match against Chelsea ... 19-year-old Jenny Agutter swims naked in *Walkabout* at cinemas ... 22-year-old Gillian Blake stars in *Follyfoot* on TV ... "You're dirty, sweet and you're my girl. Get it on. Bang a gong ..." ***Get It On*** by T-Rex (with 23-year-old Marc Bolan) is new at number one - the song is the group's second number one hit ... ***What Are You Doing Sunday?*** by Dawn is number thirteen ... Adolescent boys browse the top shelf at their local newsagents ... A new magazine called *Men Only* is on sale for 30 new pence ... Modern household gadgets are in vogue ... A Goblin *Teasmade* costs around £27.50.

Autumn 1971

I just like the things you do

The Troubles continue in Ireland ... A school girl is fatally wounded in crossfire between British soldiers and the IRA ... The Democratic Unionist Party is founded by 45-year-old Rev Ian Paisley ... A bomb explodes at the Post Office tower in London - there are no casualties ... 10-year-old schoolboy Jonathan Ross from Leytonstone stays up late to watch telly ... 50-year-old movie star Dirk Bogarde is a guest on BBC One chat show *Parkinson* ... "I remember when I was five and you were ten, boy. You knew that I was shy, so you teased and made me cry, but I loved you" - ***I'm Still Waiting*** by 27-year-old Diana Ross climbs to number one in the pop chart - and stays there for four weeks ... "I've got a never ending love for you" - ***Never Ending Song Of Love*** by the New Seekers spends five weeks at number two ... 29-year-old Geoff Hurst and 26-year-old Martin Chivers score the goals as Sir Alf Ramsey's England football team (G Banks, Lawler, Cooper, Mullery, McFarland, Moore, F Lee, Madeley, Chivers, G Hurst, Peters and substitute Radford) beats Switzerland 2-3 in Basel ... Back in Britain - the political battle between Left and Right intensifies as Edward Heath's new Industrial Relations Act becomes law - defiant union leaders say they will not comply with its conditions ... Triumph car workers at Speke and Coventry are on a go-slow in an effort to avoid being laid-off due to a lack of components ... Thousands of workers are also idle at British Leyland's Longbridge factory ... Civil servants begin working on Mr. Heath's plans for a new airport at Maplin Sands in Essex ... "You just call out my name, and you know wherever I am, I'll come running (oh yeah baby), to see you again" - ***You've Got A Friend*** by 23-year-old James Taylor is number four in the pop chart ... ***Bangla-Desh*** by 28-year-old George Harrison is number ten ... Thieves break into Lloyds Bank on Baker Street in London and steal cash and valuables from over two-hundred safe deposit boxes ... Thick fog descends on the North West ... A motorway pile-up (involving two-hundred vehicles) on the M6 at the Thelwall Viaduct near Warrington claims the lives of ten people and injures dozens more ... 45-year-old Queen Elizabeth II cuts the ribbon to officially open the new section of M62 motorway across the Pennines ... "Well I just wonder..." ***Did You Ever*** ("... all the time") by 31-year-old Nancy Sinatra and 42-year-old Lee Hazelwood is number two in the pop chart ... ***Tweedle Dee, Tweedle Dum*** by Middle of the Road is number four ... Yellow 'smiley face' images are seen everywhere ... Boys wear T shirts with the happy symbol emblazoned on the front ... Girls sew 'smiley face' badges onto their jeans ... A new series of *The Flaxton Boys* (a drama for children set in

Yorkshire in the year 1928) is on ITV ... *Blue Peter* is on BBC One on Monday and Thursday evenings. 37-year-old presenter John Noakes introduces a new pet - a young border collie, and viewers are asked to send in postcards with name suggestions for the puppy ... 25-year-old footballer 'super' Georgie Best scores a hat-trick for Manchester Utd in a 4-2 victory over West Ham Utd at Old Trafford ... 33-year-old centre-forward Derek Dougan scores a hat-trick for Wolverhampton Wanderers in a 4-2 victory over Nottingham Forest at the Molineux ... In Division Three, 25-year-old Alf Wood scores five as Shrewsbury Town thrash Blackburn Rovers 7-1 at Gay Meadow ... "You never wrote me, you never called..." ***Nathan Jones*** ("... you've been gone too long") by The Supremes is number five in the pop chart ... ***Keep On Dancing*** by The Bay City Rollers is number nine ... The *Daily Mail* reports, 'Wild scenes as MPs take big step into Europe' ... 50-year-old Roy Jenkins and many of his fellow Labour MPs defy a party whip by voting with Edward Heath's Conservative government - to approve Britain's entry into the Common Market. (A number of disgruntled Tory back-benchers are still hoping to scupper the deal before it becomes law) ... Queen Elizabeth II welcomes 70-year-old Emperor Hirohito of Japan on an official state visit to Britain ... 21-year-old Princess Anne wins the three-day horse trial event at Burghley House on *Doublet* ... 26-year-old disc jockey Dave Lee Travis presents the weekday lunch time show on Radio One ... ***Hey Girl Don't Bother Me*** ("... stay out of my arms, don't use your charms. Don't bother me") by The Tams spends three weeks at number one in the pop chart ... ***Tap Turns On The Water*** by CCS is number five ... Radio One DJ's take turns to present *Top of the Pops* on BBC One television at 7.25 p.m. on Thursday evenings ... 28-year-old Tony Blackburn hosts the show on the fourteenth of October ... 44-year-old Jimmy Savile hosts the show the following week ... Pan's People are the resident dancers ... For the first time since 1967, the clocks are moved back by one hour - as the government ends its experiment into 'British Standard Time' and reverts to 'Greenwich Mean Time' ... 30-year-old Ed 'stewpot' Stewart presents *Junior Choice* on Radio One at the weekend ... "To Bombay, a travelling circus came, they brought an intelligent elephant, and Nellie was her name" - Mandy Miller sings ***Nellie The Elephant*** ... All sixty-three people on board *BEA* Flight 706 are killed when the plane crashes over Belgium ... The Troubles continue in Northern Ireland ... 'Super' Georgie Best receives death threats from Irish Nationalists ... Police detectives from Special Branch are assigned protection duties to the 25-year-old football star ... A boardroom power struggle at Manchester City results in 44-year-old Malcolm Allison taking over from 57-year-old Joe Mercer as manager ... John Harris' Sheffield Utd lead the way in Division One after beating Jimmy Bloomfield's Leicester City 1-0 at Bramall Lane ... The names 'Best, Charlton, Law' appear together on the same score-sheet for the final time as Manchester Utd beat Huddersfield Town 3-0 with goals from 25-year-old George, 33-year-old Bobby and 31-year-old Denis

... 21-year-old actress Susan George plays a terrified babysitter in the horror film *Fright* ... "Marie, Marie da voodoo veau, she'll put a spell on you" - ***The Witch Queen Of New Orleans*** by Redbone climbs to number two in the pop chart ... ***For All We Know*** by 34-year-old Shirley Bassey is number six ... "Wake up Maggie I think I got something to say to you. It's late September and I really should be back at school" - ***Maggie May*** by 26-year-old Rod Stewart is new at number one ... The new 100 mph Triumph *Dolomite* motorcar is on display at the Earls Court Motor Show - but after recent industrial action, orders for the new car will take up to two-months to fulfill ... "Good game, good game!" - 43-year-old Bruce Forsyth presents the *Generation Game* on BBC One ... ITV broadcasts the first episode of *Upstairs Downstairs* (with 37-year-old Jean Marsh as Rose, 67-year-old Angela Baddeley as Mrs. Bridges and 47-year-old Gordon Jackson as Hudson) ... "It really doesn't matter if it's raining or it's fine, just as long as you've got time to P-L-A-Y, play-away-away-way, play-away-play-play, away-way, play-away, play-away" - 38-year-old Brian Cant introduces the first *Play Away* for younger viewers on BBC Two ... *Crystal Tipps and Alistair* is also new ... "Reggae, Reggae, Reggae. Here comes Johnny Reggae. Johnny Reggae Reggae. Lay it on me" - ***Johnny Reggae*** by The Piglets reaches number three in the pop chart ... "I won't laugh at you when you boo hoo hoo..." ***Coz I Luv You*** by Slade (with 25-year-old Noddy Holder) spends four weeks at number one ... John Lennon and The Plastic Ono Band are number one in the album chart with

Imagine ... Tape cassettes and 8-track cartridges are in demand at *The Tape Revolution Store* ... *The Old Grey Whistle Test* begins on late-night BBC Two ... 21-year-old Richard Branson's *Virgin Records* on Oxford Street is thriving ... "Don't cry. Don't raise your eye. It's only teenage wasteland" - ***Baba O'Riley*** by The Who plays on a transistor radio ... 33-year-old purple-shirted Jake Thackray appears on TV show *Braden's Week* ... 38-year-old Peter Wyngarde drives a Bentley *S2 Continental* and stars as *Jason King* on ATV ... The second, third, fourth, fifth and sixth episodes of *Upstairs Downstairs* are all transmitted in black and white due to last year's strike by ITV technicians ... Children read *Mr. Tickle* - the first of *The Mr. Men* books by Roger Hargreaves ... "There's a farmer down there with a purple face / I expect it's all that sun and the open air life, Joe / Now he's doing one of those country dances / Well, I don't think he looks very friendly / Aye, maybe you're right. 'Though it can't be anything we've done" - cartoon couple Joe and Petunia star on TV in a short public information film telling people to follow the Country Code - and close gates behind them ... There's a flurry of activity on football's transfer market ... 25-year-old striker Keith Weller leaves Dave Sexton's Chelsea and joins Jimmy Bloomfield's Leicester City for £100,000 ... 25-year-old playmaker Tony Green leaves Bob Stokoe's Blackpool and joins Joe Harvey's Newcastle Utd for £150,000 ... 19-year-old midfielder Martin O'Neill leaves Distillery in Ireland and joins Matt Gillies' Nottingham Forest for £15,000 ... The proposed transfer of Asa Hartford from West Bromwich Albion to Leeds Utd is called off when a medical reveals that the 21-year-old has a hole in his heart ... 'Super' Georgie Best scores a hat-trick as Frank O'Farrell's league-leaders Manchester Utd win 2-5 at Southampton ... 30-year-old centre-forward Andy Lochhead scores a hat-trick, and 24-year-old midfielder Bruce Rioch scores twice, as Vic Crowe's Aston Villa thrash Oldham Athletic 0-6 in Division Three ... 24-year-old Ted MacDougall scores nine goals as Bournemouth thrash Margate 11-0 in the first round of the FA Cup ... "I'm so..." ***Tired Of Being Alone*** ("... I'm so tired of on my own") by 25-year-old Al Green is number four in the pop chart ... ***The Night They Drove Old Dixie Down*** by 30-year-old Joan Baez is number six ... The national road network continues to develop and grow ... 'Spaghetti Junction' opens - and the M6 motorway links up seamlessly with the A38(M) to form a brand new express-way into Birmingham city centre ... The stylish new Vauxhall *Viva* motorcar is available as a saloon, estate or coupe. The 1100cc base model has a top speed of 78 mph and accelerates from 0-60 mph in 20 seconds ... A new television series called *The Onedin Line* (with 40-year-old Peter Gilmore, 32-year-old Anne Stallybrass and 60-year-old Howard Lang) begins on BBC One on Friday evenings ... *The Goodies* episode 'Kitten Kong' airs for the first time, with a giant pussy cat terrorising the city of London ... TV presenter Eamonn Andrews surprises 25-year-old footballer Georgie Best on *This is Your Life* ... Hilda Ogden (played by 45-year-old Jean Alexander) wins £500 of premium bonds in ITV's ever popular soap-opera

Coronation Street ... 'Mah-na, mah-na. Doo-doo, doo-doo-doo' - 47-year-old Benny Hill stars in a new edition of *The Benny Hill Show* ... 43-year-old John Collin plays DS Cecil Haggar in BBC's long-running police drama *Z Cars* ... Miss Marple features in *Nemesis* - the latest 'whodunit' novel from 81-year-old crime-writer Agatha Christie ... "Till the moon deserts the sky, till all the seas run dry, till then I'll worship you" - ***Till*** by 31-year-old Tom Jones is number two in the weekly pop chart ... ***Banks Of The Ohio*** by 23-year-old Olivia Newton-John is number six ... Modern food branding takes a step forward ... *Wotsits* are a new type of crisps ... *Golden Nuggets* are a new type of breakfast cereal.

Winter 1971 - 1972

Ernie had a rival, an evil looking man

'Everybody Out!' - Strikes at British Leyland ... Strikes at Ford ... Strikes at hundreds of engineering factories across the country ... 'Flushed with Success! The Carry On team carries on round the bend!' - *Carry On at Your Convenience* is now showing at cinemas, with 45-year-old Kenneth Williams as W.C. Boggs and 58-year-old Sid 'cor blimey' James as Sid Plummer ... ***Diamonds Are Forever*** ("... They are all I need to please me. They can stimulate and tease me") - 34-year-old Shirley Bassey sings the theme song as 41-year-old Sean Connery returns as James Bond (aka 007) in the movie, *Diamonds Are Forever.* 43-year-old Jimmy Dean plays Willard Whyte. 31-year-old Jill St John is (Bond girl) Tiffany Case. 22-year-old Lola Larson is Bambi. 23-year-old Trina Parks is Thumper ... 21-year-old Susan George from Surbiton stars alongside Dustin Hoffman in *Straw Dogs* ... 19-year-old twins Mary and Madeleine Collinson from Malta star alongside Peter Cushing in *Twins of Evil* - an 'X' rated Hammer horror film ... "They'd call us..." ***Gypsies, Tramps And Thieves*** ("... but every night all the men would come around, and lay their money down") by 25-year-old Cher is number four in the pop chart ... "You're so sweet, you're so fine. I want you all and everything just to be mine, 'cause you're my babe" - ***Jeepster*** by T-Rex (with 24-year-old Marc Bolan) is number two ... 37-year-old *Blue Peter* presenter John Noakes informs viewers that the new border collie puppy will be called 'Shep' ... 21-year-old footballer Malcolm MacDonald scores twice as Newcastle Utd beat West Bromwich Albion 0-3 at the Hawthorns ... Freezing fog rolls across the Midlands and South-East ... People stay in and watch telly ... 44-year-old Roger Moore plays Lord Sinclair and 46-year-old Tony Curtis plays Daniel 'Danny' Wilde in *The Persuaders!* on ITV ... 37-year-old Wendy Craig stars in a new series of *And Mother Makes Three* ... 21-year-old Princess Anne is voted BBC's 'Sports Personality of the Year' after winning a major equestrian event ... 12-year-old Neil Reid from Glasgow scores the highest number of points on the 'clapometer' and also obtains the most public votes to win ITV's popular talent show *Opportunity Knocks* - singing *Mother Of Mine* ... Comedians 45-year-old Frank Carson, 40-year-old Les Dawson and double act Little and Large all appear on the Christmas special *Opportunity Knocks - All Winners Show* ... 'Very Urgent' - Monty Python's *Big Red Book* is on sale in all good bookshops ... Hallmark Records release *The Best of Top of the Pops '71* - a budget priced cover-version pop compilation LP with a buxom girl pictured on the sleeve ... 24-year-old David Bowie releases the *Hunky Dory* album with the tracks

Changes and ***Life On Mars?*** on side one ... 35-year-old Gordon Honeycombe reads the news for ITN ... Inflation is rising - it now stands at 8.6% ... 55-year-old prime-minister Edward Heath is under severe pressure because of the weak economy, rising unemployment and poor relations with the unions ... "Do you want pasteurised, 'cause pasteurised is best? She said 'Ernie, I'll be happy if it comes up to me chest'" - ***Ernie (The Fastest Milkman In The West)*** by 47-year-old Benny Hill climbs to number one on the hit parade - and stays there for four weeks ... "When the day is dawning, on a Texas Sunday morning" - ***Is This The Way To Amarillo*** by Tony Christie is number eighteen ... The Troubles continue in Northern Ireland ... A bomb explosion kills fifteen people in a Belfast bar ... Footballers 29-year-old Geoff Hurst and 26-year-old Martin Chivers score the goals for Sir Alf Ramsey's England team (G Banks, Madeley, Hughes, Bell, McFarland, Moore, F Lee, Ball, Chivers, G Hurst, Peters) in a 2-0 victory over Greece ... Frank O'Farrell's Manchester Utd remain top of Division One with a 3-2 victory over Nottingham Forest ... 36-year-old Brian Clough's Derby County move up to second with a 2-0 win against Everton ... 27-year-old Franny Lee scores for Manchester City in a 1-3 away win at Stoke City ... 26-year-old Alan Ball leaves Everton and joins Arsenal for a new record transfer fee of £220,000 ... Parents take their kids to the cinema to see the latest Disney film - *Bedknobs and Broomsticks*, and to eat snacks ... *Hula-Hoops* from KP are new ... Christmas morning arrives ... *Klackers*, *Lego*, *Etch-A-Sketch*, *Fuzzy-Felts* and orange bouncy *Space Hoppers* keep the children happy ... The new *Mastermind* board game (where the aim is for one player to deduce the correct sequence of colours of his opponents four hidden pegs) is also popular ... Excited schoolboys play with Matchbox *Superfast* 'double-loop' race sets and Corgi *Whizzwheels* 'rockets' tracks ... 41-year-old Rolf Harris *Meets the Kids in Hospital* on BBC One ... 42-year-old pianist and conductor Andre Previn is a guest star on the *Morecambe & Wise Show* in the evening. During the program - Previn criticises Eric Morecambe for playing all the wrong musical notes. The 45-year-old comedian responds by saying, "I am playing all the *right* notes, but not *necessarily* in the right order" ... 52-year-old Sir Derek Ezra is the new chairman of the National Coal Board ... Production has risen slightly in 1971 with 154 million tonnes of coal being mined, but there's unrest within the National Union of Mineworkers ... A demand for a 25% pay increase is rejected and miners embark on an overtime ban ... 29-year-old Richard Roundtree stars as funky detective John Shaft at cinemas ... "Who's the black private dick that's a sex machine to all the chicks? (Shaft!) You're damn right" - The ***Theme From 'Shaft'*** by 29-year-old Isaac Hayes is number four in the pop chart ... ***No Matter How I Try*** ("... I just can't say goodbye. No matter what you say, looks like I'm here to stay") by 25-year-old Gilbert O'Sullivan is number five ... Families sit at home, watching telly and enjoying food snacks ... A packet of *Golden Wonder* crisps is 3 new pence ... A bar of Cadbury's *Old Jamaica* costs 9 new pence ... The average price of a house in the UK is now over £5,000 ... "Coo-ee! Mr. Shifter!" - the chimpanzees move a piano in a TV advert for *PG Tips* ... Coal miners go on strike ... Nationwide power cuts plunge the country into darkness ... Schools and businesses are forced to close ... 55-year-old prime-minister Edward Heath declares a State of Emergency ... Three-thousand workers are laid-off at British Leyland's Longbridge factory after two-hundred engine inspectors walk out on strike ... Unemployment tops one million for the first time in thirty years ... Frugal housewives carry out the 'weekly shop' at supermarkets ... A loaf of bread is 10p ... A pint of milk is 5p ... A small jar of *Maxwell House* coffee is 25p ... A tub of *Stork* margarine is 11½p ... A can of *Coca-Cola* is 6½p ... ***I'd Like To Teach The World To Sing (In Perfect Harmony)*** ("... I'd like to hold it in my arms, and keep it company") by The New Seekers spends four weeks at the top of the hit parade ... Families book their summer holidays at the local travel agents ... 'Go Pontin!' - a chalet at one of *Pontin's* thirteen holiday centres around Britain is available from just £13.50 per person, per week ... 'Well-to-do' middle-class families also book their summer holidays at the travel agents ... 'Pontinental' - a week in Torremolinos costs £55 per person ... "Mother of mine, you gave to me, all of my life to do as I please. I owe everything I have to you, mother, sweet..." ***Mother Of Mine*** by 12-year-old *Opportunity Knocks* winner Neil Reid is number two in the pop chart ... ***Softly Whispering I Love You*** by The Congregation is number four ... 58-year-old Sid 'cor blimey' James, 43-year-old Diana Coupland and

21-year-old Sally Geeson star in a new series of sit-com *Bless This House* on ITV ... "What's got four legs, walks peculiar, talks with all the choicest words? What's got four arms, loves to grab you? Answer is, two Liver Birds" - 30-year-old Polly James and 30-year-old Nerys Hughes star as Beryl and Sandra in a new series of *The Liver Birds* on BBC One ... 46-year-old Richard Baker presents the *Nine O'Clock News* ... Prime-minister Edward Heath travels to Brussels to sign a treaty binding Britain to Europe - and gets doused in ink by a German protestor ... 'End the Common Market!' - demonstrators take to the streets of Britain urging the government to think again and alter its course ... 11-year-old schoolboy Ian Hislop from Swansea reads the Sunday newspapers ... ***Something Tells Me (Something Is Gonna Happen Tonight)*** by 28-year-old Cilla Black is number three in the pop chart ... ***Tokoloshe Man*** by 26-year-old John Kongos moves down four places to number eleven ... The miners' strike continues ... 37-year-old picket Freddie Matthews is killed when a lorry mounts the pavement outside a power station in Lincolnshire ... 34-year-old Arthur Scargill leads thousands of miners against the police at Saltley in Birmingham, and forces the closure of a large coke depot ... Power cuts continue and families huddle around candles in cold, dim living rooms ... The Troubles in Northern Ireland reach a tragic low point on Bloody Sunday when soldiers of the British Army kill thirteen unarmed people in Derry. A fourteenth person dies four months later ... 48-year-old Jack Scott presents the weather forecast on BBC One ...

It's generally cold, wet and windy ... A film version of Dylan Thomas' *Under Milk Wood* (starring Richard Burton, Peter O'Toole and 39-year-old Elizabeth Taylor) is at cinemas ... 'Being the adventures of a young man whose principle interests are rape, ultra-violence and Beethoven' - Stanley Kubrick's ('X' rated) *A Clockwork Orange* is also now showing ... 30-year-old Fred West marries 18-year-old Rosemary Letts at Gloucester Register Office ... "Ohhh, Soley, Soley. Soley, Soley. So lay, so lay" - ***Soley Soley*** by Middle Of The Road is number five on the hit parade ... "I can't remember if I cried, when I read about his widowed bride. Something touched me deep inside, the day the music died" - ***American Pie*** by 26-year-old Don McLean is number two ... 25-year-old Manchester Utd footballer 'super' Georgie Best fails to turn up for training after his team loses 3-0 to West Ham at Upton Park and manager Frank O'Farrell drops him from the side ... Best spends the evening at *Tramp* discotheque in London - drinking Champagne with his 19-year-old girlfriend, Carolyn Moore (aka Miss Great Britain) ... 36-year-old writer David Nobbs pens humorous scripts and one-line gags for the new series of *Sez Les* on ITV ... 5-year-old Andrew Lovell spends his first day at St. Joseph's school in Rugeley ... Many school children are now being taught with 'The Wide Range Readers' blue and green books ... *Ken Dodd and the Diddymen* and *The Basil Brush Show* keep young TV viewers entertained on Sunday afternoons - before *Songs of Praise* begins ... ***Morning Has Broken*** ("... like the first morning. Blackbird has spoken, like the first bird") by Cat Stevens is number nine in the pop chart ... "I've been through the desert on a..." ***Horse With No Name*** by America is number three ... 25-year-old footballer 'super' Georgie Best returns to the Manchester Utd team and scores twice in a 4-1 win victory over Southampton at Old Trafford ... 28-year-old footballer Ronnie Radford scores a 'screamer' as non-league Hereford knock First Division Newcastle Utd out of the FA Cup ... 21-year-old Charlie George scores twice as Bertie Mee's Arsenal beat John Harris' Sheffield Utd 0-5 at Bramall Lane ... 29-year-old Alan Hinton scores twice as Brian Clough's Derby County thrash Matt Gillies' Nottingham Forest 4-0 in front of 31,801 at the Baseball Ground ... ***I Just Can't Help Believing*** ("... when she's lying close beside me, and my heart beats with the rhythm of her sighs. This time the girl is gonna stay. This time the girl is gonna stay, for more than just a day") by 37-year-old Elvis Presley is number six in the pop chart ... "Oh, I got a brand new pair of roller skates, you got a..." ***Brand New Key*** by 24-year-old Melanie is number four ... 45-year-old disc jockey Jimmy Savile is awarded an OBE ... Seven people are killed when an IRA car-bomb explodes at an army base in Aldershot ... 22-year-old Alex 'Hurricane' Higgins wins £400 in the *Park Drive* World Snooker Championship - beating John Spencer by 37 frames to 32 in the final at Selly Park British Legion in Birmingham ... 49-year-old Nicholas Parsons presents *Sale of the Century* - an exciting new TV game-show from Norwich ... The hugely popular *Upstairs Downstairs* (with 37-year-old Jean Marsh as Rose, 67-year-old Angela Baddeley as Mrs. Bridges and

48-year-old Gordon Jackson as Hudson) is now being broadcast in colour ... A new series of *Steptoe and Son* begins on BBC One with 46-year-old Harry H. Corbett and 59-year-old Wilfrid Brambell. 45-year-old Leonard Rossiter makes a guest appearance in episode seven - playing an escaped convict ... *Fingerbobs* with Yoffi is new for the children ... Glam rock thumps out (in stereo) from ITT *KP-821* record players ... "Telegram Sam, Telegram Sam, you're my main man" - T-Rex (with 24-year-old Marc Bolan) achieve their third number one hit with ***Telegram Sam*** ... "Hey, hey, hey, hey what you doin' to me? Hey, hey, hey..." ***Look Wot You Dun*** by Slade (with 25-year-old Noddy Holder) is number four ... 38-year-old Michael Caine stars alongside 39-year-old Elizabeth Taylor in *Zee and Co.* at cinemas ... 27-year-old footballer Franny Lee scores a hat-trick for Malcolm Allison's high-flying Manchester City in a 5-2 victory over Wolverhampton Wanderers at Maine Road. The win keeps City at the top of Division One, closely followed by Leeds Utd, Derby County and Liverpool ... 20-year-old Steve Perryman is on the score-sheet for Tottenham Hotspur in a 2-0 win against Manchester Utd ... 21-year-old Malcolm 'Supermac' MacDonald is on the score-sheet for Newcastle Utd in a 2-0 win against Leicester City ... A top-of-the-table Third Division clash between Vic Crowe's Aston Villa and John Bond's Bournemouth draws a crowd of 48,110. Villa achieve a 2-1 victory with goals from 30-year-old Geoff Vowden and 30-year-old Andy Lochhead ... Power cuts continue ... High streets are in darkness ... Shops run out of candles and paraffin ... 54-year-old Joe Gormely of the National Union of Mineworkers negotiates with 55-year-old prime-minister Edward Heath (over beer and sandwiches) at 10 Downing Street ... After seven weeks of strike action - the miners return to work with a 20% pay rise and a 'shopping list' of other demands fully met ... 35-year-old burglar Donald Nielson (aka the Black Panther) breaks into a sub-post office at Haywood in Lancashire and guns down postmaster Leslie Richardson ... Chelsea football supporters invade the pitch at Brisbane Road when 21-year-old Barry Fairbrother scores a last minute winner for Orient in the fifth round of the FA Cup ... In Division One, 21-year-old Kevin Keegan scores a goal as Bill Shankly's Liverpool move to the-top-of-the-table with a 3-0 victory over Manchester City ... 22-year-old centre-back Martin Buchan transfers from Aberdeen to Manchester Utd for £125,000 ... "Son of my father, molded I was folded I was preform packed. Son of my father, commanded I was branded in a plastic vac. Surrounded and confounded by statistic facts" - ***Son Of My Father*** by Chicory Tip is new at number one in the pop chart ... ***Have You Seen Her*** ("... Tell me, have you seen her?") by The Chi-Lites is number three ... Tony the Tiger advertises *Frosties* on TV - "They're g-r-r-r-eat!"

Spring 1972

Blue is the colour, football is the game

The Troubles continue in Northern Ireland ... 55-year-old prime-minister Edward Heath imposes direct rule on the province and sends more troops to patrol the streets of Belfast ... ***Got To Be There*** by 13-year-old Michael Jackson is number five in the pop chart ... ***Beg, Steal Or Borrow*** by The New Seekers climbs to number two ... Tony Waddington's Stoke City football team (with Mike Pejic, Denis Smith, Terry Conroy, Jimmy Greenhoff, John Ritchie and 34-year-old goalkeeper Gordon Banks) defeats Dave Sexton's Chelsea (with Ron 'Chopper' Harris, John Hollins, David Webb, Peter 'Ossie' Osgood, Alan Hudson and 30-year-old goalkeeper Peter 'the cat' Bonetti) by two goals to one in the League Cup final ... "Blue is the colour. Football is the game. We're all together and winning is our aim" - ***Blue Is The Colour*** by The Chelsea Football Team moves down the pop chart ... 18-year-old office junior Matthew Harding makes cups of tea at a firm of insurance brokers in London - and holds ambitions to become a successful businessman ... 11-year-old schoolboy William Hague from Rotherham completes his homework - and holds ambitions to become a politician ... A brand new comedy show begins on Radio Four called *I'm Sorry I Haven't A Clue.* 29-year-old Graeme Garden, 34-year-old Jo Kendall, 30-year-old Bill Oddie and 31-year-old Tim Brooke-Taylor are the stars. 37-year-old Barry Cryer is chairman for the first show. 50-year-old Humphrey Lyttelton then takes over in the hot seat for subsequent programs ... "Hey Mr. Dream Seller, where have you been?" - ***Meet Me On The Corner*** by Lindisfarne is number five in the pop chart ... ***It's One Of Those Nights*** by The Partridge Family (with 21-year-old heart-throb David Cassidy) climbs to number eleven ... A craze for yoga sweeps the nation ... Middle-aged folk sit cross legged on the floor and contemplate life ... Fashionable young people head off to the pub wearing flared jeans and cheese-cloth shirts - many with a yellow 'smiley face' badge sewn onto the rear pocket of their denim jeans ... Star footballer 'super' Georgie Best scores in a 2-1 win for Manchester Utd against Huddersfield Town ... The race to become champions of Division One is being contested by four teams: Manchester City, Derby County, Leeds Utd and Liverpool. Just three points separates the clubs with six games still to play ... Eamonn Andrews surprises 34-year-old England goalkeeper Gordon Banks on ITV's *This is Your Life* ... 47-year-old Kenneth Kendall reads the news on BBC One ... A motorway pile-up involving two-hundred vehicles on the M1 near Luton claims the lives of nine people and injures dozens more ... 27-year-old Detective Sergeant Derek Ridgewell of the British Transport Police arrests four innocent black men at Oval Tube station in London ... "I can't live, if living is..." ***Without You*** by 30-year-old Nilsson climbs to the top of the pop chart - and stays there for five weeks! ... ***Mother And Child Reunion*** by 30-year-old Paul Simon reaches number five ... Crowds flock to cinemas to see a new feature-length film version of the popular comedy *Steptoe & Son* - in which Harold (Harry H. Corbett) marries a stripper, and Old Man Steptoe (Wilfrid Brambell) does his best to break up the happy couple ... 19-year-old Nina Carter (34C) from Solihull is a popular new page three girl in *The Sun* newspaper ... *Cosmopolitan* magazine is new - and contains the feature, 'How to turn a man on when he's having problems in bed' ... 51-year-old Chancellor of the Exchequer Anthony Barber delivers his second Budget for Edward Heath's Conservative government ... Sweeping cuts are made in income tax ... Huge tax concessions are given to industry ... It's a high-risk budget designed to deliver immediate growth in the economy and to reverse rising unemployment ... Builders and labourers go on strike demanding higher pay and better conditions ... Flying pickets move in - and occupy construction sites around the country ... ***Hold Your Head Up*** ("... high") by Argent is number five in the pop chart ... "I want to live. I want to give. I've been a miner for a heart of gold. It's these expressions I never give, that keep me searchin' for a..." ***Heart Of Gold*** by 26-year-old Neil Young is number ten ... American spacecraft *Apollo 16* (with astronauts: John Young, Tom Mattingly and Charles Duke) lands on the Moon and stays for three days ... "And I think it's gonna be a long, long time, till touch down brings me round again to find, I'm not the man they think I am at home. Oh, no, no, no" - ***Rocket Man*** by 25-year-old Elton John reaches number two in the pop chart ... *Apollo 16* makes a safe return to Earth - splashing down successfully in the Pacific Ocean ... Back in England - 36-year-old footballer Jack Charlton scores a goal on his 600th appearance for Leeds Utd in a 1-0 victory over Coventry City at Elland Road ... 27-year-old maverick footballer Rodney Marsh leaves Queens Park Rangers and joins high-flying Manchester City for £200,000. (Marsh scores his first two goals for City in a 3-1 win against West Ham Utd) ... With just four matches remaining, City are equal on points with Liverpool, one point behind Leeds Utd and two points behind Division One leaders Derby County ... New TV drama *The Brothers* (with Jean Anderson as Mary Hammond, Glyn Owen as Edward Hammond, Richard Easton as Brian Hammond, Robin Chadwick as David Hammond and 27-year-old Gabrielle Drake as Jill Williams) grips the nation on Friday evenings ... Emily Nugent (played by 40-year-old Eileen Derbyshire) marries Ernest Bishop (played by 46-year-old Stephen Hancock) in ITV's ever popular soap-opera *Coronation Street* ... "You bloody nig-nog!" - 40-year-old Jack Smedhurst is Eddie 'Honky' Booth and 32-year-old Rudolph Walker is Bill 'Chalky' Reynolds in *Love Thy Neighbour* ... "Oh, come on. Stop messin' about" - 46-year-old Kenneth Williams, 50-year-old Hattie Jacques and 34-year-old Barbara Windsor (36-23-34) star in *Carry*

On Matron at cinemas ... "Ask yourself one question, 'Do I feel lucky?' Well do ya punk?" - 41-year-old Clint Eastwood stars in *Dirty Harry* ... ***Saturday Night At The Movies*** ("... who cares what picture you see?") by The Drifters is number three in the pop chart ... ***Sweet Talking Guy*** by The Chiffons is number four ... Footballers 25-year-old 'super' Georgie Best and 34-year-old Bobby Charlton are on the score-sheet for Frank O'Farrell's Manchester Utd in a 3-0 victory over Stoke City. Utd finish the season in eighth position ... Brian Clough's Derby County defeat Liverpool 1-0 in their final game of the season, and 'The Rams' are champions of Division One - but only just! Colin Boulton, Ron Webster, John Robson, Roy McFarland, Colin Todd, Alan Durban, Terry Hennessey, Archie Gemmill, John O'Hare, Kevin Hector, John McGovern and 29-year-old top scorer Alan Hinton have all been outstanding. Just one point separates Derby from three other teams: Don Revie's hard-tackling Leeds Utd (with Sprake, Reaney, Charlton, Hunter, Cooper, Bremner, Madeley, Lorimer, Clarke, Giles, Jones and Gray); Bill Shankly's Liverpool (with Clemence, Lawler, Lloyd, Hughes, Lindsay, Smith, Ross, Hall, Whitham, Keegan, Heighway, Toshack and Callaghan); and Malcolm Allison's Manchester City (with Corrigan, Book, Doyle, Booth, Oakes, Donachie, Summerbee, Bell, Davies, Lee, Mellor, Towers and Marsh) ... 31-year-old John Craven presents *John Craven's Newsround* - a new (twice-weekly) TV program for sensible children ... 11-year-old schoolboy William Hague from Rotherham watches avidly, then completes his homework ...

Amazing Grace by The Pipes and Drums and Military Band of the Royal Scots Dragoon Guards spends five weeks at number one on the hit parade ... People purchase the latest 7-inch singles at *Woolworths* for 50 new pence ... "Could it be forever, or is my mind just rambling on? Touched you once, kissed you once, now I feel like you're mine" - ***Could It Be Forever / Cherish*** by 22-year-old heart-throb David Cassidy is number two in the pop chart ... "We may as well go home, as I did on my own..." ***Alone Again (Naturally)*** by 25-year-old Gilbert O'Sullivan is number three ... Bomb disposal experts from the SAS and Royal Marines are scrambled to deal with a bomb scare on board the *QE2* ocean liner as the luxury vessel is sailing between New York and Southampton. No explosives are found. The incident is a hoax ... 25-year-old footballer Allan 'sniffer' Clarke scores the only goal as Leeds Utd beat Bertie Mee's Arsenal 1-0 in the FA Cup final. 29-year-old Billy Bremner (captain of the 'All Whites') lifts the famous silver trophy. A ticket for the standing enclosure at the Empire Stadium in Wembley costs £1.00 ... 41-year-old Roy Sproson plays his final game for Port Vale - a 1-2 defeat against Rotherham Utd in Division Three ... Martin Chivers scores twice and Alan Mullery scores once as Bill Nicholson's Tottenham Hotspur beat Bill McGarry's Wolverhampton Wanderers 3-2 on aggregate over two legs to win the UEFA Cup ... "Wake up, meat head. Don't pretend that you are dead. Get yourself up off the cart" - ***Back Off Boogaloo*** by 31-year-old Ringo Starr is number two on the hit parade ... 27-year-old maverick striker Rodney

Marsh, 26-year-old Colin Bell and 24-year-old Emlyn Hughes score the goals (and 22-year-old centre-forward Malcolm 'Supermac' MacDonald makes his debut) for Sir Alf Ramsey's England team in a 0-3 victory over Wales at Ninian Park. England's full line-up for the match is: G Banks, Madeley, Hughes, Storey, McFarland, Moore, Summerbee, Bell, MacDonald, Marsh and Hunter ... ***Stir It Up*** ("... little darling") by 31-yearold Johnny Nash is number thirteen in the pop chart ... "Oh..." ***Deborah*** ("... always look like a zeb-o-ra") by Tyrannosaurus Rex is number seven ... The final section of M6 motorway opens - linking 'Spaghetti Junction' with the existing carriageway - and motorists can now travel uninterrupted for 226 miles between Rugby and Carlisle ... The Triumph *Dolomite* motorcar has a top speed of 100 mph and accelerates from 0-60 mph in 11.3 seconds. The popular car (known affectionately as the 'dolly') costs £1,399 (plus delivery) and comes with fully reclining front seats as standard ... More and more foreign cars are being sold in the UK ... The latest Datsun *100A Cherry* costs £765.63 (plus delivery) and comes with hazard warning lights and two speed wipers ... Fashion conscious home owners install multi coloured 'crazy paving' on their driveways ... 33-year-old disc jockey Terry Wogan leaves Radio One to become the new host of Radio Two's breakfast show ... 44-year-old Alan 'Fluff' Freeman replaces Wogan at Radio One ("Not 'arf!") ... ***Come What May*** ("... I will love you forever, and forever my heart belongs to you") by 22-year-old Vicky Leandros is number two in the pop chart ... "You can't see it with your eyes, hold it in your hand, but like the wind it covers our land. Strong enough to move the heart of any man, this thing called love" - ***A Thing Called Love*** by 40-year-old Johnny Cash is number four ... 25-year-old Lesley Judd is a new presenter on BBC One's children program *Blue Peter* ... Ford launches the *Consul* and *Granada* range of motorcars as a replacement for the ageing *Zephyr* and *Zodiac*. The new 2000cc *Consul* has a top speed of 92 mph and accelerates from 0-60 mph in 16.5 seconds. The new 2500cc *Granada* has a top speed of 106 mph and accelerates from 0-60 mph in 11.6 seconds ... Prince Edward, Duke of Windsor, dies aged 77 in Paris. The duke's wife, 75-year-old Wallis, Duchess of Windsor, is at his side ... Back in England - a twenty-foot tall statue of King Kong is erected near the Bull Ring in Birmingham ... Recently married couple Fred and Rosemary West move into a house at 25 Cromwell Street in Gloucester ... *Texas Homecare* 'Do-It-Yourself' stores are new ... Woodchip wallpaper is all the rage ... "Can you ride tandem?" - The *PG Tips* chimpanzees are back on ITV.

Summer 1972

Jesus Christ, Superstar

The sun shines ... Girls wear hotpants ... Boys strip to the waist and swim in rivers ... *Shandy Bass* is a refreshing new drink ... Discarded ring-pulls from drinks cans litter public parks and communal spaces ... "He rocks in the tree tops all day long, hoppin' and a-boppin' and singing his song" - ***Rockin' Robin*** by 13-year-old Michael Jackson is number three in the pop chart ... ***Oh Babe, What Would You Say*** by 48-year-old Hurricane Smith is number four ... The funeral of Prince Edward, the Duke of Windsor, takes place at the Frogmore burial ground near Windsor Castle. Queen Elizabeth II, the Duke of Edinburgh, Prince Charles, Edward Heath and a small number of other distinguished guests gather to pay their respects - alongside 75-year-old Wallis, the Duchess of Windsor ... Children break up from school ... *The Adventures of Robinson Crusoe* - a black and white TV program (first shown in 1965) is broadcast during the summer holiday ... "Down in the meadow where the wind blows free, in the middle of a field stands a lightning tree. It's limbs all torn from the day it was born, for the tree was born in a thunderstorm. Grow, grow, the lightning tree. It's never too late for you and me" - a second series of *Follyfoot* is on ITV ... The sun continues to shine ... White dog poo is seen on pavements ... Boys play with pen-knives ... Girls play with *Klackers* ... Raleigh introduces the *Tomahawk* bicycle ... "Metal guru is it you? Metal guru is it you? Sitting there in your armour plated chair" - ***Metal Guru*** by T-Rex is top of the pop chart - the record is the group's fourth number one hit ... ***Song Sung Blue*** ("... everybody knows one") by 31-year-old Neil Diamond is number fourteen ... David Bowie releases *The Rise and Fall of Ziggy Stardust and the Spiders from Mars* album, which peaks at number five ... Manchester Utd's 26-year-old 'super' Georgie Best announces his retirement from football whilst on holiday in Marbella. Six weeks later, Best changes his mind and says he'll continue playing for Utd ... 36-year-old jockey Lester Piggott rides *Roberto* to victory in the Epsom Derby ... Retail prices continue to rise ... 51-year-old Chancellor of the Exchequer Anthony Barber decides to float the pound. Almost immediately, sterling plummets in value ... Long-term price inflation has become a major threat to the economy ... The House of Commons votes in favour of Britain's entry into the European Common Market - membership will begin at the start of next year ... Industrial disputes continue ... More than two-thousand production workers walk out at British Leyland's Morris engine plant in Coventry ... Flying pickets hold up construction work as the builders' strike continues ... Dockworkers also come out on strike and there's fear of food shortages in shops ... 56-year-old Conservative prime-minister Edward Heath declares a State of Emergency - it's the second in just eight months ... 41-year-old Peter Woods reads the news on BBC One ... 14-year-old schoolgirl Judith Roberts is battered to death at Tamworth in Staffordshire ... "Starry, starry night. Paint your palette blue and grey. Look out on a summer's day, with eyes that know the darkness in my soul" - ***Vincent*** by Don McLean is new at number one in the pop chart ... ***I Can See Clearly Now*** ("... the rain has gone") by Johnny Nash is number five ... 24-year-old footballer Trevor Cherry leaves Huddersfield Town and joins Don Revie's hard-tackling Leeds Utd for £100,000 ... 30-year-old Geoff Hurst leaves West Ham Utd and joins Tony Waddington's Stoke City for £80,000 ... Cricketers 31-year-old Geoffrey Boycott and 34-year-old John Edrich stride out together to open the batting for England in the first Test against Ian Chappell's Australia at Old Trafford. Boycott scores 8 runs. Edrich makes 49 before being run out. 25-year-old all-rounder Tony Greig makes a half-century and England win the match by 89 runs. 27-year-old bowler Derek Underwood takes 6 for 45 in the fourth Test at Headingley, and 40-year-old captain Ray Illingworth scores 57 runs, as England gain the victory needed to retain the Ashes. G Boycott, J H Edrich, B W Luckhurst, B Wood, M J K Smith, P H Parfitt, B L D'Oliveira, K W R Fletcher, A W Greig, J H Hampshire, A P E Knott (wk), R Illingworth (cpt), J A Snow, N Gifford, G G Arnold, J S E Price and P Lever have all contributed to keeping the Ashes in England ... Conservative prime-minister Edward Heath makes changes to his Cabinet - Robert Carr takes over from Reg Maudling as Home Secretary ... Trade unions reject the prime-minister's wage restraint plan ... One-hundred and eighteen people die when *BEA* Flight 548 crashes near the town of Staines after taking off from Heathrow - an investigation into the accident concludes that pilot error was partly to blame ... 40-year-old Elizabeth Taylor stars alongside her 46-year-old husband Richard Burton in *Hammersmith is Out* at cinemas - the movie is not a huge success ... A repeat of *The Monkees* is broadcast on BBC One television on Friday evenings ... 8-year-old Jarvis Cocker from Sheffield dreams of one day becoming a famous popstar ... "Can you still recall, in the juke box hall, when the music played. And the world span round to a brand new sound in those far off days. In their blue-suede shoes they would scream and shout, as they sang the blues, let it all hang out. Rock 'n' ro-o-oll, rock 'n' roll!" - ***Rock And Roll (Parts 1 & 2)*** by 28-year-old Gary Glitter is number two in the pop chart ... "And it was alright, yeah it was alright" - ***Take Me Bak 'Ome*** by Slade (with 26-year-old Noddy Holder) spends a week at number one ... 29-year-old entertainer Freddie Starr makes the nation laugh with his hilarious impersonations of Elvis Presley, Mick Jagger, Norman Wisdom and Hitler on ITV's *Who Do You Do?* ... Window cleaner Stan Ogden (played by 57-year-old Bernard Youens) is accused of being a Peeping Tom in ITV's ever popular soap-opera *Coronation Street* ... Sandy Richardson (played by 26-year-old Roger Tonge) is in a coma after being critically injured in a car crash in *Crossroads* ... "'Cause Little Willy, Willy won't go home! But you can't push Willy 'round, Willy won't go" - ***Little Willy*** by The Sweet is number four in the pop chart ... 42-year-old Stuart Hall is the new presenter of *It's a Knockout* on BBC One. 57-year-old referee Arthur Ellis ensures fair play between the teams, and keeps order with his dipstick. Millions tune-in on Friday evenings to watch as a team from Salisbury gains a victory over a team from Exeter (by twelve points to nine) ... In the following weeks, a team from Banbury beats a team from Congleton (by twelve points to ten) ... A team from Folkestone beats a team from Canterbury (by thirteen points to seven) ... A team from Dalkeith beats a team from Lanark (by thirteen points to eight) ... A team from Lincoln beats a team from Nottingham (by fourteen points to eight) ... A team from Luton thrashes a team from Watford (by sixteen points to four) ... The Troubles continue in Northern Ireland ... The IRA plants twenty-two bombs at various locations around Belfast on Friday the twenty-first of July - killing nine people and injuring one-hundred and thirty ... "I've got a..." ***Silver Machine*** by Hawkwind reaches number three in the pop chart ... ***10538 Overture*** by the Electric Light Orchestra is number nine ... 'L' reg cars go on sale ... An Austin *Mini 1275 GT* costs £973 ... The new Ford *Consul 2000L* saloon costs £1,350 ... A vinyl roof is extra ... Jaguar announces the *XJ12* with a 5.3 litre engine and a top speed of 140 mph ... Four star leaded petrol is 35 new pence a gallon ... 45-year-old Jimmy Savile OBE is back on TV reminding motorists - "Clunk, click, every trip" ... Racing driver Jackie Stewart finishes second in the British Grand Prix at Brands Hatch in a Tyrrell-Ford. Emerson Fittipaldi from Brazil wins the race in a Lotus ... "And they called it puppy love, I guess they'll never know" - ***Puppy Love*** by 14-year-old Donny Osmond is a smash hit - the song stays at the top of the pop chart for five weeks! ... "Sylvia's mother says, Sylvia's busy, too busy to come to the phone. Sylvia's mother says, Sylvia's tryin' to start a new life of her own" - ***Sylvia's Mother*** by Dr. Hook and the Medicine Show is number two ... 32-year-old disc jockey John Peel presents *Sounds of the Seventies* on Radio One on Tuesday nights ... "There's a starman waiting in the sky, he'd like to come and meet us, but he thinks he'd blow our minds" - 25-year-old David Bowie performs ***Starman*** on *Top of the Pops* and becomes an instant figure of inspiration to thousands of confused teenagers ... 48-year-old Larry Grayson stars in *Shut That Door!* on ATV ... It's estimated that there are now 1.5 million colour TV sets in the UK. Most families rent from *Visionhire*, *Rediffusion*, *Radio Rentals* or the *Co-op* - where it costs around £80 a year to hire a 22-inch set ... The Munich Olympics are marred by a terrorist attack - which leads to the death of seventeen people including five Israeli athletes. The Games continue ... 33-year-old Mary Peters from Halewood wins a gold medal in the pentathlon ... 21-year-old Alan Minter from Crawley wins a bronze in boxing ... 25-year-old Brian Jacks from London wins a bronze in judo ... 18-year-old David Wilkie from Scotland wins a silver in swimming ... David Hemery, David Jenkins, Alan Pascoe and Martin Reynolds win silver in the 4x400m relay ... The musical ***Jesus Christ Superstar*** ("... do you think you're what they say you are?") debuts in the West End, with

27-year-old Paul Nicholas in the title role ... 46-year-old Rock Hudson stars alongside 26-year-old Susan Saint James in *McMillan and Wife* on TV ... 24-year-old footballer David Nish leaves Jimmy Bloomfield's Leicester City and joins Brian Clough's Derby County for a new record transfer fee of £225,000 ... 39-year-old Graham Parker presents the weather forecast on BBC One ... The sun shines ... A fresh breeze keeps temperatures cool ... "School's out for summer... ***School's out*** ("... for ever") by 24-year-old Alice Cooper moves to the top of the pop chart ... "Sunbathe now on the beach. Here is the man who sells ice-cream" - ***Sea Side Shuffle*** by Terry Dactyl and the Dinosaurs is number two ... The infectious instrumental ***Popcorn*** by Hot Butter climbs to number five ... Teenagers hang out at fun-fairs, and queue for a turn on the Parachutes ... Candyfloss costs 6p ... A toffee-apple is 8p ... The new football season gets underway ... 20-year-old centre-forward Joe Jordan scores his first league goals for Don Revie's hard-tackling Leeds Utd - netting twice in a 3-3 draw against Bobby Robson's Ipswich Town ... 27-year-old Alan Ball scores from the penalty spot as Bertie Mee's Arsenal defeat Ron Greenwood's West Ham Utd 1-0 at Highbury ... Adolescent boys find pornographic magazines in the bushes near canal tow-paths ... 'New Andrex goes a long, long way' - The 'Andrex' Labrador Retriever puppy is used for the first time in television adverts ... A pack of twenty Player's *No. 6* cigarettes costs 20½p ... A pint of mild in the Red Lion is 13p.

Autumn 1972

Hiawatha didn't bother too much

32-year-old John Craven presents *John Craven's Newsround* on BBC One on Tuesday and Thursday evenings ... Unemployment continues to rise and so does inflation ... A *Mars* bar costs 5 new pence ... A packet of spicy tomato *Snaps* (crisps) is 5 new pence ... A can of *Coca-Cola* is 7 new pence ... Property prices have also increased, with the average cost of a house now standing at over £6,000 ... 56-year-old prime-minister Edward Heath and his 52-year-old Chancellor of the Exchequer Anthony Barber call for a 'national crusade' against inflation ... Despite pressure from the unions, the government introduces statutory controls to restrict pay increases and hold retail prices ... Wages are frozen for ninety days ... Workers at Jaguar's car factory in Coventry go on strike for more money ... The builders' strike continues ... Twenty-four flying pickets are arrested in Shrewsbury and two of the men (34-year-old Des Warren from Chester and 33-year-old Ricky Tomlinson from Liverpool) are given prison sentences ... 25-year-old Newcastle Utd footballer Tony Green is injured in a match against Crystal Palace.

(It's an injury that will end Green's playing career) ... 21-year-old Kevin Keegan scores a penalty (and is man-of-the-match) as Bob Shankly's Liverpool thrash John Harris' Sheffield Utd 5-0 at Anfield ... ***All The Young Dudes*** ("... carry the news. Boog-a-loo dudes, carry the news") by Mott the Hoople is number three in the pop chart ... ***Layla*** ("... you've got me on my knees") by Derek and the Dominoes is number seven ... 'Keep Britain White' - 38-year-old John Tyndall becomes leader of the National Front. 28-year-old Martin Webster organises rallies for the extreme, right-wing fascist group ... A new series of *Love Thy Neighbour* is on ITV with 40-year-old Jack Smethurst as 'Chalky' and 33-year-old Rudolph Walker as 'Honky' ... Innocent men Winston Trew, Sterling Christie, Omar Boucher and George Griffiths (aka 'The Oval Four') are sentenced to two years in prison after being 'fitted-up' by bent copper DS Derek Ridgewell ... ***You Wear It Well*** ("... a little old fashioned but that's all right") by 27-year-old Rod Stewart spends a week at number one in the pop chart ... "What's her name..?" ***Virginia Plain*** by Roxy Music reaches number four ... A new series of *The Onedin Line* (with 41-year-old Peter Gilmore, 33-year-old Anne Stallybrass and 61-year-old Howard Lang) begins on BBC One ... Comedians 42-year-old Ronnie Barker and 41-year-old Ronnie Corbett play the roles of bumbling private detectives Piggy Malone and Charley Farley in the latest series of *The Two Ronnies* ... A new series of *Upstairs Downstairs* (with 38-year-old Jean Marsh as Rose, 68-year-old Angela Baddeley as Mrs. Bridges and

48-year-old Gordon Jackson as Hudson) begins on ITV ... 38-year-old Wendy Craig stars as Sally Harrison in *And Mother Makes Three* ... 19-year-old student Tony Blair goes up to Oxford to read Jurisprudence ... Girls (and boys!) wear glittery make-up and outlandish clothes - flares and platform shoes are very much in vogue ... "Don't stop now, ah c'mon. Another drop now, ah c'mon. I wanna lot now, so c'mon. That's right, that's right. I said... ***Mama Weer All Crazee Now*** by Slade (with 26-year-old Noddy Holder) is new at number one in the pop chart ... ***Wig-Wam Bam*** ("... gonna make you my man. Wam-bam bam, gonna get you if I can") by Sweet is number four ... 33-year-old racing driver Jackie Stewart wins the Canadian Grand Prix in a Tyrrell-Ford. 43-year-old Graham Hill is eighth in a Brabham-Ford ... Back in Britain - 22-year-old footballer Malcolm 'Supermac' MacDonald scores a hat-trick as Newcastle Utd beat Coventry City 0-3 at Highfield Road ... 28-year-old Martin Peters scores all four goals for Tottenham Hotspur in a 1-4 victory over Manchester Utd at Old Trafford ... 23-year-old centre-forward Stuart Pearson scores four goals as Hull City beat Portsmouth 5-1 in Division Two ... 20-year-old goalkeeper David Icke keeps a clean sheet as Hereford Utd beat Aldershot 1-0 in Division Four ... Teenage boys play conkers ... Teenage girls hang glossy posters of David Cassidy on their bedroom walls ... ***How Can I Be Sure*** ("... I really, really, really wanna know. I really, really, really wanna know") - the latest single from the 22-year-old heart-throb climbs to number one - and stays at the top of the pop chart for two weeks ... ***John, I'm Only Dancing*** ("... She turns me on") by 25-year-old David Bowie peaks at number twelve ... 25-year-old entrepreneur Alan Sugar changes the name of his thriving electrical company to A. M. S. Trading (Amstrad) ... *Access* credit cards are new ... Conservative prime-minister Edward Heath meets with his ambitious Minister for Education and Science, 46-year-old Margaret Thatcher, at Number 10 Downing Street ... The school leaving age is raised from 15 to 16 ... "Up above the streets and houses, rainbow climbing high. Everyone can see it smiling over the sky. Paint the whole world with a..." *Rainbow*, with Bungle the Bear and 32-year-old David Cook, is a new program for children on ITV ... The fifth series of *Dad's Army* begins on BBC One on Friday evenings. The opening episode sees Captain Mainwaring's home-guard platoon trapped inside a pumping station ... Television soap-operas are hugely popular ... Sandy Richardson comes out of his coma in ATV's *Crossroads* - but is now confined to a wheelchair ... Yorkshire Television broadcasts the first episode of *Emmerdale Farm* and introduces the characters Annie Sugden (played by 53-year-old Sheila Mercier), Joe Sugden (28-year-old Frazer Hines) and Amos Brearly (52-year-old Ronald Magill) ... ***Mouldy Old Dough*** by Lieutenant Pigeon climbs to number one in the pop chart - and stays at the top for four weeks ... "No, you won't fool the..." ***Children Of The Revolution*** by T-Rex reaches number two ... Thomas and Peggy Gallagher of Longsight in Manchester are proud parents of newborn son, Liam - a little brother for 5-year-old Noel ... 17-year-old soldier Andrew Evans is charged with the murder of schoolgirl Judith Roberts in Tamworth ... Forty-two football hooligans are arrested at a Second Division football match between Nottingham Forest and Aston Villa ... Seventy-five football hooligans are arrested at a First Division match between Manchester Utd and Liverpool ... "Clair, the moment I met you, I swear. I felt as if something, somewhere, had happened to me, which I couldn't see" - ***Clair*** by 25-year-old Gilbert O'Sullivan is top of the hit parade ... ***I'm Stone In Love With You*** by The Stylistics climbs to number nine ... 40-year-old Reginald Bosanquet reads the news for ITN ... Iceland extends its territorial fishing waters around its shoreline to fifty nautical miles. (Previously, it was twelve). British trawlers continue to operate in the disputed zone and political tensions rise between prime-minister Edward Heath and Kristjan Eldjarn the president of Iceland. The 'Cod Wars' begin when an Icelandic gunboat chases sixteen British and German trawlers from the area ... "I've started so I'll finish" - 42-year-old Magnus Magnusson presents *Mastermind* on TV ... 39-year-old Barry Norman presents the late night movie review program *Film 72* on BBC One ... "I'm gonna make him an offer he can't refuse..." 48-year-old Marlon Brando stars as Don Vito Corleone in *The Godfather* at cinemas ... *The Joy Of Sex* - a gourmet guide to lovemaking is now available in book shops - the popular publication features graphic lined-drawings of a bearded (ape-like) man performing sex acts with a dark haired woman ... Mrs. Slocombe tells tales about her pussy in a new TV comedy called *Are You Being Served?* ... 49-year-old Eric Sykes and 50-year-old Hattie Jacques star in a new series of *Sykes* on BBC One ... *The Adventures of Black Beauty*, with 18-year-old Judi Bowker as Vicky, begins on ITV ... Labour MP Jack McCann dies aged 61 - triggering a by-election in Rochdale. 44-year-old Liberal Cyril Smith (29 stone) wins the seat, with a five-thousand majority over Lawrence Cunliffe the Labour candidate. Jim Merrick (chairman of the British Campaign to Stop Immigration) comes last ... "My ding-a-ling, my ding-a-ling, I want you to play with..." ***My Ding-A-Ling*** by 46-year-old Chuck Berry is new at number one in the pop chart ... "Crazy horses (Wah! Wah!)" - ***Crazy Horses*** by The Osmonds is number two ... 33-year-old Jackie Stewart wins the American Grand Prix in a dark blue (Elf sponsored) Tyrrell-Ford racing car ... *Matchbox* die-cast model toys bring out a futuristic wedge shaped car called the *Soopa Coopa* ... 22-year-old boxer Joe Bugner defeats Jurgen Blin in eight rounds at Wembley to become the new European heavy-weight champion ... 34-year-old Stoke City and England goalkeeper Gordon Banks is injured in a car crash after losing control of his Ford *Consul*. (24-year-old Ray Clemence of Liverpool will take over for the next international game)... 23-year-old striker Mick Channon makes his debut for Sir Alf Ramsey's England team against Yugoslavia - the match ends in a 1-1 draw ... 21-year-old Kevin Keegan makes his debut for England against Wales - the match ends in a 1-0 victory to England, with Colin Bell scoring the winning goal ... 24-year-old Stan Bowles transfers from Second

Division Carlisle Utd to Second Division Queens Park Rangers for £110,000 ... 22-year-old speedy winger Dave Thomas also joins QPR - signing from Burnley for £165,000... "I'll say... ***Goodbye To Love*** ("... No one ever cared if I should live or die. Time and time again the chance for love has passed me by, and all I know of love, is how to live without it") by The Carpenters is number nine in the pop chart ... "I met him at the candy store. He turned around and smiled at me. You get the picture? That's when I fell for the..." ***Leader Of The Pack*** by The Shangri-Las is number three ... Frank O'Farrell's Manchester Utd football team (with 35-year-old Bobby Charlton, 32-year-old Denis Law, 26-year-old 'super' Georgie Best, and new signings 30-year-old Wyn Davis and 25-year-old Ted MacDougall) is struggling near the bottom of Division One after a 3-0 defeat to Malcolm Allison's Manchester City ... Bill Shankly's Liverpool are top, after 26-year-old Peter Cormack scores the only goal in a 1-0 victory over Harry Catterick's Everton ... Second Division Sunderland sack manager Alan Brown and appoint Bob Stokoe ... "If you're the tallest, the smallest, if you beat them all" - *Record Breakers* with 40-year-old Roy Castle, and 47-year-old twin brothers Norris and Noel McWhirter, is on TV ... Hartley the Hare is up to no good in *Inigo Pipkin* ... Cheeky 41-year-old comedian Les Dawson is up to no good in the latest series of *Sez Les* ... Sunday drivers take to the roads at weekends as families enjoy a spin in the motorcar ... A new Austin *1100* has a top speed of 80 mph and can accelerate from 0-60 mph in 19.7 seconds ... "If you mix cross-ply and radial tyres on the same axel, or use cross-ply on the rear, when you've radials on the front, you might not live to regret it!" - a short, hard-hitting public information film for motorists is shown on TV ... 33-year-old Roger Clark wins the RAC Rally in a Ford *Escort* (registration LVX 942J) ... The three-millionth *Mini* motorcar rolls off the production line at Longbridge, and British Leyland chairman, Lord Stokes, drives it to the Earls Court Motor Show as a publicity stunt ... ***Gudbuy T' Jane*** ("... Gudbuy t' Jane. She's a dark horse, see if she can") by Slade (with 26-year-old Noddy Holder) is number two in the pop chart ... "I remember when rock was young. Me and Susie had so much fun" - ***Crocodile Rock*** by 25-year-old Elton John is number five ... Schools organise coach trips ... Children trudge around Blackpool Zoo (with a packed lunch), looking at the monkeys ... 26-year-old footballer 'super' Georgie Best scores a goal for Manchester Utd in a 2-2 draw against Leicester City. Frank O'Farrell's Utd team remains at the bottom of the league, and relegation is looking increasingly likely ... Millions of people enjoy a night in, watching telly ... Eamonn Andrews surprises 49-year-old Pat Phoenix (who plays Elsie Howard in ITV's soap-opera *Coronation Street*) on *This is Your Life* ... 37-year-old Rod Hull and his uncontrollable puppet, Emu, appear in front of the Queen Mother at the Royal Variety Show ... Middle-class people enjoy a night in, with a good book ... Popular fictional detective Hercule Poirot features in *Elephants Can Remember* - the latest 'whodunit' novel from 82-year-old crime-writer Agatha Christie ... Working class men enjoy an evening out at the cinema ... Actresses 28-year-old Gabrielle Drake and 20-year-old Me Me Lay appear stark naked in *Au Pair Girls* ... A pair of *Wilkinson Sword* garden shears cost £2.75 at hardware shops ... "She flies like a bird in the sky" - adverts say, '*Nimble* - real bread but lighter' ... A return flight from London to New York on *BOAC* costs £85.05.

Winter 1972 - 1973

A very merry Christmas and a happy new year

Mornings are cold and frosty ... Green 'snorkel' parker coats, with fur-lined hoods, keep schoolboys warm and dry ... TV adverts say, '*Ready Brek* - central heating for kids' ... "Get down Shep!" - 38-year-old John Noakes, 33-year-old Peter Purves and 26-year-old Lesley Judd present *Blue Peter* on BBC One ... Viewers are asked to donate old watch straps and key-rings to help raise money for specially equipped vans to deliver hot dinners to elderly people ... 33-year-old Olympic champion Mary Peters is BBC's 'Sports Personality of the Year' ... "I'll be your..." ***Long Haired Lover From Liverpool*** ("... and I'll do anything you say") by 9-year-old Little Jimmy Osmond climbs to number one in the pop chart - and stays there for five weeks! ... Schoolboys run to the shops to spend their pocket-money ... *The Beano Book* costs 50p at newsagents ... The Christmas edition of *Mayfair* magazine also costs 50p ... Football matches draw crowds of men to the terraces each Saturday afternoon ... 25-year-old right-winger Ray Graydon scores twice for Aston Villa in a 2-2 draw away against Sheffield Wednesday in

Division Two ... 26-year-old left-winger Tony Field scores twice for Blackburn Rovers in a 2-1 victory over Southend Utd in Division Three ... Industrial unrest prevails as powerful trade unions fight for the rights of their members ... Eleven-thousand British Leyland car workers at Cowley join a national strike of engineers protesting against a fine imposed on the AUEW ... Coal production is at an all time low, after recent strike action by the NUM. Just 127 million tonnes have been produced in 1972 ... NCB chairman Sir George Ezra seeks to improve industrial relations and increase production ... Approximately one-million people in the UK are unemployed ... The individual weekly dole payment currently stands at £6.75 ... A pack of twenty *Benson & Hedges* is 22½p ... The Troubles continue in Northern Ireland ... 54-year-old Secretary of State for Northern Ireland Willie Whitelaw holds top-secret meetings with IRA representatives ... The 'Cod Wars' continue in the seas off the coast of Iceland ... Icelandic patrol boats cut the lines of nets on British trawlers, and valuable hauls of cod and other fish are lost ... ***Stay With Me*** by Blue Mink is number eleven in the pop chart ... ***Keeper Of The Castle*** by The Four Tops is number eighteen ... K-tel's compilation *20 All Time Hits of the 50s* is the number one LP ... Hallmark Records release *The Best of Top of the Pops '72* - a budget priced cover-version pop compilation record with a pretty blonde girl pictured on the sleeve ... "And so this is Christmas, and what have you done? Another year over, and a new one just begun" - John and Yoko and the Plastic Ono Band sing

Happy Xmas (War Is Over) ... Ladies accompany their men to the pub and say, 'I'd Love a Babycham' ... *Bontempi* electronic organs are popular gifts for lucky children ... Also in demand is the wonderful game of *Crossfire* from Ideal, and the new *Big League* table-top football game from Chad Valley ... Soap-on-a-Rope is a common stocking filler ... 34-year-old Tony Lewis is England's cricket captain for a tour of India and Pakistan ... New BBC drama series *Colditz* (with 42-year-old Jack Hedley and 39-year-old David McCallum) grips the nation for an hour on Thursday evenings ... 18-year-old actress Anne Kirkbride makes her first appearance as Deirdre Hunt in ITV's ever popular soap-opera *Coronation Street* ... 26-year-old footballer 'super' Georgie Best walks out on struggling Manchester Utd and is seen in the early hours in a London nightclub ... "But I can't get no satisfaction, all I want is easy action!" - ***Solid Gold Easy Action*** by T-Rex is number two in the pop chart ... "I'll never let you go. Why? Because I love you" - ***Why*** by 15-year-old Donny Osmond is number three ... Bill Shankly's Liverpool are three points clear at the top of Division One ... 23-year-old John Toshack scores twice, and 21-year-old Kevin Keegan is man-of-the-match, as 'The Reds' beat Coventry City 2-0 at Anfield ... *Apollo 17* (with astronauts: Eugene Cernan, Ron Evans and Harrison Schmitt) lands on the Moon and stays for three days. (This will be the final moon landing of the Apollo space program) ... "A jumped up pantry boy, who never knew his place" - 39-year-old Michael Caine and 65-year-old Lord Olivier (Laurence Olivier) star in *Sleuth* at cinemas ... Men in long, grubby 'macs' loiter outside seedy picture houses ... 'How far does a girl have to go to untangle her tingle?' - 23-year-old Linda Lovelace stars in *Deep Throat* ... 39-year-old Frank Bough presents *Nationwide* on TV ... 'The Holiday of a Laugh time!' - 59-year-old Sid 'cor blimey' James is Vic Flange, and 35-year-old Barbara Windsor (36-23-34) is Sadie Tomkins, in *Carry On Abroad* - a low-budget film with Mediterranean scenes shot on a car-park at Pinewood Studios ... ITV television programmes on Friday evenings include: *Danger Man* (a repeat) - starring Patrick McGoohan; *The Forest Rangers*; *Magpie* - presented by 34-year-old Susan Stranks, 25-year-old Douglas Rae and 26-year-old Mick Robertson; *The Flintsones*; *Crossroads* - with Roger Tonge as Sandy Richardson, Noele Gordon as Meg Richardson and 69-year-old Ann George as Amy Turtle; *The Sky's the Limit* - hosted by 52-year-old Hughie Green; and *The Protectors* - starring 40-year-old Robert Vaughn ... 22-year-old footballer Malcolm 'Supermac' MacDonald scores a goal for Newcastle Utd in a 4-1 victory over Sheffield Utd - and 'The Toon' move up to fifth in Division One ... Manchester Utd are second from bottom after losing 5-0 against Crystal Palace ... 26-year-old 'super' Georgie Best is no longer in the team and has been placed on the transfer list ... Utd sack manager Frank O'Farrell and appoint 44-year-old Tommy Docherty as replacement ... 'The Doc' immediately signs 29-year-old George Graham from Arsenal, 20-year-old Alex Forsyth from Partick Thistle and 23-year-old Lou Macari from Celtic

... "The Jean Genie lives on his back. The Jean Genie loves chimney stacks. He's outrageous, he screams and he bawls. Jean Genie, let yourself go, woah" - ***The Jean Genie*** by 25-year-old David Bowie reaches number two in the pop chart ... Private Pike and Private Walker (played by 26-year-old Ian Lavender and 43-year-old James Beck) cause a large radio-controlled wheel (loaded with explosives) to go out of control in *Dad's Army* on BBC One ... 'Mah-na, mah-na. Doo-doo, doo-doo-doo' - 48-year-old Benny Hill stars in a new edition of *The Benny Hill Show* on ITV ... 'Weebles wobble but they don't fall down' - is the advertising strap-line for a range of new toys ... 'If you like a lot of chocolate on your biscuit join our club' - is the advertising strap-line used by Jacobs *Club* ... 56-year-old prime-minister Edward Heath gives his authorisation for construction work to begin on a new airport at Maplin Sands in Essex ... Children buy *Fruit Salads* and *Black Jacks* from the sweet shop ... The cost of living is on the increase ... The average price of a house in the UK has risen to £7,400 ... A pint of milk is 5½p ... A loaf of bread is 11p ... New year arrives ... There's snow across much of the country, with the heaviest falls occurring in East Anglia, the Midlands and the Home Counties ... Traffic is disrupted and some schools and factories close temporarily because of the cold weather ... Milk bottles freeze on doorsteps, and silver tops are pushed upwards by the iced milk ... The European community expands from six member states to nine - as Britain, Ireland and Denmark join West Germany, France, Italy, the Netherlands, Belgium and

Luxembourg in the Common Market ... The value of the (recently floated) pound falls against other currencies - such as the franc, the deutsche mark and the lire ... Conservative prime-minister Edward Heath and his Chancellor of the Exchequer Anthony Barber are forced to defend their economic record in the House of Commons ... "You better beware. You better take care. You better watch out if you've got long black hair. He'll come from behind, you'll go out of your mind. You'd better not go, you never know what you'll find" - ***Blockbuster*** by Sweet is a number one smash hit - the record stays at the top of the pop chart for five weeks! ... "You walked into the party, like you were walking onto a yacht. Your hat strategically dipped below one eye, your scarf it was apricot" - ***You're So Vain*** by 27-year-old Carly Simon is number three ... 21-year-old footballer Kevin Keegan scores for Bill Shankly's high-flying Liverpool in a 0-1 victory over West Ham Utd ... The 'Cod Wars' continue in the seas off the coast of Iceland ... British trawlers are forced to retreat from the disputed waters after Icelandic patrol boats successfully cut the fishing lines on eighteen vessels ... Back in England - A national strike by BRS lorry drivers disrupts the supply of components to British Leyland car factories ... Production of *Minis*, *1100s*, *1300s* and *1800s* at Longbridge in Birmingham comes to a halt ... Production of Jaguar *XJ6s* and *XJ12s* comes to a halt in Coventry ... 59-year-old Sid 'cor blimey' James, 44-year-old Diana Coupland and 22-year-old Sally Geeson star in the third series of sit-com *Bless This House* on ITV ... The second series of family drama *The Brothers* grips the nation on Sunday evenings on BBC One ... 'Hell, Upside Down' - cinema goers flock to see 43-year-old Gene Hackman, 30-year-old Carol Lynley and 20-year-old Pamela Sue Martin in *The Poseidon Adventure* ... 19-year-old Jilly Johnson (34A) from Woking is a popular new page three girl in *The Sun* ... "What a fool I've been to fall in love again. Love, love, when will it ever end?" - ***Ball Park Incident*** by Wizzard is number six in the pop chart ... "Daniel my brother, you are older than me. Do you still feel the pain of the scars that won't heal?" - ***Daniel*** by 25-year-old Elton John climbs to number four ... 22-year-old boxer Joe Bugner beats Rudi Lubbers in fifteen rounds at the Royal Albert Hall to retain his European heavy-weight title ... 24-year-old American George Foreman knocks out Smokin' Joe Frazier in Jamaica to become the new heavy-weight champion of the world ... Back in England - 11-year-old Frank Bruno from Wandsworth plays out with his friends ... 51-year-old Raymond Baxter and 29-year-old Michael Rodd present *Tomorrow's World* on BBC One ... A new concept called the 'digital watch' will soon be available, but, at around £150, is far too expensive for most people ... ***Sylvia***, a progressive rock instrumental, by Focus reaches number four in the pop chart ... ***Looking Through The Eyes Of Love*** by The Partridge Family (with 22-year-old heart-throb David Cassidy) is number nine ... "A house - with a door. One-two-three-four. Ready to play - what's the day?" - 39-year-old Brian Cant and 32-year-old Toni Arthur present *Play School* on BBC Two ... Children have hours of fun playing out on pogo-sticks ... England football manager Sir Alf Ramsey loses patience with 29-year-old maverick striker Rodney Marsh in a match against Wales and threatens to pull him off at half-time. Marsh tells Sir Alf he only gets an orange when he plays for Manchester City ... Troublesome footballer 26-year-old 'super' Georgie Best remains on the transfer list at Manchester Utd ... Manager Tommy 'The Doc' Docherty says he'll consider offers of around £300,000 for Best ... 35-year-old Bobby Charlton scores twice for Utd in a 2-1 win over Wolverhampton Wanderers, and 'The Reds' begin to climb the league table ... "Would you like to ride my..." ***Paper Plane*** by Status Quo reaches number eight in the pop chart ... "Wack for my daddy-oh, there's..." ***Whisky In The Jar*** ("...oh") by Thin Lizzy peaks at number six ... Alan Ball and John Radford score the goals as Bertie Mee's Arsenal defeat Bill Shankly's Liverpool 0-2 at Anfield in a top-of-the-table clash ... Don Revie's hard-tackling Leeds Utd lose 2-0 at Filbert Street against Jimmy Bloomfield's Leicester City ... 27-year-old West Ham Utd striker Pop Robson is the leading goal scorer in Division One ... 24-year-old Mick Channon scores his first international goal in England's 0-5 victory over Scotland at Hampden Park - the other four goals come from 26-year-old Allan 'sniffer' Clarke (2), 27-year-old Martin Chivers and an own goal by Peter Lorimer. England's full line-up for the match is: Shilton, Storey, Hughes, Bell, Madeley, Moore, Ball, Channon, Chivers, Clarke and Peters ... 26-year-old Bob Harris presents *The Old Grey Whistle Test* on BBC Two on Tuesday nights at 10.45 p.m. ... "Yo-de-oh-da-dodie, oh-da-dodie, oh-da-dodie, oh-da-dodie, oh-da-dodie, oh-da-um-ba-bah!" - ***Hocus Pocus*** by Focus climbs to number twenty in the pop chart ... 38-year-old American pop legend Elvis Presley and his 27-year-old wife Priscilla announce their separation ... "On Wimbledon Common, where the Wombles live, Bungo and Orinoco are tidying up" - 44-year-old Bernard Cribbins narrates *The Wombles* - a new teatime TV show for children on BBC One ... "Do you wanna touch? (Yeah). Do you wanna touch? (Yeah). Do you wanna touch me there?" - ***Do You Wanna Touch Me? (Oh Yeah)*** by 28-year-old Gary Glitter reaches number two on the hit parade - and stays there for two weeks ... 36-year-old Gordon Honeycombe reads the news for ITN ... BRS lorry drivers continue their industrial action ... The distribution of goods to shops and factories slows down ... Rail workers also come-out strike ... "You don't get me, I'm part of the union. You don't get me, I'm part of the union. You don't get me, I'm part of the union. Till the day I die, till the day I die" - ***Part Of The Union*** by The Strawbs reaches number two on the hit parade - and stays there for three weeks ... Civil servants go on strike ... "Oh, what happened to you? Whatever happened to me? What became of the people, we used to be? " - 37-year-old James Bolam and 35-year-old Rodney Bewes return to TV screens, after a gap of six years, in *Whatever Happened To The Likely Lads* ... "Oooh, Betty" - 30-year-old Michael Crawford plays Frank Spencer in *Some Mothers Do 'Ave 'Em* ... A 22-inch *PYE* colour TV set costs £258 ... The average price of a house in the UK has risen to £8,500 ... The number of *Wimpy* hamburger bars has risen to one-thousand ... 56-year-old prime-minister Edward Heath and his Conservative government set up the Maplin Development Authority - a new body to oversee the construction of an international airport on the Essex coast ... 22-year-old boxer Joe Bugner takes on Muhammad Ali in Las Vegas - Bugner loses by a unanimous decision after twelve rounds ... 40-year-old Stan Anderson resigns as football manager of Second Division Middlesbrough ... 28-year-old defender Cyril Knowles scores a 'nice one' as Tottenham Hotspur beat non league Margate 0-6 in the FA Cup third round ... 23-year winger Don Givens is on the score-sheet as Queens Park Rangers defeat Burnley 2-0 in a top-of-the-table clash in Division Two ... 35-year-old Stoke City and England goalkeeper Gordon Banks remains optimistic of making a return to football after his recent car accident ... The government imposed wage restraint program continues ... Working families begin to feel the pinch ... A loaf of bread goes up in price to 12p ... The clocks go forward an hour - and the evenings stay lighter for longer ... Youngsters congregate on street corners ... The sound of glam rock blares from transistor radios ... Freaky people in tanktops and loons 'score' gallons of juice in the pub, man ... A pint of *Skol* in the Red Lion is 14p.

Spring 1973

You're a bad dog, baby

"So, cum on feel the noise. Girls grab the boys. We get wild, wild, wild" - ***Cum On Feel The Noize*** by Slade (with 26-year-old Noddy Holder) enters the pop chart at number one - and stays there for four weeks ... ***Nice One Cyril*** ("... nice one son. Nice one Cyril, let's have another one") by the Cockerel Chorus is number fourteen ... "In the..." ***Avenues And Alleyways*** by Tony Christie is number twenty-seven ... Robert Vaughn and Nyree Dawn Porter star in *The Protectors* on ATV ... Patrick Cargill stars in *Father, Dear Father* on LWT ... Approximately 18 million people watch *Coronation Street* each week - in the current storyline, Hilda Ogden (played by 47-year-old Jean Alexander) is embarrassed because her house (at number 13) requires fumigation ... Millions also tune-in to see *It's A Knockout* on BBC One on Friday evenings. Presenter Stuart Hall laughs so much as he's describing events in a contest between Bicester and Woodstock, that he's unable to speak - 62-year-old co-commentator, Eddie Waring, steps in when needed. (Bicester win by fourteen points to eight) ... 'The antidote to panel games' - a new series of *I'm Sorry I Haven't A Clue* begins on Radio Four, with panelists Graeme Garden, Jo Kendall, Bill Oddie and Tim Brooke-Taylor, and with 51-year-old Humphrey Lyttelton in the chair ... Retail prices continue to rise ... Prime-minister Edward Heath and his Cabinet are under severe pressure ... The Trade Union Congress calls for a one day strike to protest against the government's pay restraint program ... The manufacturing sector, rail travel and postal service are all severely affected ... Construction work begins on the new airport at Maplin Sands - 60,000 tonnes of stone and gravel are deposited on the mudflats of the Thames estuary to create a protective bank for the new complex ... Harold Wilson (leader of the opposition Labour party) is against the multi-million pound project ... 54-year-old Shadow Environment Secretary Anthony Crosland describes Maplin as a "thoroughly bad site" to build a new international airport ... A national environmental campaign encourages people to 'Plant a Tree in '73' ... 11-year-old schoolboy Richard Coles from Northampton plays out with his friends, before going to church ... "Feel..." ***Feel The Need In Me*** by The Detroit Emeralds climbs to number four on the hit parade ... ***Roll Over Beethoven*** by The Electric Light Orchestra is number six ... 35-year-old centre-forward Derek Dougan bags a hat-trick, and his strike partner John Richards scores twice, as Wolverhampton Wanderers thrash Manchester City 5-1 at the Molinuex ... 45-year-old Malcolm Allison resigns as football manager of City and takes over at Crystal Palace -

on a salary reputed to be £13,000, plus bonuses. Allison's first game in charge produces a 2-0 victory over Chelsea - but Palace remain near the bottom of the First Division table ... 48-year-old Kenneth Kendall reads the news on BBC One ... Two IRA bombs explode in London killing two people and injuring hundreds ... Edward Heath's Conservative government brings in 'trial without jury' for terrorist offences in Northern Ireland ... 46-year-old Queen Elizabeth II opens the new London Bridge ... Retail prices go up again, as a 10% Value Added Tax comes into effect ... The 'Cod Wars' continue in the seas off the coast of Iceland ... Royal Navy frigates escort British trawlers back into the disputed waters so that fishing can be resumed ... Icelandic people are angered by the Royal Navy's intervention. The British Embassy in Reykjavic is attacked and its windows smashed ... Back in England - 31-year-old Fred West and his 19-year-old wife Rosemary murder 19-year-old Lynda Gough and bury her body beneath their house at 25 Cromwell Street in Gloucester ... "Hey! Hey! Hey! And it's..." ***All Because Of You*** ("... baby") by Geordie is number six in the pop chart ... "I may seem a fool to you, for everything I say or think or do" - ***Pyjamarama*** by Roxy Music (featuring 27-year-old Bryan Ferry) is number ten ... 'Introducing Allegro. The new driving force from Austin' - after eleven years in production, Austin *1100* and *1300* motorcars are replaced by the all new *Allegro*, with its revolutionary hydragas suspension and a 'Quartic' (square-shaped) steering wheel. A new *Allegro 1100 De-luxe* costs £1,009. A new *Allegro 1500 Super De-luxe* is £1,200 ...

The Beatles *Red* and *Blue* albums are released - three years after the 'Fab Four' went their separate ways ... *Hickory House* (featuring 36-year-old Alan Rothwell and a talking cushion called Humphrey) is new on TV for children ... The fourth series of *The Flaxton Boys* (a drama set in Yorkshire in the year 1945) is broadcast on Sunday afternoons on ITV ... "It's Friday. It's five o'clock and it's..." *Crackerjack* (hosted by 40-year-old Michael Aspel, and featuring comedians Don MacLean and Peter Glaze) is on BBC One ... 26-year-old footballer Ralph Coates comes on as substitute to score the only goal as Bill Nicholson's Tottenham Hotspur beat Ron Saunders' Norwich City 1-0 in the League Cup final at Wembley ... Joint favourite *Red Rum* (ridden by Brian Fletcher) makes a late run to win the Grand National at Aintree ... Cambridge win the Boat Race for the sixth consecutive year - beating Oxford by thirteen lengths ... "You ask how long I'll love you. I'll tell you true. Until..." ***The Twelfth Of Never*** ("... and that's a long, long time") by 15-year-old Donny Osmond spends a week at number one ... "Yeah, I'm your toy, your..." ***20th Century Boy*** by T-Rex reaches number three ... 38-year-old writer David Nobbs drinks wine and works on his fourth novel - a dark comedy called *The Death of Reginald Perrin* ... 32-year-old Cliff Richard finishes third at the Eurovision song contest in Luxembourg singing *Power To All Our Friends* ("... to the music that never ends. To the people we want to be. Baby, power to you and me") ... 40-year-old Ray 'Dracula' Reardon wins the *Park Drive* World Snooker Championship - beating

Graham Miles from Birmingham by 22 frames to 12 in the final at Belle Vue in Manchester ... "Told you once before, and I won't tell you no more. Get down, get down, get down. You're a bad dog baby, but I still want you around" - ***Get Down*** by 26-year-old Gilbert O'Sullivan spends two weeks at the top of the pop chart ... "Tweedle, tweedle, tweedle doh. I'm a lucky so and so' - ***Tweedle Dee*** by 9-year-old Little Jimmy Osmond is number four ... 56,202 football spectators are at Anfield on Saturday the twenty-eighth of April to see Bill Shankly's Liverpool gain a point (from a 0-0 draw against Leicester City) and become the new champions of Division One. Ray Clemence, Chris Lawler, Alec Lindsay, Tommy Smith, Larry Lloyd, Phil Thompson, Emlyn Hughes, Brian Hall, Steve Heighway, John Toshack, Peter Cormack, Ian Callaghan, Phil Boersma and 22-year-old Kevin Keegan have all been outstanding for 'The Reds' ... Bertie Mee's Arsenal (with Bob Wilson, Geoff Barnett, Pat Rice, Bob McNab, Peter Storey, Frank McLintock, Jeff Blockley, Peter Simpson, Alan Ball, George Armstrong, John Radford, Eddie Kelly and 21-year-old Ray Kennedy) are runners-up ... Don Howe's West Bromwich Albion finish bottom of the table and are relegated along with Malcolm Allison's Crystal Palace ... After serving his club for twenty years, 35-year-old Bobby Charlton makes his final appearance for Manchester Utd in a 1-0 defeat against Chelsea ... 27-year-old Bob Harris, 34-year-old John Peel and 33-year-old Annie Nightingale take turns presenting *Sounds of the 70s* on Radio One at 10 p.m. on weekday nights ... "It's a crash course for the ravers.

It's a..." ***Drive-In Saturday*** by 26-year-old David Bowie is number three in the singles chart ... Bowie's new LP, *Aladdin Sane*, is number one in the album chart ... Jimmy Adamson's Burnley football team (with Keith Newton, Martin Dobson, Paul Fletcher and 20-year-old Leighton James) finishes top of Division Two and gains promotion to Division One alongside Gordon Jago's Queens Park Rangers (with Gerry Francis, Dave Thomas, Don Givens and 24-year-old Stan Bowles) ... 27-year-old midfielder Ian Porterfield scores the only goal as Bob Stokoe's Second Division Sunderland shock the football world with a surprise FA Cup final victory over Leeds Utd of the First Division. A ticket for the standing enclosure at the Empire Stadium in Wembley costs £1.00 ... "Oh, I was just a boy..." ***Giving It All Away*** by 29-year-old Roger Daltrey is number five in the pop chart ... ***I'm A Clown / Some Kind Of Summer*** by 23-year-old heart-throb David Cassidy is number three ... 38-year-old Jack Charlton is the new football manager of Second Division Middlesbrough ... 35-year-old Bobby Charlton is the new football manager of Second Division Preston North End ... 32-year-old Esther Rantzen presents the first edition of *That's Life* on TV ... 37-year-old John Inman declares, "I'm Free!" in *Are You Being Served?* ... Alf Roberts (played by 41-year-old Bryan Mosley) and Annie Walker (played by 74-year-old Doris Speed) are the new Mayor and Mayoress of Weatherfield in ITV's ever popular soap-opera *Coronation Street* ... 60-year-old Jimmy Chipperfield opens the West Midland Safari Park near Kidderminster, and families travel from all around to see the monkeys ... "I'm coming home, I've done my time, and I've got to know what is and isn't mine" - ***Tie A Yellow Ribbon Round The Old Oak Tree*** ("... it's been three long years, do you still want me?") by Dawn is new at number one in the pop chart ... "Hello, hello. It's good to be back. It's good to be back. Did you miss me (yeah) while I was away?" - ***Hello Hello I'm Back Again*** by 29-year-old Gary Glitter is number two ... Bill Shankly's Liverpool football team wins the UEFA Cup - defeating Borussia Monchengladbach 3-2 on aggregate (over two legs). 24-year-old goalkeeper Ray Clemence saves a penalty and 22-year-old Kevin Keegan and 24-year-old Larry Lloyd score the goals for high-flying Liverpool ... 29-year-old outside-left Martin Peters scores the only goal as England (with Peter Shilton, Emlyn Hughes and 32-year-old Bobby Moore) beat Scotland (with Ally Hunter, Lou Macari and 30-year-old Billy Bremner) 1-0 in front of 95,950 spectators at Wembley ... Petrol prices are rising ... The fuel economy of motorcars is becoming more and more important ... A Hillman *Imp* (which has been in production for ten years) returns 32.4 mpg ... An Austin *Allegro 1100* (which has just been launched) returns 33 mpg ... "Look out! Look out! Your mamma will shout, you might as well go home" - ***See My Baby Jive*** by Wizzard (with 26-year-old lead singer Roy Wood) reaches number one in the pop chart ... "Plucked her eyebrows on the way, shaved her legs and then he was a she. She said, hey babe, take a..." ***Walk On The Wild Side*** by 31-year-old Lou Reed reaches number ten ... The new LP *Tubular Bells* by 20-year-old

Mike Oldfield is the first release on 22-year-old Richard Branson's *Virgin Record* label ... Sally Harrison (played by 38-year-old Wendy Craig) marries David Redway (played by 43-year-old Richard Coleman) in the new series of *And Mother Makes Three* on ITV ... 41-year-old Jack Smethurst and 33-year-old Rudolph Walker star as 'Chalky' and 'Honky' in a new series of *Love Thy Neighbour* ... John Tyndall's National Front party takes 16% of the vote at a by-election in West Bromwich, but 43-year-old Betty Boothroyd manages to hold the seat for Labour ... "She's a hell raiser, star chaser, trail blazer, natural born raver, yeah! Yeah! Yeah! Yeah! Yeah!" - ***Hell Raiser*** by Sweet (with 27-year-old lead singer Brian Connolly) is number two in the pop chart ... ***And I Love You So*** ("... The people ask me how, how I've lived till now") by 60-year-old Perry Como is number three ... 'Admittance Restricted' - 49-year-old Marlon Brando and 21-year-old Maria Schneider get raunchy in a new movie called *Last Tango In Paris* ... Half a pound of *Lurpak* butter costs 11p at *Fine-Fare*.

Summer 1973

You got rude talk, you got one walk.
All your jokes are blue

The sun shines, but temperatures remain cool ... 'Stop Me and Buy One' - children purchase *Screwballs*, *Funny Feet* and *99s* from the ice-cream man ... The first edition of *Why Don't You Just Switch Off Your Television Set and Go and Do Something Less Boring Instead?* is on TV ... Children play out ... Girls wear cheese-cloth tops with tie waists ... Boys ride bikes ... A Mark II Raleigh *Chopper* costs £33.75 and is available in three colours: Infra Red, Ultra Violet or Fizzy Lemon ... 11-year-old schoolboy Phillip Schofield from Oldham in Lancashire stays in to watch telly ... "Oooh, hello honky tonks" - 58-year-old Dick Emery stars in *The Best of Dick Emery* on BBC One ... The first ever Radio One Roadshow is broadcast from Fistral Beach at Newquay in Cornwall - 46-year-old disc jockey Alan 'Fluff' Freeman is the host ("Not 'arf!") ... "So make a stand for your man honey, try to can the can. Put your man in the can honey, get him while you can..." ***Can The Can*** by 23-year-old Suzi Quatro is new at number one in the pop chart ... "Clowns to the left of me, jokers to the right. Here I am..." ***Stuck In The Middle***

With You by Stealers Wheel is number eight ... 40-year-old Dickie Bird stands as umpire for the first time in an international cricket Test Match - Ray Illingworth's England team beats Bevan Congdon's New Zealand by 38 runs ... The 'Cod Wars' continue in the seas off the coast of Iceland ... Icelandic patrol boats employ a new tactic of ramming into British Royal Navy frigates ... Back in England - heated debate takes place in the House of Commons over the high inflation rate and rising food costs ... Harold Wilson's Labour opposition pushes for food subsidies to be given to the less well off, but Conservative Chancellor of the Exchequer Anthony Barber resists ... The number of road accidents in the UK is on the increase ... It's now compulsory for motorcyclists to wear crash-helmets ... The latest Suzuki *GT250* has a top speed of 90 mph ... Crowds flock to cinemas to see *Steptoe & Son Ride Again* - in which Old Man Steptoe (Wilfrid Brambell) fakes his own death so that son Harold (Harry H. Corbett) can cash in on a life insurance policy ... Don Revie's hard-tackling Leeds Utd are fined by the Football Association for their poor disciplinary record last season ... Derby County's outspoken manager Brian Clough says Leeds' punishment should have been relegation to Division Two ... 28-year-old Alan Ball is sent-off for fighting as Sir Alf Ramsey's England team (Shilton, Madeley, Hughes, Storey, McFarland, Moore, Ball, Bell, Chivers, A Clarke, Peters) loses 2-0 in Poland ... ***You Are The Sunshine Of My Life*** ("... That's why I'll always be around") by 23-year-old Stevie Wonder is number seven in the pop chart ... ***Touch Me In***

the Morning by 29-year-old Diana Ross is number nine ... Cricketers 32-year-old Geoffrey Boycott and 30-year-old Dennis Amiss stride out together to open the batting for England against the West Indies at the Oval. Boycott scores 97 runs. Amiss makes 29. Clive Lloyd hits 132 and Alvin Kallicharran scores 80 as the touring West Indians triumph by 158 runs. In the third Test at Lord's, an IRA bomb scare halts play for almost two hours before the West Indians complete an easy 2-0 series victory over Ray Illingworth's team ... "Load up, load up, load up with..." ***Rubber Bullets*** by 10cc spends a week at the top of the pop chart ... "Ten, twenty, thirty, forty, fifty or more. The Bloody Red Baron was rollin' out the score. Eighty men died tryin' to end that spree, of the Bloody Red Baron of Germany" - ***Snoopy vs The Red Baron*** by The Hotshots is number four ... 42-year-old Peter Woods reads the news on BBC One ... 22-year-old David McGreavy is sentenced to life imprisonment for the brutal murders of three young children in Worcester ... 18-year-old Andrew Evans is sentenced to life imprisonment for the brutal murder of schoolgirl Judith Roberts in Tamworth ... 'M' reg cars go on sale ... 'Well-to-do' young men drive fast on motorways in sporty saloon cars ... The Triumph *Dolomite Sprint* has a top speed of 115 mph and accelerates from 0-60 mph in 9.1 seconds ... The Vauxhall *Firenza 2300 SL* has a top speed of 120 mph and accelerates from 0-60 mph in 8 seconds ... Sensible family men consider the options for a new motorcar ... Economical hatchbacks are popular, with more and more foreign cars being purchased ... A

Datsun *Cherry* costs £884 and can achieve 34.8 mpg ... A Fiat *127* costs £978 and returns 32 mpg ... The new Renault *5TL* costs £929 and returns 26.5 mpg ... Four star leaded petrol has risen to 39p a gallon ... Actor James Beck (who plays Private Walker in the hit television comedy *Dad's Army*) dies aged 44 in Roehampton ... 43-year-old Ronnie Barker is Fletcher, and 50-year-old Fulton Mackay is Mr. Mackay, in *Prisoner and Escort* - a one-off comedy written by Dick Clement and Ian La Frenais for BBC's *Seven Of One* series ... 26-year-old footballer Fabio Capello scores a goal past Peter Shilton as Italy beat Sir Alf Ramsey's England 2-0 in Torino. England's full line-up for the match is: Shilton, Madeley, Hughes, Storey, McFarland, Moore, Currie, Channon, Chivers, A Clarke and Peters ... 33-year-old Denis Law leaves Manchester Utd and joins Manchester City on a free transfer ... 28-year-old Peter Noble leaves Swindon Town and joins Burnley for £40,000 ... 24-year-old Noel Edmonds takes over from Tony Blackburn as presenter of the Radio One breakfast show ... "You know how to skweeze me. Whoa-ah! You know how to pleeze me. Whoa-ah!" - ***Skweeze Me Pleeze Me*** by Slade (with 27-year-old Noddy Holder) comes straight into the pop chart at number one - and stays at the top for three weeks ... Slade's drummer Don Powell is badly injured, and his girlfriend Angela Morris is killed in a car crash ... "Every sha-la la-la, every wo-oh wo-oh still shines. Every shing-a-ling-a-ling, that they're starting to sing's so fine. When they get to the part, where he's breaking her heart, it can really make me cry, just like before. It's..." ***Yesterday Once More*** by The Carpenters is number two ... 23-year-old boxer Joe Bugner loses to former world champion Smokin' Joe Frazier in a closely fought contest at Earls Court ... 31-year-old tennis player Roger Taylor from Sheffield loses to Jan Kodes in the semi-finals of the men's singles championship at Wimbledon ... 28-year-old Virginia Wade from Bournemouth loses to Evonne Goolagong in the quarter-finals of the ladies' singles ... Nine racing cars crash at Woodgate Corner on the first lap of the British Grand Prix at Silverstone - and the race has to be restarted. Peter Revson (from the USA) is the eventual winner ... Two weeks later, 34-year-old Jackie Stewart wins the Dutch Grand Prix, and extends his lead to ten points over Emerson Fittipaldi in the drivers' championship ... "Good evening. The name's Bond, you have a reservation for me" - The film *Live And Let Die* is now showing at cinemas, with 45-year-old Roger Moore as the new James Bond (aka 007). 22-year-old Jane Seymour plays the role of Solitaire. 65-year-old Bernard Lee is M. 46-year-old Lois Maxwell is Miss Moneypenny ... "When you were young, and your heart was an open book, you used to say, live and let live. (You know you did - you know you did - you know you did). But in this ever changin' world in which we live in, makes you give in, and cry. Say..." ***Live And Let Die*** by Paul McCartney and Wings is number seven in the pop chart ... "Welcome home. (Welcome). Come on in, and close the door" - ***Welcome Home*** by Peters and Lee is number one for a week ... Families sit together and watch TV ... An *ITT CK702* 26-inch colour set costs £292.00 including VAT ... A *Ferguson* 12-inch portable black and white set costs £56.05 including VAT ... *Man About the House* is a great new sit-com - starring 23-year-old Paula Wilcox, 23-year-old Sally Thomsett and 29-year-old Richard O'Sullivan ... Rita Littlewood (played by 39-year-old Barbara Knox) and Mavis Riley (played by 44-year-old Thelma Barlow) serve customers at 'The Kabin' - a brand new newsagents - in *Coronation Street* ... Children enjoy a new show called *Michael Bentine's Potty Time* ... 21-year-old Hereford Utd goalkeeper David Icke is forced to retire from football because of arthritis in his knees ... "Come on - come on! Come on - come on! Come on - come on - come on! D'ya wanna be in my gang, my gang, my gang?" - ***I'm The Leader Of The Gang (I Am)*** by 29-year-old Gary Glitter is number one for four weeks ... "48 crash, 48 crash. Come like a lightning flash, a lightning flash. And it's a silk sash bash, a silk sash bash. That's the..." ***48 Crash*** by 23-year-old Suzi Quatro is number three ... Teenage tearaways smoke cigarettes in the park ... A pack of twenty Player's *No. 6* cigarettes is 21p ... Ace racing driver Jackie Stewart wins the German Grand Prix at the Nurburgring - and extends his lead to fifteen point in the Formula One drivers' championship ... Back in England - the new football season gets underway ... 23-year-old Malcolm 'Supermac' MacDonald scores twice as Newcastle Utd beat West Ham Utd 2-1 in front of 28,169 spectators at St. James' Park ... Billy Bremner, Johnny Giles and Mick Jones are on the score-sheet as Leeds Utd beat Everton 3-1 in front of 39,325 at Elland Road.

(Leeds players have a new club badge on their jerseys - the letters L and U joined together in a yellow bubble, reminiscent of the ubiquitous 'smiley face' symbol) ... "Oh man, wonder if he'll ever know, he's in the freakiest show. Is there..." ***Life On Mars*** by 26-year-old David Bowie reaches number three on the weekly hit parade ... "Blue..." ***Spanish Eyes*** ("... Prettiest eyes in all of Mexico") by 45-year-old Al Martino is number five ... "Ying tong, ying tong, ying tong, ying tong, ying tong, iddle I po" - ***The Ying Tong Song*** by The Goons is number nine ... *Jollees* nightclub opens in Stoke-on-Trent ... Customers enjoy chicken-in-a-basket whilst being entertained by upcoming comedians Little & Large ... 35-year-old Stoke City and England goalkeeper Gordon Banks announces his retirement from football after being blinded in one eye in a car accident last year ... "I'm a secret lemonade drinker. R Whites. R Whites. I've been tryin' to give it up but it's one of those nights" - *R Whites* advertise lemonade on TV.

Autumn 1973

I was working in the lab, late one night

47-year-old Queen Elizabeth II opens Sydney Opera House in Australia - the impressive new building has taken fourteen years to complete ... Back in Britain - people watch telly ... 37-year-old comedian Dave Allen stars in *Dave Allen at Large* on BBC One on Friday evenings ... 39-year-old Jean Marsh (Rose), 69-year-old Angela Baddeley (Mrs. Bridges) and 49-year-old Gordon Jackson (Hudson) star in a new series of *Upstairs Downstairs* on ITV on Saturday evenings ... "They say for every boy and girl, there's just one love in this whole world, and I-I-I know I-I-I've found mine" - ***Young Love*** by 15-year-old heart-throb Donny Osmond reaches number one in the pop chart ... "Don't wanna say good night..." ***Dancing On A Saturday Night*** by 22-year-old Barry Blue is number two ... 11-year-old schoolboy Micky Flanagan from Whitechapel in East London plays out-out with his mates ... Children return to school after the summer holidays ... Those aged ten or eleven with neat hand-writing are permitted to use an ink cartridge *Parker* pen instead of a pencil - in preparation for Secondary School ... "You can do magic, baby..." ***You Can Do Magic*** ("... magic") by Limmie and the Family Cookin' is number three on the hit parade ... ***The Dean And I*** by 10cc is number ten ... The IRA steps up it's bombing campaign in England ... There are explosions at King's Cross Station, Euston Station, Oxford Street, Sloane Square and also in Manchester ... An agreement over fishing rights is reached between Iceland and the UK and the 'Cod Wars' come to an end. A zone of fifty nautical miles from the coastline of Iceland is established, with British trawlers being granted limited rights to fish within the newly defined area ... 40-year-old Barry Norman presents the late night movie review program *Film 73* on BBC One ... 32-year-old Ryan O'Neal stars as Moses and 9-year-old Tatum O'Neal stars as Addie in *Paper Moon* at cinemas ... 25-year-old Captain Mark Phillips wins the three-day horse trial event at Burghley House on *Maid Marion* ... 23-year-old boxer Joe Bugner defeats Giuseppe Ros on points at the Royal Albert Hall to retain his European heavy-weight title ... 20-year-old footballer Paul Mariner scores two goals on his debut for Plymouth Argyle in a 5-0 victory over Rochdale in Division Three ... "Are you ready Steve? Uh-huh. Andy? Yeah. Mick? Okay. Alright fellas, let's go!" - ***Ballroom Blitz*** by The Sweet is number two in the pop chart ... ***Angie*** ("... I still love you. Remember all those nights we cried") by The Rolling Stones is number five ... Supersonic airplane Concorde makes its first non-stop crossing of the Atlantic - and completes the trip in a record breaking time of just 3 hours and 32 minutes ... 57-year-old prime-minister Edward Heath and his Conservative government push ahead with their plans for a new international airport at Maplin Sands in Essex - even though estimated costs for the project have risen to over £1,000 million ... Inflation stands at 8.8% ... Chancellor of the Exchequer Anthony Barber ignores calls to put the brakes on the economy and says, "I believe our present path of expansion is sustainable and my conclusion is that it would be wrong now to check it" ... Tensions are growing between the National Coal Board (led by 54-year-old Sir Derek Ezra) and the National Union of Mineworkers (led by 56-year-old Joe Gormley) ... Coal miners begin an overtime ban ... Housewives go shopping on crowded high streets ... *Green Shield Stamps* catalogue stores are now called *Argos* ... A *Russell Hobbs* electric kettle costs £6.10 ... A *Morphy Richards* hair-dryer costs £3.25 ... A red *Tonka Toy* fire-engine is £4.95 ... ***Angel Fingers*** ("... Angel fingers, how I sing for the things you do") by Wizzard (with 26-year-old lead singer Roy Wood) spends a week at number one in the pop chart ... "Hey kid, rock and roll..." ***Rock On*** ("... Ooh, my soul") by 26-year-old David Essex reaches number three ... Fashions move on ... The Swinging Sixties seem like a distant memory ... Carnaby Street in London is pedestrianised ... Thirty-four football hooligans are arrested at a First Division match between Huddersfield Town and Leeds Utd ... Ace racing driver Jackie Stewart is in blistering form! The 34-year-old Scot charges through a pack of cars at the Italian Grand Prix and moves up from twentieth position to fourth - gaining enough points to become Formula One world champion for the third time in his career ... Emerson Fittipaldi from Brazil is runner up in the drivers' championship and Ronnie Peterson of Sweden is third ... Back in England - young men dream of owning a fast car ... The latest Ford *Escort RS2000* has a top speed of 108 mph and can reach 60 mph in 9 seconds ... The latest Hillman *Avenger Tiger* has a top speed of 106 mph and can reach 60 mph in 9.5 seconds ... The all new Reliant *Robin* three-wheeler replaces the Reliant *Regal* ... Schoolboys crave the new *Matchbox* die-cast model of the *Boss Mustang* car in yellow with a black (opening) bonnet ... "Der-de-de-der, de-de, de-de, de-de, de-de. Der-de-de-de-de-der" - ***Eye Level*** by The Simon Park Orchestra spends four weeks at number one in the pop chart ... 41-year-old actor Barry Foster plays Dutch detective *Van der Valk* on Wednesday evenings on ITV ... A new series of *The Onedin Line* (with 42-year-old Peter Gilmore, 34-year-old Anne Stallybrass and 62-year-old Howard Lang) is on BBC One on Sunday evenings ... The character Sgt Bert Lynch (played by 42-year-old Jimmy Ellis) is promoted to the rank of Inspector in long-running police drama *Z Cars* ... 15-year-old Stacy Dorning is Jenny Gordon in a new series of *The Adventures of Black Beauty* on ITV ... Elsie Howard (played by 49-year-old Pat Phoenix) and her husband, Alan, leave the ever popular soap-opera *Coronation Street* to begin a new life in Newcastle ... 45-year-old Jimmy Hill is the new presenter of *Match of the Day* ... "I was working in the lab, late one night, when my eyes beheld an eerie sight. For my monster from his slab, began to rise and suddenly to my surprise, he did the mash. He did the…" ***Monster Mash*** by Bobby 'Boris' Pickett and the Crypt-Kickers reaches number three in the pop chart ... "'Ello darlin'!" - 32-year-old Ed 'stewpot' Stewart presents *Junior Choice* on weekend mornings on Radio One ... "Oh! The runaway train came down the track and she blew. The runaway train came down the track and she blew. The runaway train came down the track, her whistle wide and her throttle back, and she blew-oo-oo-oo-oo" - Michael Holliday sings ***The Runaway Train*** ... Sir Alf Ramsey's England football team is out of next year's world cup. Mistakes by 29-year-old defender Norman Hunter and 24-year-old goalkeeper Peter Shilton allow Poland to score a goal in a match at Wembley - and a sixty-third minute penalty equaliser by Allan 'sniffer' Clarke is not enough. The game ends in a 1-1 draw - and England needed to win. Shilton, Hunter and Clarke - along with Paul Madeley, Roy McFarland, Emlyn Hughes, Colin Bell, Tony Currie, Martin Peters, Mick Channon, Martin Chivers and Kevin Hector all miss out on the chance to play in the finals in West Germany ... 38-year-old manager Brian Clough shocks the football world by walking out on Derby County ... "I'm just a daydreamer. I'm walkin' in the rain, chasin' after rainbows I may never find again" - ***Daydreamer*** by 23-year-old heart-throb David Cassidy is top of the hit parade ... "Come on sweet Caroline. You're my sweet…" ***Caroline*** by Status Quo is number five ... 26-year-old Uri Geller bends spoons on TV and the nation tries to emulate him ... Captain Mainwaring says, "Don't tell him, Pike!" in the opening episode of a new series of *Dad's Army* ... The recently deceased James Beck (who plays Private Walker) appears in six of the shows - which were recorded just weeks before his death ... ***For The Good Times*** by 61-year-old Perry Como is number seven in the pop chart ... "They call it... ***Nutbush City Limits*** by 41-year-old Ike Turner and his wife, 33-year-old Tina, is number three ... 17-year-old footballer Liam Brady makes his debut for Arsenal - coming on as a substitute in a 1-0 victory over Birmingham City ... 23-year-old Malcolm 'Supermac' MacDonald scores twice as Newcastle Utd beat Chelsea 2-0 in front of 32,154 spectators at St. James' Park ... After a year out of the game, 27-year-old 'super' Georgie Best asks Manchester Utd manager Tommy 'The Doc' Docherty if he can return to the team ... 'Super' Georgie resumes training and is called up to play in a First Division match against Tottenham Hotspur at White Hart Lane - where he scores Utd's goal in a 2-1 defeat ... "Cheeky little thing! I'd like to put her across my knee" - *Carry On Girls* is now showing at cinemas with 54-year-old Peter Butterworth as 'the old admiral', 60-year-old Sid 'cor blimey' James as Sidney Fiddler and 36-year-old Barbara Windsor (36-23-34) as Hope Springs ... "We're still together, after all that we've been through. They tried to tell you, I was not the boy for you. They didn't like my hair, the clothes I love to wear. They didn't realise that I was strong enough for two" - ***I Love, You Love, Me Love*** by 29-year-old Gary Glitter enters the pop chart at number one - and stays there for four weeks ... "Ah-won't you be..." ***My Coo-Ca Choo*** by 31-year-old Alvin Stardust is number two ... 28-year-old maverick striker Rodney Marsh scores for Manchester City, and 24-year-old Mick Channon scores for Southampton, in a 1-1 draw at Maine Road ... Millions fill in their weekly football pools coupon - hoping for eight score-draws ... *Littlewoods* introduce 'Spot the Ball' ... Don Revie's hard-tackling Leeds Utd are the early leaders in Division One ... 27-year-old striker Allan 'sniffer' Clarke scores twice for Leeds in a 1-2 away victory at Southampton - to make it seven consecutive wins for the 'All Whites' ... 21-year-old Steve Perryman is on the score-sheet for Tottenham Hotspur in a 1-1 against Everton at Goodison Park ... 40-year-old John Bond replaces Ron Saunders as manager of Norwich City ... 32-year-old Fred West and his 19-year-old wife, Rosemary, murder 15-year-old Carol Ann Cooper and bury her body beneath their house at 25 Cromwell Street in Gloucester ... "Won't you plea-ea-ease..." ***Let Me In*** ("... Let me in your arms again") by The Osmonds peaks at number two in the pop chart ... "I'm on top of the world looking down on creation and the only explanation I can find, is the love that I've found, ever since you've been around, your love's put me at the..." ***Top Of The World*** by The Carpenters is number five ... "Oooh, Betty" - 31-year-old Michael Crawford plays Frank Spencer in a new series of *Some Mothers Do 'Ave 'Em* ... Ken Barlow (played by 41-year-old Bill Roache) marries Janet Reid (played by 30-year-old Judith Barker) in *Coronation Street* ... 23-year-old Princess Anne marries 25-year-old Captain Mark Phillips at Westminster Abbey. The young Princess' wedding dress is designed by 52-year-old Maureen Baker ... ***Paper Roses*** ("... Paper roses. Oh, how real those roses seem to me") by 14-year-old Marie Osmond climbs to number two in the pop chart ... Vauxhall announce the new *Magnum* motorcar (a sporty version of the *Viva*) with *Rostyle* wheels and a choice of 1800cc or 2300cc engine ... Children rush to the sweet-shop after school for a *Sherbet Fountain* and then go home to watch *Animal Magic* on TV ... Dad's carry out tricky DIY jobs ... Adverts say, 'Do It Well With Polycell'.

Winter 1973 - 1974

It's Christmas!

'Mah-na, mah-na. Doo-doo, doo-doo-doo' - 49-year-old Benny Hill stars in a new edition of *The Benny Hill Show* on ITV ... 50-year-old Jack Scott presents the weather forecast on BBC One ... There's snow in the air ... "Are you hanging up a stocking on your wall? It's the time that every Santa has a ball" - ***Merry Xmas Everybody*** by Slade (with 27-year-old Noddy Holder) enters the pop chart at number one! ... 32-year-old footballer Bobby Moore makes his 108th (and final) appearance for England in a 0-1 defeat against Italy at Wembley. (27-year-old Fabio Capello scores Italy's goal two minutes before full-time). England's line-up for the match is: Shilton, Madeley, Hughes, Bell, McFarland, Moore, Currie, Channon, Osgood, Clarke, Peters and substitute Hector ... "Ooh, baby would I look right, climbing up the drainpipe? Baby, would it feel right, if I stayed all night?" - ***Lamplight*** by 26-year-old David Essex is number seven in the pop chart ... "Won't you..." ***Roll Away The Stone*** ("... Why be cold and so alone?") by Mott the Hoople is number eight ... 26-year-old footballer Peter 'Ossie' Osgood scores a goal for Chelsea in a 3-2 victory over Leicester City at Stamford Bridge. (25-year-old Frank Worthington is on the score-sheet for Leicester) ... 34-year-old world champion racing driver Jackie Stewart is BBC's 'Sports Personality of the Year' ... Stan and Hilda Ogden celebrate their thirtieth wedding anniversary in ITV's ever popular soap-opera *Coronation Street* ... 31-year-old actor John Thaw marries 40-year-old Sheila Hancock in Cirencester ... People post their Christmas cards in plenty of time before the big day ... A first class postage stamp costs 3½p ... A second class stamp is 3p ... The IRA bombing campaign continues - a device is detonated outside the Home Office at Millbank in London and sixty people are injured ... Children rush to the cinema to see the matinee showing of *Digby the Biggest Dog in the World* - starring Jim Dale, Angela Douglas and 55-year-old Spike Milligan ... 35-year-old disc jockey Terry Wogan attracts millions of listeners to his morning show on Radio Two ... 48-year-old Pete Murray entertains housewives on his mid-morning show, before *Waggoners' Walk* ... 47-year-old Jimmy Savile OBE presents *Savile's Travels and Speakeasy* on Sundays on Radio One ... "Baby! Although I chose this lonely life, it seems it's strangling me now" - ***The Show Must Go On*** by 25-year-old Leo Sayer is number two in the pop chart ... "Step into Christmas, let's join together, we can watch the snow fall for ever and ever " - ***Step Into Christmas*** by 26-year-old Elton John is number eleven ... Hallmark Records release *The Best of Top of the Pops '73* - a budget priced cover-version pop compilation LP with a 'knowing' blonde girl on the sleeve ... Coal miners hold firm with their overtime ban ... The Conservative government imposes restrictions on the 'non-essential' use of electricity ... Football clubs are banned from using floodlights - and all matches have to be played in daylight hours ... Jack Charlton's Middlesbrough are top of Division Two after a 3-0 win against Bobby Charlton's Preston North End ... 55-year-old Willie Whitelaw is the new Secretary of State for Employment in Edward Heath's Cabinet ... Francis Pym is the Secretary of State for Northern Ireland ... BBC One TV programs on a Saturday night include: *Dr. Who* - starring 54-year-old Jon Pertwee; *Wonderful World of Disney*; *Bruce Forsyth and The Generation Game* - with 45-year-old Bruce and 25-year-old Anthea Redfern; *The Harry Secombe Show*; and *Match of the Day* - introduced by 45-year-old Jimmy Hill ... 22-year-old Kevin Keegan and 26-year-old Steve Heighway score the goals as Bill Shankly's Liverpool beat Tommy 'The Doc' Docherty's Manchester Utd 2-0 at Anfield ... Opposing football fans taunt George Best with, "Georgie Best. Superstar. Walks like a woman and he wears a bra" ... Don Revie's hard-tackling Leeds Utd remain unbeaten - and are seven points clear at the top of Division One ... 23-year-old Terry Yorath scores the only goal as Leeds beat John Bond's Norwich City 1-0 in front of 34,747 at Elland Road ... 37-year-old Lawrie McMenemy takes over from Ted Bates as manager of Southampton ... 38-year-old Brian Clough is the new manager of Third Division Brighton and Hove Albion ... 16,017 spectators turn out at the Goldstone Ground for Cloughie's first game in charge - a 0-0 draw against York City ... Roxy Music (with 28-year-old lead singer Bryan

Ferry) perform their new single, ***Street Life*** ... 27-year-old Gilbert O'Sullivan sings ***Why, Oh Why, Oh Why*** ... 60-year-old Robert Dougall and 40-year-old Richard Whitmore read the news on BBC One ... 53-year-old Chancellor of the Exchequer Anthony Barber refuses to budge from the path he's set for speedy economic expansion ... Inflation has now rocketed to 10.6% and food prices are at an all-time high ... To compound the government's woes, the coal miners come out on strike and the country is plunged into darkness ... Fuel shortages and power cuts follow ... Shops run out of candles ... Schools are without heating and are forced to close ... 57-year-old prime-minister Edward Heath introduces a three-day working week ... (132 million tonnes of coal have been mined in 1973 - just 5 million more than the all time low of last year) ... The oil crisis escalates in the Middle East and petrol prices sore ... Four star is now 59p a gallon ... Two star is 57p ... Lines of stationary Morris *1100s*, Ford *Escorts*, Hillman *Avengers* and Vauxhall *Vivas* clog the roads outside garage forecourts ... A 50 mph speed limit is imposed on motorists in an effort to conserve fuel ... A limited edition Ford *Capri RS3100* goes on sale - with a (petrol thirsty) V6 engine - and sales of the new car are slow ... A strike at British Leyland's car body factory at Llanelli affects production at Longbridge and Cowley - with many workers being laid-off ... The nights are cold and foggy ... Brave courting couples venture out for an evening at the local cinema ... 31-year-old Britt Ekland (34-24-33) dances naked in *The Wicker Man* ... 41-year-old Elizabeth Taylor stars alongside Henry Fonda in *Ash Wednesday* ... 32-year-old Bill Oddie, 30-year-old Graeme Garden and 33-year-old Tim Brooke-Taylor star in *The Goodies and the Beanstalk* - a one-off TV special shown on Christmas Eve ... "So here it is, 'Merry Christmas', everybody's havin' fun" - ***Merry Xmas Everybody*** by Slade remains at number one in the pop chart ... "Oh, well..." ***I Wish It Could Be Christmas Everyday*** ("... when the kids start singing and the band begins to play") by Wizzard (with 27-year-old lead singer Roy Wood) is number four ... Schoolboys ask Santa Claus for a 5-speed racer bicycle with *Huret* speedometer ... Pocket calculators and a new board game called *Escape From Colditz* are also in demand ... 'You'll find what you want in a box of Week-End' - millions of people give Mackintosh's *Week-End* assorted chocolates as gifts ... 10-year-old James May from Bristol receives an *Airfix* model from his auntie ... The power cuts continue and families huddle around candles in cold, dim living rooms ... Don Revie's hard-tackling, top-of-the-table Leeds Utd football team beats Newcastle Utd 0-1 on Boxing Day with a goal from 29-year-old Paul Madeley ... Bill Shankly's second placed Liverpool lose 1-2 at Burnley ... 57-year-old prime-minister Edward Heath and his Cabinet review their plans for a new international airport at Maplin Sands in Essex - the project now seems a little extravagant in light of the current economic climate ... "Charley and I were in the park. Then this man came up and said would I like to see some puppies and I said 'yes,' and I was going to go, but Charley stopped me" - A cartoon cat called Charley tells the public not to go anywhere with men or ladies they don't know ... 32-year-old Fred West and his 20-year-old wife Rosemary murder 21-year-old Lucy Partington and bury her body beneath their house at 25 Cromwell Street in Gloucester ... "We've got a thing that's called radar love. We've got a wave in the air..." ***Radar Love*** by Dutch rock group Golden Earring is number seven in the pop chart ... Housewives go shopping on Saturday afternoons ... Instant puddings sell well at *VG Food Stores* ... Banana flavour *Angel Delight* tastes great ... 'Stork SB margarine helps a good mum becomes a super mum' - 45-year-old Bruce Forsyth promotes margarine on TV ... 38-year-old David Vine introduces the first *Superstars* TV program - Bobby Moore (footballer), Joe Bugner (boxer), Jackie Stewart (racing driver), Roger Taylor (tennis player), David Hemery (runner), Tony Jacklin (golfer) and Barry John (rugby player) all take part ... 29-year-old David Hemery is the eventual winner ... The new year brings cold dark nights, power cuts and a three-day working week ... 'Who rules Britain? Heath or the miners?' ... A general election is called and people go to the polls on the twenty-eighth of February ... When all counts are completed, the Conservatives are four seats behind Labour. (Labour: 301 seats, Conservatives: 297 seats, Liberals: 14 seats). Sitting Conservative prime-minister Edward Heath fails to form a coalition with Jeremy Thorpe's Liberals ... Labour's leader Harold Wilson becomes prime-minister in a hung parliament ... 30-year-old Conservative candidate John Major loses in St. Pancras North ... 43-year-old Douglas Hurd is the new

Conservative MP for Mid Oxfordshire ... 48-year-old John Stonehouse is the new Labour MP for Walsall North ... ***You Won't Find Another Fool Like Me*** ("... babe") by The New Seekers is new at number one in the pop chart ... ***Dance With The Devil*** by Cozy Powell is number three ... Tanktops are in fashion ... 35-year-old Barbara Edwards presents the weather forecast on BBC One ... It's generally mild, wet and windy with some sleet on high ground ... Housewives cook food in the kitchen and distribute it to their waiting families through a 'serving-hatch' in the wall ... *Findus* Crispy Pancakes are delicious ... 32-year-old Polly James, 32-year-old Nerys Hughes and a pregnant pet hamster star in the first of a new series of *The Liver Birds* on BBC One ... 24-year-old Paula Wilcox, 23-year-old Sally Thomsett and 29-year-old Richard O'Sullivan star in the second series of *Man About the House* on ITV ... Eamonn Andrews surprises 35-year-old footballer Derek Dougan on *This is Your Life* ... 29-year-old footballer Kevin Hector scores a hat-trick, and 25-year-old Jeff Bourne scores twice, as Dave Mackay's Derby County thrash Jimmy Adamson's Burnley 5-1 at the Baseball Ground ... 43-year-old Chelsea manager Dave Sexton falls-out with star players Alan Hudson and Peter 'Ossie' Osgood - and puts both men on the transfer list ... 27-year-old 'super' Georgie Best plays his final match for Manchester Utd - a 3-0 defeat against Queens Park Rangers ... "That's neat, that's neat, that's neat, that's neat. I really love your..." ***Tiger Feet*** by Mud climbs to number one in the pop chart - and stays there for four weeks ... "So recognise your age it's a teenage rampage. Turn another page on the..." ***Teenage Rampage*** ("... now, now, now, now, now, now, now, now") by Sweet is number two ... A strike by British Leyland workers at Cowley brings production of the Austin *Maxi* motorcar to a halt ... More and more foreign cars are being sold in the UK ... The latest Renault *5TL* costs £1,086 and has a top speed of 87 mph ... A smart, new Volkswagen *Passat L 1300* costs £1,686 and has a top speed of 92 mph ... 37-year-old burglar Donald Nielson (aka the Black Panther) breaks into a post office at Harrogate in Yorkshire and murders sub-postmaster Donald Skepper ... BRMB radio station launches in Birmingham ... 38-year-old Tony Butler keeps listeners up to date with the local football news ... 23-year-old footballer Bob Latchford leaves Birmingham City and joins Everton for a new record transfer fee of £350,000 ... Second Division Aston Villa achieve a 2-0 victory over First Division Arsenal in an FA Cup fourth round replay at Villa Park - Alun Evans and Sammy Morgan score the goals ... "Bagpuss, dear Bagpuss, old fat furry Catpuss" - a children's TV show called *Bagpuss* is new on BBC One ... "Meet the gang 'cause the boys are here, the boys to entertain you" - *It Ain't Half Hot Mum* (a sit-com set in the Burmese jungle during World War II), starring 43-year-old Windsor Davies as Sergeant Major, 40-year-old Don Estelle as Lofty and 38-year-old Melvyn Hayes as Gloria, is also new ... 60-year-old Sid 'cor blimey' James, 45-year-old Diana Coupland and 23-year-old Sally Geeson star in the fourth series of popular ITV sit-com *Bless This House* ... "So, come alive! Come alive! Down in..." ***Devil Gate Drive*** by 23-year-old Suzi Quatro climbs to number one in the pop chart ... "Underground, overground, wombling free. The Wombles of Wimbledon Common are we" - ***The Wombling Song*** by The Wombles is number four ... People enjoy an evening out at the pictures... '... all it takes is a little Confidence' - 48-year-old Paul Newman and 37-year-old Robert Redford star in Hollywood movie *The Sting* ... A shocking new film called *The Exorcist* (starring 14-year-old Linda Blair as possessed schoolgirl Regan MacNeil) is banned in some cinemas, after public protests ... 45-year-old Alastair Burnet reads the news for ITN ... Nine British soldiers and three civilians lose their lives when an IRA bomb explodes on a coach travelling on the M62 in Yorkshire ... 17-year-old cemetery keeper Stephen Downing is sentenced to life imprisonment for the brutal rape and murder of Wendy Sewell at Bakewell in Derbyshire ... Police detective Jack Slipper of the Yard meets 44-year-old fugitive Ronnie Biggs in Copacabana but is unable to extradite him back to the UK ... 25-year-old Lulu sings ***The Man Who Sold The World*** ... 46-year-old Andy Williams sings ***Solitaire*** ... 22-year-old footballer Joe Jordan scores twice as Don Revie's hard-tackling Leeds Utd defeat Arsenal 3-1 to stay seven points clear at the top of Division One ... Kevin Keegan and Alec Lindsay score the goals as Bill Shankly's Liverpool beat Joe Mercer's Coventry City 2-1 at Anfield to stay second ... 22-year-old Alan Hudson leaves Chelsea and signs for Stoke City for £240,000 ... Peter 'Ossie' Osgood remains on the transfer list at Stamford Bridge ...

26-year-old Ray Graydon scores the winning goal for Vic Crowe's Aston Villa in a 0-1 victory over Cardiff City in Division Two ... 27-year-old Chris Tarrant presents a new program called *Tiswas* on ATV - and Saturday morning telly for children in the Midlands is never the same again ... "Goodnight John Boy" / "Goodnight Mary Ellen" - *The Waltons* begins on BBC Two ... The third series of TV drama *The Brothers* grips the nation on Sunday evenings ... On-going industrial action by workers at British Leyland's Cowley factory slows production of the *Maxi* and *Marina* motorcars ... ***Living For The City*** by 23-year-old Stevie Wonder is number fifteen in the pop chart ... ***All Of My Life*** by 29-year-old Diana Ross is number nine ... "Sha-la-la-la-la-la-la-la, sho-be-do-ay. Remember all the little things we used to say" - ***Remember (Sha-La-La)*** by The Bay City Rollers is number six ... Peter and Janet Williams from Stoke-on-Trent are proud parents of newborn son, Robbie ... 'Where did it all go wrong?' - 27-year-old wayward footballer Georgie Best spends an evening drinking Champagne with Marjorie Wallace (aka Miss World) at his own nightclub, *Slack Alice*, in Manchester ... 26-year-old footballer Bruce Rioch transfers from Second Division Aston Villa to First Division Derby County for £200,000 ... The Ford *Capri Mk II* motorcar (with a contemporary 'hatchback' boot design) is launched ... The *1300 L* model costs £1,731 and has a top speed of 87 mph. The *3000 Ghia* costs £3,109 and has a top speed of 120 mph ... Inflation continues to rise under Harold Wilson's Labour government ... A loaf of bread is 13p.

Spring 1974

Ma, he's makin' eyes at me

"Kids in water, they love it" - 43-year-old Rolf Harris presents a short public safety broadcast on TV promoting, 'Teaching children to swim' ... "Ma! Ma! He's makin' eyes at me. Ma, he's awfully nice to me" - 10-year-old Lena Zavaroni wins ITV's Opportunity Knocks for five weeks running. Her song, ***Ma He's Making Eyes At Me***, reaches number ten in the pop chart ... ***Jet*** ("... I can almost remember their funny faces") by Paul McCartney and Wings is number seven ... "Ah-oh! It's just my..." ***Jealous Mind*** by 31-year-old Alvin Stardust is number one ... There's a flu bug going around ... Poorly school children sit at home sipping Lucozade, drawing pictures with Crayola crayons and watching television ... 31-year-old Geoffrey Hayes is the new presenter of Rainbow on ITV. Bungle, Zippy and George are Geoffrey's housemates ... 44-year-old Leonard Parkin reads the lunchtime news for ITN ... A Turkish Airlines flight from Istanbul to London crashes near Paris killing all 346 people on board - it's the world's worst aviation disaster ... The airlines BOAC and BEA merge to form British Airways ... French president

Georges Pompidou dies aged 62 in Paris. Prime-minister Harold Wilson and leader of the opposition Edward Heath attend the funeral along with dozens of other political leaders including Willy Brandt of West Germany and Richard Nixon of the USA ... Back in Britain - striking miners return to work after an improved pay offer from Harold Wilson's Labour government ... The three-day working week comes to an end ... Full production resumes at British Leyland's Cowley plant - but Austin Maxi and Morris Marina motorcars remain in short supply ... 56-year-old Chancellor of the Exchequer Denis Healey delivers his first Budget ... The basic rate of income tax rises from thirty percent to thirty-three percent ... A pint of beer increases by one penny ... Spirits are increased by twenty pence ... 32-year-old Fred West and his 20-year-old wife Rosemary murder 21-year-old Therese Siegenthaler and bury her body beneath their house at 25 Cromwell Street in Gloucester ... "Goodbye Joe, you gotta go, me oh, my oh. He gotta go pole the pirogue, down the bayou" - ***Jambalaya (On The Bayou)*** by The Carpenters reaches number twelve on the hit parade ... "Emmalene..." ***Emma*** ("... Emmalene, I'm gonna write your name high on that silver screen") by Hot Chocolate is number three ... 27-year-old wayward footballer Georgie Best is charged (and later acquitted) with stealing a fur coat from Marjorie Wallace (aka Miss World) ... 46-year-old Bill McGarry's Wolverhampton Wanderers defeat 41-year-old Ron Saunders' Manchester City 2-1 in the League Cup final at Wembley - with 23-year-old Kenny Hibbitt and 23-year-old John

Richards scoring the goals ... "Billy don't be a hero, don't be a fool with your life. Billy don't be a hero, come back and make me your wife. And as Billy started to go, she said, keep your pretty head low, oh, oh..." ***Billy Don't Be A Hero*** ("... come back to me") by Paper Lace is number one in the pop chart ... ***Seven Seas Of Rhye*** by Queen climbs to number ten ... ***Candle In The Wind*** by 27-year-old Elton John reaches number eleven ... ATV's programs on a Saturday night include: Reg Varney - a musical variety show featuring 57-year-old Reg Varney, with Henry McGee and Pat Coombs; Sale of the Century - hosted by 50-year-old Nicholas Parsons; Candid Camera - with Peter Dulay and Arthur Atkins; and The Saturday Night Film ... Oxford win the Boat Race for the first time in seven years ... A naked 25-year-old Michael O'Brien streaks across Twickenham rugby pitch before being caught by a policeman - who covers the young man's embarrassment with his helmet ... ***Rebel Rebel*** ("... you've torn your dress. Rebel, rebel, your face is a mess") by 27-year-old David Bowie is number five in the pop chart ... "Let it rip! And then the cat crept in, and crept out again" - ***The Cat Crept In*** by Mud climbs to number two ... 32-year-old footballer Bobby Moore leaves First Division West Ham Utd (after eighteen years) and transfers to Second Division Fulham for £25,000 ... 31-year-old Des Lynam presents Sports Report on Radio Two on Saturday afternoons ... Fans protest outside Stamford Bridge football ground when Chelsea manager Dave Sexton sells 27-year-old Peter 'Ossie' Osgood to Southampton for £275,000 ... "We're gonna win the league! We're gonna win the league! And now you're gonna believe us!" - Don Revie's hard-tackling Leeds Utd finish the season five points ahead of Bill Shankly's Liverpool to become champions of Division One ... 27-year-old Peter Lorimer scores twice as Leeds beat Sheffield Utd 0-2 and then two more victories over Ipswich Town (3-2) and Queens Park Rangers (1-0) ensure that Leeds finish top-of-the-table ... Liverpool are runners-up ... Dave Mackay's Derby County are third. Leeds players: David Harvey, Trevor Cherry, Paul Reaney, Paul Madeley, Gordon McQueen, Norman 'Bites Yer Legs' Hunter, Johnny Giles, Billy Bremner, Terry Yorath, Peter Lorimer, Mick Jones, Allan 'sniffer' Clarke and 22-year-old Joe Jordan have all been outstanding ... 34-year-old Denis Law scores in a 0-1 win for Manchester City at Old Trafford and Tommy 'The Doc' Docherty's Manchester Utd are relegated to Division Two ... "We had joy we had fun, we had seasons in the sun, but the hills that we climbed, were just seasons out of time" - ***Seasons In The Sun*** by 30-year-old Terry Jacks spends four weeks at number one in the pop chart ... ***I'm Gonna Knock On Your Door*** ("... ring on your bell, tap on your window too. If you don't come out tonight, when the moon is bright, I'm gonna knock and ring and tap until you do") by 11-year-old Little Jimmy Osmond is number eleven ... 54-year-old Sir Alf Ramsey is sacked as England manager, and Joe Mercer is appointed on a temporary basis ... Mick Channon and Frank Worthington score the goals as England (with a line-up of: Shilton, Hughes, Lindsay, Todd, Watson, Bell, Keegan, Channon,

Worthington, Weller, Brooking) draw 2-2 in a friendly against Argentina at Wembley ... The Wonderloaf Gang charges down the grass bank at St. Joseph's Junior School in Rugeley - in pursuit of the Freedom Fighter Gang. (Headmaster Mr. 'Percy' Edwards is not amused) ... Families gather together to watch television in the evenings ... 39-year-old Wendy Craig stars in ITV's new sit-com And Mother Makes Five - which picks up the storyline from last year's And Mother Makes Three ... 49-year-old Kenneth Kendall reads the news on BBC One ... Michael Barratt, Frank Bough, Bob Wellings and 27-year-old Sue Lawley present Nationwide ... A kidnap attempt is made on Princess Anne and Captain Mark Phillips - it fails ... "Hey, did you happen to see..." ***The Most Beautiful Girl*** ("... in the world") by 40-year-old Charlie Rich climbs to number two in the pop chart ... ***You're Sixteen*** ('... you're beautiful, and you're mine") by 32-year-old Ringo Starr reaches number four ... Red Rum (ridden by Brian Fletcher) wins the Grand National at Aintree for the second year in succession ... The Eurovision Song Contest (with 47-year-old Katie Boyle as compare) takes place in Brighton on the sixth of April. Britain's entry, ***Long Live Love*** by 25-year-old Olivia Newton-John, finishes in fourth position. Sweden's entry, ***Waterloo*** by Abba, is the winning song ... The Lamborghini Countach sports car is launched with a top speed of 192 mph and capable of 0-60 mph in 5.4 seconds ... Citroen launch its range of CX executive cars, with hydro-pneumatic suspension and a top speed of 108 mph ... "Waterloo, I was defeated, you won the war. Waterloo, promise to love you forever more" ***Waterloo*** by Abba (with 27-year-old Benny, 29-year-old Bjorn, 28-year-old Anni-Frid and 24-year-old Agnetha) moves up to number one in the pop chart ... ***Remember You're A Womble*** ("... Remember you're a Womble. Remember, 'member, 'member what a Womble, Womble, Womble you are") by The Wombles is number three ... 23-year-old footballer Kevin Keegan scores twice as Bill Shankly's Liverpool beat Joe Harvey's Newcastle Utd 3-0 in the FA Cup final. (26-year-old Steve Heighway is also on the score-sheet). 43-year-old Gordon Kew from South Shields is referee. A ticket for the standing enclosure at the Empire Stadium in Wembley costs £1.00 ... Relegated Manchester Utd sign 24-year-old centre-forward Stuart Pearson from Hull City for £200,000 ... "Sugar baby love..." ***Sugar Baby Love*** by The Rubettes shoots up the pop chart from number twenty-seven to number two, and moves up to top spot the following week ... "Well, we sang shang-a-lang as we ran with the gang, doin' doo wop be dooby do aye. We were all in the news with our blue suede shoes, and our dancin' the night away" - ***Shang-a-Lang*** by The Bay City Rollers reaches number two ... Glossy, colour posters of Eric, Les, Woody, Alan and Derek adorn the bedroom walls of teenage girls ... Children watch The Wombles on TV ... Glossy, colour posters of Orinoco, Tobermory, Bungo, Wellington and Great Uncle Bulgaria adorn the bedroom walls of young school children ... Public Notices remind people to, 'Keep Britain Tidy'.

Summer 1974

I'm taking the Costa Brava plane

It's a dull and drizzly summer ... School children stay indoors watching *Wacky Races*, *Whirlybirds*, *Adventures of Tintin* and *Daktari* on television ... "Heartbeat, increasing heartbeat" - ***This Town Ain't Big Enough For The Both Of Us*** by Sparks climbs to number two in the pop chart ... "Wo-oh, wo-oh. Jet plane flying high above me..." ***Don't Stay Away Too Long*** by Peters and Lee peaks at number three ... 44-year-old Stuart Hall presents *It's A Knockout* on BBC One on Friday evenings. A team representing Skegness beats a team from Mablethorpe and Sutton-on-Sea, after competing in events: Canoe Race, Water Netball, Pyjama Race, Island Crossing, Boat Sinking, Netting the Ball and Raft Pyramid ... 24-year-old boxer Joe Bugner beats Piermario Baruzzi by a Technical Knock-out in round ten in Copenhagen to retain his European heavy-weight title ... 43-year-old Peter Woods reads the news on BBC One ... Hospital services are disrupted as disgruntled NHS staff stage a number of walk-outs, sit-ins and go-slows ... White collar workers go on strike at Triumph's car factory in

Coventry ... Production workers walk-out at Rover's factory in Solihull ... "Come on follow the Geordie boys, they'll fill your heart with joy. They're marching for their freedom now" - ***Jarrow Song*** by Alan Price climbs from number eighteen to number eight in the pop chart ... ***Judy Teen*** by Cockney Rebel is number seven ... Adverts for *Coca-Cola* proclaim, 'It's the real thing. Coke' ... Discarded ring-pulls from drinks cans litter public parks and communal spaces ... The campaign to 'Keep Britain Tidy' intensifies ... Violence breaks out at Red Lion Square in central London when members of the National Front are confronted by demonstrators from the Liberation group ... Mounted police charge into the crowd and 20-year-old student Kevin Gately dies after receiving a blow to the head ... An explosion at a chemical plant in Flixborough on Humberside kills twenty-eight people ... Sugar is in short supply due to low stocks of sugar cane at refineries - long queues form outside shops ... 7-year-old Helen Hinks makes her First Holy Communion at St. Joseph & St. Etheldreda's church in Rugeley ... 42-year-old Elizabeth Taylor and 48-year-old Richard Burton divorce after ten years of marriage ... "Oh yes, they call him the streak. Bug-idee. Bug-idee" - ***The Streak*** by Ray Stevens is the new number one pop song ... ***There's A Ghost In My House*** ("... the ghost of your memories. The ghost of the love you took from me") by R Dean Taylor is number three ... 46-year-old Terry Scott and 48-year-old June Whitfield star in *Happy Ever After* on BBC One ... 43-year-old Les Dawson from Manchester appears in ITV's hit comedy *Sez Les* - some of the show's jokes and sketches are written by 39-year-old David Nobbs from Orpington ... "I know, you know, I'll never, never let you go" - ***Always Yours*** by Gary Glitter is number one on the hit parade ... ***Hey Rock And Roll*** ("... Bring it to town, let's stroll!") by Showaddywaddy is number two ... Cricketers Geoffrey Boycott and Dennis Amiss stride out together to open the batting for England against India at Old Trafford. Boycott makes 10 runs. Amiss hits 56. 30-year-old batsman Keith Fletcher scores 123 not out. 25-year-old fast bowler Bob Willis takes 4 for 64, and England win the match ... 21-year-old Jimmy Conners uses a new-fangled metal framed tennis racket, instead of the traditional wooden instrument, and defeats 39-year-old Ken Rosewall 6-1, 6-1, 6-4 in the men's singles final at Wimbledon ... ***Kissin' In The Back Row Of The Movies*** ("... on a Saturday night with you. Holdin' hands together, you and I, holdin' hands together") by The Drifters peaks at number two in the pop chart ... "I was..." ***Born With A Smile On My Face*** ("... the whole of my life's been a pantomime") by Stephanie de Sykes (with Rain) also reaches number two ... Chancellor of the Exchequer Denis Healey reduces the standard rate of VAT from 10% to 8%, but introduces a new higher rate of 12.5% on petrol ... An IRA bomb explodes at the Houses of Parliament - injuring eleven people ... 'N' reg cars go on sale ... High-flying businessmen in dark pinstriped suits, with extensive lapels and flared trousers, collect their brand new car from the showroom ... The new Ford *Capri MKII 3000 GT* has a top speed of 120 mph and can reach 60 mph in 8.4

seconds ... The latest BMW *2002 Turbo* has a top speed of 130 mph and can reach 60 mph in 7.5 seconds ... 32-year-old Geoffrey Hayes makes his final appearance as DC Dave Scatliffe in BBC's long-running police drama *Z Cars* ... 16-year-old actress Helen Worth makes her first appearance as Gail Potter in ITV's ever popular soap-opera *Coronation Street* ... "She, may be the face I can't forget, a trace of pleasure or regret, maybe my treasure or the price I have to pay" - ***She*** by Charles Aznavour is new at number one in the pop chart ... "Well, I'm a one man band. Nobody knows nor understands" - ***One Man Band*** by 26-year-old Leo Sayer is number six ... Radio One's weekday schedule of disc jockeys is - Noel Edmonds (7 a.m. to 9 a.m.), Tony Blackburn (9 a.m. to 12 noon), Johnnie Walker (12 noon to 2 p.m.), 'Diddy' David Hamilton (2 p.m. to 5 p.m.) and 47-year-old Alan 'Fluff' Freeman (5 p.m. to 7 p.m.) ... 40-year-old actor Tom Baker takes over from 55-year-old Jon Pertwee as *Dr. Who* on TV ... 'All for one, one for all!' - 32-year-old Michael York is d'Artagnan playing alongside Oliver Reed, Frank Finlay and Richard Chamberlain in *The Three Musketeers* at cinemas ... 'Dick Turpin Carries On with his Flintlock Cocked!' - 61-year-old Sid 'cor blimey' James is 'Big Dick' Turpin and 36-year-old Barbara Windsor (36-23-34) is his partner-in-crime in *Carry On Dick* ... "Woman, take me in your arms..." ***Rock Your Baby*** by George McCrae spends three weeks at number one in the pop chart ... ***Beach Baby*** ("... Beach Baby, give me your hand. Give me something that I can remember") by First Class is number thirteen ... A bomb explodes at the Tower of London - killing one person and injuring forty-one ... The chief of Scotland Yard's Bomb Squad says, "It was an indiscriminate attack designed to create as much trouble and injury as possible. It is the sort of target the IRA would pick" ... Fears are high that more terror atrocities are to follow ... 46-year-old Don Revie is appointed as the new football manager of England ... 39-year-old Brian Clough takes over at Leeds Utd and tells his new players they can throw their medals in the bin because they've all been won by cheating ... Bill Shankly retires as Liverpool manager and is replaced by 55-year-old Bob Paisley ... 41-year-old Ron Saunders is the new manager of Second Division Aston Villa ... 34-year-old John Lyall is the new manager of First Division West Ham Utd ... "Oh this year we're off to sunny Spain..." ***Y Viva Espana*** by Sylvia is number four in the pop chart ... "And you can run in the sun, having fun with the one that you really love. Walk in the sand, hand in hand, with the boy that you met on vacation. And on a warm summer night, it's alright when he says, 'Baby I love you'. Then, boy oh boy, you're enjoying that summerlove sensation" - Tartan-clad teenage girls go wild with joy as ***Summerlove Sensation*** by The Bay City Rollers climbs to number two ... 27-year-old cricketer David Lloyd scores an unbeaten 214 at Edgbaston and Mike Denness' England win the Test series 3-0 against India ... 48-year-old Richard Baker reads the news on BBC One ... Richard Nixon is forced to resign over the Watergate scandal and 60-year-old Gerald Ford becomes the new president of the USA ...

Back in England - The headless body of a woman is found near Swaffham in Norfolk ... 33-year-old Esther Rantzen presents *That's Life* on TV - aided by reporters Glyn Worsnip, Kieran Prendiville and 61-year-old Cyril Fletcher - who delivers odd little odes at the end of the show ... "H-ooh-ooh. H-aah-aah. H-aah-aah. H-ooh-ooh. Precious moments..." ***When Will I See You Again*** by The Three Degrees reaches number one in the pop chart ... ***I Shot The Sheriff*** ("... but I did not shoot the deputy") by 29-year-old Eric Clapton is number nine ... There's a flurry of activity on football's transfer market ... 23-year-old Ray Kennedy leaves Arsenal and joins Liverpool for £180,000 ... 25-year-old Brian Kidd transfers from Manchester Utd to Arsenal for £110,000 ... 25-year-old Larry Lloyd leaves Liverpool and joins Coventry City for £240,000 ... 30-year-old Franny Lee leaves Manchester City and joins Dave Mackay's Derby County for £100,000 ... 28-year-old 'super' Georgie Best is released from his contract at Manchester Utd ... People buy the latest 7-inch singles at *W. H. Smith & Son* for 55p ... "Oh, Liverpool Lou, lovely..." ***Liverpool Lou*** by The Scaffold is number seven in the pop chart ... "And the jailer man and sailor Sam were searching everyone, for the..." ***Band On The Run*** by Paul McCartney and Wings is number three ... ***I'm Leaving It (All) Up To You*** ("... ooh-ooh-ooh") by 16-year-old Donny Osmond and 14-year-old Marie Osmond is number two ... The new football season gets underway ... 31-year-old Billy Bremner of Leeds Utd and 23-year-old Kevin Keegan of Liverpool fight on the pitch in the Charity Shield at Wembley

... Football fans wear flared jeans, platform shoes, denim jackets and tie their club coloured scarves around their wrists ... Hooligans riot at Ashton Gate as Bristol City beat Cardiff City 2-1 in the League Cup ... Other instances of football violence occur throughout the country ... A tragic low point is reached when 17-year-old Kevin Olsson is stabbed to death at a match between Blackpool and Bolton Wanderers ... "Don't love me for fun girl, let me be the one girl. Love me for a reason, and let the reason be love" - ***Love Me For A Reason*** by The Osmonds is top of the pop chart ... "Big wheels keep on turning, carry me home to see my kin" - ***Sweet Home Alabama*** by Lynyrd Skynyrd is number twenty-one ... 54-year-old wartime football legend Tommy Lawton is found guilty of obtaining goods by deception ... 54-year-old Bill Nicholson resigns as manager of Tottenham Hotspur. Nicholson had been with Spurs for thirty-eight years - serving first as a trainee, then as a player and finally as the manager ... 25-year-old Joe Royle scores twice for Billy Bingham's Everton in a 2-1 win over Stoke City in a First Division match at Goodison Park ... 20-year-old Gerry Daly scores a hat-trick for Tommy 'The Doc' Docherty's Manchester Utd in a 4-0 win over Millwall in a Second Division match at Old Trafford ... ***Rock The Boat*** ("... Don't rock the boat, baby. Rock the boat. Don't tip the boat over") by The Hues Corporation reaches number six in the pop chart ... "I know..." ***It's Only Rock And Roll*** ("... but I like it, I like it, yes I do") by The Rolling Stones is number ten ... 21-year-old Mary Connors is fired from a cannon at Tewkesbury in an attempt to cross the River Avon. She fails, and has to be rescued from the water by a diver ... 'Our Barest Beach Girls' - *Mayfair* magazine costs 40p at newsagents ... A pack of twenty Player's *No. 6* cigarettes is 25½p ... Prices continue to rise and people of Britain are becoming anxious ... 56-year-old Shadow Home Secretary Keith Joseph warns that, "Inflation is threatening to destroy our society" ... The average price of a house in the UK has now risen above £10,000 ... 'The antidote to panel games' - a new series of *I'm Sorry I Haven't A Clue* begins on Radio Four, with panelists Graeme Garden, Barry Cryer, Willie Rushton and Tim Brooke-Taylor, and with 53-year-old Humphrey Lyttelton in the chair ... Adverts say, '*Tetley* make teabags make tea!'

Autumn 1974

Those kicks were fast as lightning

11-year-old Nick Robinson from Macclesfield in Cheshire rushes home from school to watch *John Craven's Newsround* on BBC One ... Chancellor of the Exchequer Denis Healey doubles the higher rate of VAT ... Four star petrol rises sharply in price - it's now a staggering 75p per gallon! ... A new ring-road opens in Coventry ... The traditional metal and chrome bumpers on the MG *B* and MG *Midget* sports cars are replaced by modern rubber bumpers ... An unofficial walk-out by engineering inspectors at British Leyland's factory in Solihull leads to four-thousand workers being laid off ... Fighting breaks out on the terracing at a Second Division football match between West Bromwich Albion and Manchester Utd ... Fighting breaks out on the terracing at a First Division football match between Chelsea and Arsenal ... "Everybody was..." ***Kung Fu Fighting*** ("... those kicks were fast as lightning. In fact it was a little bit frightening, but they fought with expert timing") by Carl Douglas is number one in the pop chart ... "She keeps the Moet et Chandon in her pretty cabinet. 'Let them eat cake' she says, just like Marie Antoinette" - ***Killer Queen*** by Queen is number two ... *Rising Damp* is a brand new sit-com on ITV - with Frances de la Tour, Richard Beckinsdale, Don Warrington and starring 47-year-old Leonard Rossiter as Rigsby ... The third series of *Man About the House* begins - starring 24-year-old Paula Wilcox, 24-year-old Sally Thomsett and 30-year-old Richard O'Sullivan as flat mates - with the Ropers (48-year-old Yootha Joyce and 42-year-old Brian Murphy) as nosy neighbours ... The latest series of *Upstairs Downstairs* (with 40-year-old Jean Marsh as Rose, 70-year-old Angela Baddeley as Mrs. Bridges, 50-year-old Gordon Jackson as Hudson and 20-year-old Lesley-Anne Down as Georgina Worsley) depicts life in an aristocratic London house during World War One ... "You fill up my senses, like a night in the forest, like the mountains in springtime, like a walk in the rain" - ***Annie's Song*** by John Denver spends a week at number one on the hit parade ... 38-year-old burglar Donald Nielson (aka the Black Panther) breaks into a post office at Baxenden in Lancashire and murders Derek Astin ... 54-year-old football legend Tommy Lawton carries out two-hundred hours of community service - after his recent conviction for obtaining goods by deception ... 32-year-old Terry Neill is the new manager at Tottenham Hotspur ... 22-year-old Nenad 'Pop' Popovic is the new PE teacher at Cardinal Griffin school in Cannock ... 18-year-old student Teresa Brasier from Eastbourne goes up to Oxford to read Geography ... ***Sad Sweet Dreamer*** ("... it's just one of those things we put down to experience") by Sweet

Sensation spends a week at number one in the pop chart ... ***Rock Me Gently*** by Andy Kim from Canada reaches number two ... 58-year-old Harold Wilson calls the second general election of the year ... People cast their votes on the tenth of October and Wilson wins another term as prime-minister - gaining a small majority over Edward Heath. (Labour: 319 seats, Conservatives: 277 seats, Liberals: 13 seats) ... 31-year-old Conservative candidate John Major loses for a second time in St. Pancras North ... One-thousand workers go on strike at British Leyland's factory in Castle Bromwich - slowing production of *Jaguar* and *Mini* motor cars ... 39-year-old football manager Brian Clough is sacked after just forty-four days in charge at Leeds Utd ... 20-year-old striker Trevor Francis scores a hat-trick for Freddie Goodwin's Birmingham City in a 1-3 win over Harry Haslam's Luton Town ... Three days later, Francis scores again as Birmingham beat reigning champions Leeds Utd 1-0 in front of 36,513 at St. Andrew's ... 24-year-old Malcolm 'Supermac' MacDonald scores twice as Newcastle Utd thrash Chelsea 5-0 at St. James' Park ... 22-year-old midfielder Terry McDermott leaves Newcastle and joins Liverpool for £175,000 ... 25-year-old goalkeeper Peter Shilton leaves Leicester City and joins Stoke City for £325,000 ... 19-year-old defender Sam Allardyce makes his debut for Second Division Bolton Wanderers in a 1-3 defeat against Notts County ... Pubs are forced to close and shops are boarded up as Millwall play host to Manchester Utd in Division Two - Gerry Daly scores in a 0-1 win for Utd ... 36-year-old Ian St.

John is appointed manager of Portsmouth football club ... ***The Bitch Is Back*** by 27-year-old Elton John is number fifteen in the pop chart ... ***Hang On In There Baby*** ("... Hang on in there darlin'. I'm gonna give you more than you ever dreamed possible") by Johnny Bristol is number three ... "Who loves ya, baby?" - Telly Savalas is *Kojak* on TV ... 33-year-old Fred West and his 20-year-old wife, Rosemary, murder 15-year-old Shirley Hubbard and bury her body beneath their house at 25 Cromwell Street in Gloucester ... 'Rollermania' causes pandemonium as teenage girls 'go crazy' for their favourite pop star heart-throbs ... 14-year-old Kora Blake from Desborough faints in the crowd when The Bay City Rollers (20-year-old Eric Faulkner, 18-year-old Les McKeown, 17-year-old Stuart 'Woody' Wood, 26-year-old Alan Longmuir and 23-year-old Derek Longmuir) take to the stage at the Granada Theatre in Kettering ... "But I said it before, and I'll say it again, and again, and again, and again..." ***All Of Me Loves All Of You*** ("... and every little thing you do") by 'The Rollers' climbs to number four in the pop chart ... "And I would give anything I own. Give up my life, my heart, my home" - ***Everything I Own*** by 26-year-old Ken Boothe is number one ... The IRA's terror campaign intensifies ... Five people are killed and forty-four are injured in pub bombings in Guildford ... A British soldier and a civilian are killed by a bomb in Woolwich ... Another twenty-one people are killed and almost two-hundred injured by bombs detonated in two Birmingham pubs ... 54-year-old Home Secretary Roy Jenkins signs his approval for the

Prevention of Terrorism Act - giving police the right to arrest, detain and question suspects for a period of up to seven days, with the further sanction of deportation back to Ireland ... Public outrage over the indiscriminate bombings leads to the ostracisation of many Irish people living in England, with some being assaulted in the street and refused service in shops, cafes and pubs ... ***Oh Yes! You're Beautiful*** by 30-year-old Gary Glitter moves up to number three on the hit parade ... "Oh, oh, oh. It's magic, you know. Never believe it's not so" - ***Magic*** by Pilot is number eleven ... 'Rumble in the Jungle' - 32-year-old boxer Muhammad Ali regains the world heavy-weight title by knocking out 25-year-old George Foreman in the eighth round in Kinshasa, Zaire ... Back in England - the High Street in West Bromwich is pedestrianised ... Young TV viewers are enthralled by a crazy new cartoon called *Roobarb* ... 'Here Be Sea Monsters' - a colour version of *Captain Pugwash* (with pirates Willy and Barnabas, cabin boy Tom and captain Horatio Pugwash) is also new ... "Norman Stanley Fletcher, you have pleaded guilty to the charges brought by this court and it is now my duty to pass sentence" - *Porridge*, with 44-year-old Ronnie Barker as Fletcher and 27-year-old Richard Beckinsale as Godber, debuts on BBC One ... A new series of the hugely popular *Dad's Army* begins on Friday evenings ... "We can rebuild him. We have the technology" - schoolboys all around the country try to emulate *The Six Million Dollar Man* - as 35-year-old Lee Majors stars as the bionic Steve Austin ... 27-year-old Jenny Hanley replaces 35-year-old Susan

Stranks on *Magpie* ... 44-year-old Bernard Manning is compare at *The Wheeltappers and Shunters Social Club* - where 43-year-old Colin Crompton wears a flat cap and rings his bell... "On behalf of the committ-ee!!" ... 29-year-old house-keeper Sandra Rivett is found murdered in Belgravia and 39-year-old Lord Lucan disappears - never to be seen again ... 41-year-old Barry Norman presents the late night movie review program *Film 74* on BBC One ... "This is your life Timmy Lea" - *Confessions of a Window Cleaner* is now showing at cinemas, starring 24-year-old Robin Askwith as Timmy Lea ... Men in long, grubby 'macs' loiter outside seedy picture houses ... 22-year-old Sylvia Kristel stars in *Emmanuelle* - an erotic, French film ... "Opal Fruits, made to make you mouth water" - *Opal Fruits* are advertised on TV ... The first *McDonalds* hamburger restaurant opens at Woolwich ... A *Big Mac* costs 45p ... 'Regular' *French Fries* are 12p ... Tottenham Hotspur footballers Steve Perryman (aged 22) and Martin Chivers (aged 29) score the goals to give Spurs a 2-0 victory over North London rivals Arsenal in Division One ... 27-year-old Ray Graydon scores a hat-trick as Aston Villa beat Millwall 3-0 in Division Two ... 17-year-old violinist Nigel Kennedy busks on Fifth Avenue in New York ... "Well, I know I've been out of style for a short while, but I don't care how cold you are. I'm coming home soon. I'm..." ***Gonna Make You A Star*** ("Yeah!") by 27-year-old David Essex climbs to number one in the pop chart - and stays there for three weeks ... ***No Honestly*** ("... I know we were meant to be") by 26-year-old Lynsey De Paul is number seven ... Racial tensions remain high in London ... 40-year-old National Front leader, John Tyndall, is ousted as chairman by 38-year-old John Kingsley Read ... People from ethnic minorities are abused frequently in the street by right wing extremists ... Hundreds of council tenants in North Kensington return home from work each day to their new accommodation at Grenfell Tower - a modern 'hi-rise' tower block ... Richard Baker and Kenneth Kendall present the *9 O'Clock News* on BBC One ... 49-year-old Labour MP John Stonehouse is presumed dead (by drowning) after his clothes are found on a beach in Miami ... 38-year-old burglar Donald Nielson (aka the Black Panther) breaks into a post office at Langley in the West Midlands and shoots dead Sidney Grayland ... An evil rapist terrorises young women in Cambridge. Police are hunting for a short, stocky man who has struck three times in the past few weeks ... 60-year-old British Leyland chairman Lord Stokes meets with Labour's 49-year-old Industry Secretary, Anthony Wedgwood Benn, to discuss a possible government bail-out for the ailing car manufacturer ... "On your last trip, did you discover what the Earth people eat? / They eat a great many of these. [Shows a potato] "They peel them with their metal knives. Boil them for twenty of their minutes. Then they smash them all to bits. (Ha-ha-ha). They are clearly a most primitive people" - 'For Mash Get *Smash*' - the Martians are on ITV.

Winter 1974 - 1975

Come up and see me, make me smile

The weather is mild and breezy ... Aran jumpers and wide-flared jeans are in fashion ... Children devour *Fizzy Lemonade* flavoured *Spangles* ... "We got it together didn't we? We've definitely got our thing together, don't we baby?" - ***You're The First The Last My Everything*** by 30-year-old Barry White is number one on the hit parade ... 33-year-old Ed 'stewpot' Stewart presents *Junior Choice* on weekend mornings on Radio One ... "Three wheels on my wagon, and I'm still rollin' along. The Cherokees are chasin' me. Arrows fly right on by, but I'm singin' a happy song" - The New Christy Minstrels sing ***Three Wheels On My Wagon*** ... Rock band Stray play a gig at the Oldham College of Technology - and go down a storm with the students ... 23-year-old footballer Bob Latchford scores his seventh goal of the season as Billy Bingham's Everton beat Derby County 0-1 to remain top of Division One ... 25-year-old Stuart Pearson scores his eleventh goal of the season as Tommy 'The Doc' Docherty's Manchester Utd beat York City 0-1 to remain top of Division Two ... 38-year-old Gordon Honeycombe reads the news for ITN ... The IRA's bombing campaign continues ... Seventeen people are injured when a device explodes amongst shoppers in Bristol ... Bombs are also detonated outside *Selfridges* and *Harrods* in London; and at the home of Edward Heath in Belgravia - thankfully, there are no casualties ... The so-called Cambridge Rapist strikes again - breaking into the homes of two women in the city and committing savage and brutal attacks. Police continue their search for the evil perpetrator ... An industrial dispute at British Leyland in Coventry sees thousands of assembly workers laid-off ... Cash is tight for tens of thousands of parents in working-class families ... Those that can afford it, take their children to matinee films at the local cinema during the Christmas holiday ... Walt Disney's *Herbie Rides Again* is now showing ... "It's behind you!" - Middle-class families enjoy an evening at the Pantomime ... 59-year-old comedian Dick Emery appears in *Goldilocks and the Three Bears* at the Wimbledon Theatre ... 61-year-old Sid 'cor blimey' James, 46-year-old Diana Coupland and 24-year-old Sally Geeson star in the fifth series of popular ITV sit-com *Bless This House* ... 40-year-old John Noakes, 35-year-old Peter Purves and 27-year-old Lesley Judd present *Blue Peter* on BBC One. The Christmas Appeal is underway with thousands of children sending in old buttons, buckles and badges to help raise money for new guide dogs for blind people ... 26-year-old athlete Brendan Foster (world record holder in the 3000 metre running event) is BBC's 'Sports Personality of the Year' ... "It'll be..." ***Lonely This Christmas***

("... without you to hold") by Mud spends four weeks at number one in the pop chart ... "We wish you a..." ***Wombling Merry Christmas*** by The Wombles is number two ... ***The Inbetweenies / Father Christmas Do Not Touch Me*** by The Goodies is number seven ... A Thomas Salter *Adventure Kit* at £4.99 (including water bottle, torch, camera, compass and penknife) is an exciting Christmas gift for schoolboys ... A *Hornby* electric train set is £10.95 from *Argos* ... The 'World Cup Striker' table-top football game from *Palitoy* now comes with floodlights ... Families gather around television sets in their G-Plan furnished living rooms ... A 'room divider' unit (supplied as a 'flat-pack') costs £22.50 ... *The Likely Lads* Christmas TV special sees Bob and Thelma attend a fancy dress party with Terry as their mini cab driver ... "Who's going to see the Queen?" - In *Some Mothers Do 'Ave 'Em*, Frank and Betty spend their first Christmas with baby, Jessica ... Eamonn Andrews surprises 74-year-old entertainer Arthur Askey on ITV's *This is Your Life* ... The latest series of TV drama *The Brothers* continues to grip the nation on Sunday evenings ... The all new *MKII* Ford *Escort* motorcar is now in showrooms. The range of cars (which will be available in the new year) is *Popular*, *L*, *GL*, *Ghia* and *RS*. The 1100cc models have a top speed of 81 mph. The 1300cc models have a top speed of 87 mph ... Hallmark Records release *The Best of Top of the Pops 1974* - a budget priced cover-version pop compilation LP with a sensual blonde girl pictured on the sleeve ... 22-year-old Helen Morgan from Barry wins the Miss World contest but is forced to resign when it's revealed she's a single mum ... "You keep buying and they'll keep the prices down! Alright!?" - Radio One disc jockey Alan 'Fluff' Freeman is on TV advertising sheets and blankets for *Brentford Nylons* ... Tony Waddington's Stoke City (with Shilton, Pejic, Greenhoff and Hudson) move to the top of Division One, after winning four of their last five league games ... Alan Ashman's Carlisle Utd (with Ross, Gorman, Train and Laidlaw) are in the relegation zone, after losing five of their last six games ... Birmingham City move up to fourteenth with a 3-1 victory over Liverpool in front of 23,608 at St. Andrew's - Gordon Taylor, Howard Kendall and 27-year-old Bob Hatton score the goals for 'The Blues' ... 28-year-old Leicester City striker Keith Weller is placed on the transfer list after refusing to play in the second half of a match against Ipswich Town ... "There's a new dance that is going around, called the bump. Do..." ***The Bump*** by Kenny is number three in the pop chart ... "Come on baby do the..." ***Juke Box Jive*** by The Rubettes is number five ... 49-year-old Labour MP John Stonehouse is caught and arrested in Australia - after faking his own death last month ... 28-year-old cricketer Tony Greig scores a century for England in the opening Test of the Ashes series in Brisbane, but Australia go on to win the match. 31-year-old Dennis Amiss and 27-year-old David Lloyd stride out together to open the batting for England in the Boxing Day Test at Melbourne. Amiss scores 4 runs. Lloyd makes 14. The match ends in a draw ... Back in Britain - Millions enjoy an evening at the cinema ... An all star cast including 50-year-old Lauren

Bacall, 59-year-old Ingrid Bergman 44-year-old Sean Connery and 38-year-old Albert Finney appear in *Murder on the Orient Express* ... "Goodnight! Goodnight! / Good night, sir" - 47-year-old Roger Moore stars as James Bond (aka 007) in *The Man With The Golden Gun*. 32-year-old Britt Ekland (32-24-33) is Bond's beautiful assistant, Mary Goodnight. 66-year-old Bernard Lee is M. 52-year-old Christopher Lee is Bond's arch enemy, Scaramanga ... "So how can you tell me you're lonely and say for you that the sun don't shine. Let me take you by the hand and lead you through the..." ***Streets Of London*** ("... I'll show you something, to make you change your mind") by Ralph McTell climbs to number two in the pop chart ... 31-year-old DJ Tony Blackburn presents the weekday mid-morning show on Radio One ... 47-year-old DJ Alan 'Fluff' Freeman presents the afternoon show on Saturdays ... Football hooligans invade the pitch, and fighting breaks out at Hillsborough as Sheffield Wednesday draw 4-4 with Manchester Utd in Division Two ... 25-year-old striker Joe Royle transfers from Billy Bingham's Everton to Tony Book's Manchester City for £200,000 ... Industrial unrest prevails ... The coal mining industry is at an all time low. The National Coal Board has produced just 110 million tonnes this year (down 46 million tonnes from five years ago) ... Inflation has risen again - it now stands at 17.2% and Harold Wilson's Labour government is under severe pressure ... A packet of McVities *Jaffa Cakes* is 11½p ... A jar of *Nescafe* coffee is 34p ... A two-piece *Terylene* suit costs £28.95 ... A pair of *Hush Puppies* is £4.99 ... Millions watch as David Vine and Ron Pickering present *Superstars* on TV. 30-year-old David Hemery (athlete), 26-year-old Mick Channon (footballer), 23-year-old John Conteh (boxer), 28-year-old Colin Bell (footballer), 24-year-old John H. Stracey (boxer), 34-year-old Chay Blyth (yachtsman) and 28-year-old Tony Greig (cricketer) take part. John Conteh is the eventual winner ... People attend New Year's Eve parties, and enjoy cubed pieces of cheese with pineapple on sticks ... Golden Wonder *Kung Fuey* crisps are new ... Adverts say, 'Try a taste of Martini, the most beautiful drink in the world. It's the bright one, the right one, it's Martini' ... The new year arrives ... Long-haired rockers wear blue denim jackets and studded leather bands on their wrists ... ***Down Down*** ("... deeper and down") by Status Quo spends a week at number one in the pop chart ... "B-b-b-baby, you just ain't seen n-n-nothin' yet. Here's something that you're never gonna forget" - ***You Ain't Seen Nothing Yet*** by Bachman Turner Overdrive reaches number two ... Harold Wilson's Labour government is poised to nationalise the troubled car manufacturer British Leyland. Workers are told to stop going on strike, or risk the bail-out deal being cancelled ... "Meet the gang 'cause the boys are here, the boys to entertain you" - A new series of *It Ain't Half Hot Mum* begins on BBC One with 44-year-old Windsor Davies as Sergeant Major, 41-year-old Don Estelle as Lofty and 39-year-old Melvyn Hayes as Gloria ... ***Morning Side Of The Mountain*** by 17-year-old Donny Osmond and 15-year-old Marie Osmond climbs to number five in the pop chart ... ***Never Can Say***

Goodbye by 31-year-old Gloria Gaynor is number four ... 13-year-old Simon Weston from Caerphilly in Glamorgan plays out with his friends ... 49-year-old Margaret Thatcher becomes leader of the Conservative party ... 'Who will survive and what will be left of them?' - *The Texas Chain Saw Massacre* is now showing at cinemas ... *Hong Kong Phooey* - ('Number One Super Guy') is on TV ... 29-year-old DJ Tom Browne presents the Top 20 chart rundown (in VHF stereo) on Radio One on Sunday evenings ... "Oooh-ooh-ooh..." ***Ms Grace*** by The Tymes is number one for a week ... ***January*** ("... sick and tired of you picking on me") by Pilot is number one for three weeks ... "All alone, once more..." ***Angie Baby*** by 33-year-old Helen Reddy peaks at number five ... A new seven part drama for children called *The Secret Garden* airs on Wednesday evenings at 5.15 (after *John Craven's Newsround*) ... The recent *Blue Peter* Appeal has been a resounding success - almost six million envelopes full of buttons, buckles and badges have been donated and eleven Labrador puppies will now be trained to become guide dogs for blind people ... Bread is in short supply after a recent strike by bakers - long queues form outside shops ... 18-year-old Ava Cadell (34D) from Budapest is a popular new page three girl in *The Sun* ... "Is this the end for our two heroes? Find out next week in another exciting episode" - 45-year-old Ronnie Barker and 44-year-old Ronnie Corbett star as private detectives Piggy Malone and Charley Farley in a new series of *The Two Ronnies* on BBC One ... "Shut it!" - 32-year-old John Thaw and 26-year-old Dennis Waterman star as Reagan and Carter in *The Sweeney* on ITV ... The latest three-litre Ford *Granada GXL* motorcar has a top speed of 113 mph and is capable of 0-60 mph in 9 seconds ... 42-year-old Reginald Bosanquet reads the *News at Ten* for ITN ... 17-year-old Lesley Whittle is kidnapped from her home near Bridgnorth ... Forty-three people are killed in a tube-train crash at Moorgate station ... Andrew Newton shoots dead a dog called Rinka in a botched murder attempt. The intended victim, 34-year-old Norman Scott, a secret former lover of Liberal leader Jeremy Thorpe MP, is unharmed ... ***Sugar Candy Kisses*** ("... Sugar honey love") by Mac and Katie Kissoon is number three in the pop chart ... ***Your Kiss Is Sweet*** ("... as sweet as candy, but honey beats your kisses by a million miles") by 28-year-old Syreeta is number twelve ... England cricket captain Mike Denness scores 188 runs and Keith Fletcher scores 146 in the final Test of the Ashes series at Sydney. England win the match, but Ian Chappell's Australia (with fast-bowlers Jeff Thompson and Dennis Lillee and wicket-keeper Rodney Marsh) win back the Ashes with a 4-1 series win. D L Amiss, B W Luckhurst, D Lloyd, J H Edrich, M C Cowdrey, M H Denness (cpt), K W R Fletcher, A W Greig, A P E Knott (wk), P Lever, D L Underwood, F J Titmus, R G D Willis, M Hendrick, C M Old and G G Arnold are all downcast by such a resounding Ashes defeat ... Back in England - energetic young dancers twist, spin, flip and drop at the *Wigan Casino* nightclub ... ***Footsee*** by Wigan's Chosen Few climbs to number nine in the national pop chart ... "Woah, yeah! Wait a minute Mr. Postman" - ***Please Mr. Postman*** by The Carpenters is to number two ... People stay up late to watch *Parkinson* on BBC One on Saturday nights ... 33-year-old world heavy-weight boxing champion Muhammad Ali is interviewed by 39-year-old Michael Parkinson ... "Sing, Muhammad, Muhammad Ali. He floats like a butterfly and stings like a bee" - ***Black Superman (Muhammad Ali)*** by Johnny Wakelin and the Kinshasa Band is a top ten hit record ... Footballers 30-year-old Franny Lee and 30-year-old Henry Newton score the goals as Dave Mackay's Derby County beat Bob Paisley's Liverpool 2-0 at the Baseball Ground ... "Ahhh-a-ah!! Ahhh-ahhh!!" - 36-year-old Ron Ely stars as *Tarzan* on Saturday morning television ... 66-year-old Magnus Pyke presents ITV's science program *Don't Ask Me* ... 29-year-old Tom Browne presents the *Top 20* countdown on Radio One on Sunday afternoons ... "Oh, baby! I'm losing sleep over..." ***The Secrets That You Keep*** by Mud is new at number twenty-six ... "Just a new man. Yes, you made me live again" - ***Now I'm Here*** by Queen is number eleven ... "I say good-bye my love..." ***Goodbye My Love*** ("... till we meet once again") by The Glitter Band is number two ... Billy Bingham's Everton football team moves back to the top of Division One with a 0-3 victory over Birmingham City - 24-year-old Bob Latchford scores two of Everton's goals against his former club ... Dave Mackay's Derby County move up to fifth with a 0-1 victory over Wolverhampton Wanderers at the Molineux ... 39-year-old Brian Clough is appointed manager of Second Division Nottingham Forest -

Clough signs midfielder John McGovern and striker John O'Hare from Leeds Utd ... 19-year-old winger Steve Coppell transfers from Tranmere Rovers to Manchester Utd ... "(Oooh-oooh, la-la-la). Blue eyes, blue eyes. (Oooh-oooh, la-la-la). How can you tell so many lies?" - ***Make Me Smile (Come Up And See Me)*** by Steve Harley and Cockney Rebel climbs to number one ... "I said..." ***Shame Shame Shame*** ("... Shame on you, if you can't dance too") by Shirley and Company is number six ... The *J. Lyons & Co* teashop on South Street in Worthing closes down ... A new coal-fired power station is now operational at Long Drax in Yorkshire ... Middle-class families replace old-fashioned blankets and eiderdowns on their beds with modern Continental Quilts ... "Charley says that if you ever see a box of matches lying around, tell mummy because they can hurt you" - a cartoon cat called Charley tells the public not to play with matches ... 'One tiny spark becomes a night of blazing suspense' - 49-year-old Paul Newman and 44-year-old Steve McQueen star in *The Towering Inferno* at cinemas ... Teenage boys lie about their age in the hope of gaining access to the local *Odeon* to see *Eskimo Nell* ... Author P.G. Wodehouse dies aged 93 in New York ... 24-year-old boxer Joe Bugner beats Dante Cane by a technical knock-out in round five in Bologna to retain his European heavy-weight title ... Back in England - Labour's 50-year-old Secretary of State for Industry, Anthony Wedgwood Benn, asks 58-year-old Sir Don Ryder to report on the future of troubled car manufacturer British Leyland ... Grown-ups stay up late, watching television ...

57-year-old Googie Withers plays the role of Faye Boswell, a governor at a women's prison, in *Within These Walls* on ITV on Friday nights ... ***Girls*** ("... Love the things they know. Love the things they show. Have to be where they go") by Moments & Whatnauts enters the pop chart at number thirty-five ... ***Only You Can*** ("... oh-oh, oh-oh. Only you") by Fox is number three ... Housewives go shopping at *Presto* or *Liptons* supermarkets ... A loaf of bread costs 15p ... A jar of lemon curd is 10p ... A pint of milk is 6p ... Adverts warn, 'Watch out, watch out! There's a Humphrey about!'

Spring 1975

If you hate me after what I say

Four-hundred members of the National Front march through London demonstrating against Britain being part of the European Common Market ... 11-year-old Nigel Farage from Farnborough plays out, alone ... "If a picture paints a thousand words, then why can't I paint you?" - ***If*** by 53-year-old Telly Savalas is number one in the pop chart ... "Young American, young American. She wants the Young American" - ***Young Americans*** by 28-year-old David Bowie is number eighteen ... 85-year-old actor Charlie Chaplin is knighted by 48-year-old Queen Elizabeth II at Buckingham Palace ... Heavy snow disrupts the Easter holidays ... Children enjoy snowball fights ... 11-year-old Michael Edwards (aka Eddie the Eagle) from Cheltenham slides down a steep, snow covered hill on his mother's metal baking tray ... Two thousand workers go on strike at British Leyland's Cowley plant ... The Transport and General Workers Union call for a 'One Out, All Out' policy, and a further two-thousand indirect workers linked to the plant also go on strike ... The unemployment figure currently stands at one million ...

Labour prime-minister Harold Wilson is under pressure ... Inflation continues to rise ... The Budget is presented by 57-year-old Chancellor of the Exchequer Denis Healey ... Taxes are raised for the second year running ... MPs vote in favour of holding a referendum on Britain's membership of the European Common Market ... Opposition leader Margaret Thatcher pays a visit to Scotland ... "You're the one girl in town I'd marry" - ***Bye Bye Baby*** ("... baby, goodbye") by The Bay City Rollers climbs to number one in the pop chart - and stays there for six weeks! ... Tartan scarves, flared trousers and high platform shoes are worn with pride. Teenage girls chant, "B-A-Y, B-A-Y, B-A-Y-C-I-T-Y, with an R-O double-L, E-R-S, Bay City Rollers are the best!" ... 24-year-old Barry Sheene suffers horrendous injuries when he crashes his Suzuki motorcycle at 170 mph at Daytona in the United States ... Back in England - the evil Cambridge Rapist strikes twice more, brutally attacking women in their homes ... "One day while I was not at home, while she was there and all alone, the angels came" - A re-issue of ***Honey*** by Bobby Goldsboro reaches number two in the pop chart ... Meg Richardson (played by 55-year-old Noele Gordon) marries Hugh Mortimer (played by 58-year-old John Bentley) in ITV's popular tea-time soap-opera, *Crossroads*, and 51-year-old comedian Larry Grayson makes a guest appearance as chauffeur of the wedding car ... 27-year-old footballer Ray Graydon scores the only goal of the game (smashing in the rebound from a saved penalty) as Ron Saunders' Second Division Aston Villa defeat John

Bond's Second Division Norwich City in the League Cup final at Wembley ... 21-year-old Paul Mariner scores twice as Plymouth Argyle beat Preston North End 2-1 in front of 22,063 spectators in a Third Division match at Home Park ... Families sit together watching TV in the evenings ... The fourth series of popular sit-com *Man About the House* is on ITV - starring 25-year-old Paula Wilcox, 24-year-old Sally Thomsett and 30-year-old Richard O'Sullivan ... Trendy young people boogie the night away at discos ... Dance floors are packed as DJs play ***Express***, the funky new single from BT Express ... ***Pick Up The Pieces*** by The Average White Band is also popular ... Richard Hittleman presents *Yoga For Health* on Sunday mornings on ITV ... Kenneth Kendall and Richard Whitmore present the *Nine O'Clock News* on weekday evenings on BBC One ... The body of Lesley Whittle is discovered in Staffordshire ... 33-year-old George Davis from Bletchley in Kent is sentenced to twenty years imprisonment for an armed payroll robbery in Ilford ... Sir Don Ryder reports back to Harold Wilson's Labour government, and recommends that state intervention is the only way to save ailing car manufacturer British Leyland ... ***There's A Whole Lot Of Loving*** ("... going on in my heart, it's a feeling I'm feeling through and through") by Guys 'n' Dolls is number two in the pop chart ... ***Only Yesterday*** ("... when I was sad and lonely, you showed me the way to leave the past behind me") by The Carpenters is number seven ... 43-year-old Jack Smethurst and 35-year-old Rudolph Walker star as 'Chalky' and 'Honky' in a new series of *Love Thy*

Neighbour on ITV ... 'You'll like what's happening at Vauxhall' - The brand new *Chevette* 'hatchback' motorcar from Vauxhall is launched - it has a heated rear window, reclining front seats and costs £1,593 ... *Red Rum* finishes second in the Grand National behind *L'Escargot* ... Cambridge win the Boat Race ... Football hooligans invade the pitch and fighting breaks out at White Hart Lane as Tottenham Hotspur beat Chelsea 2-0 in Division One ... Football hooligans invade the pitch and fighting breaks out at the City Ground as Nottingham Forest lose 0-1 to Manchester Utd in Division Two ... 24-year-old Roger Davies scores all five goals as Dave Mackay's Derby County thrash Luton Town 5-0 at the Baseball Ground in Division One ... Malcolm 'Supermac' MacDonald is on the score-sheet for Newcastle Utd in a 3-1 victory over Arsenal ... Tony Curry of Sheffield Utd and Alan Birchenhall of Leicester City kiss during a football match in front of the *Match of the Day* cameras ... ***Oh Boy*** ("... when you're with me, oh boy. The world will see that you, were meant for me") by Mud is new at number one in the weekly pop chart ... "And it hurts so good, don't let me know" - ***Hurt So Good*** by 23-year-old Susan Cadogan is number four ... Families sit in front of Ferguson *3713* 19-inch colour television sets and argue about who's going to 'turn over.' (Switching channels involves getting up from the settee!) ... 28-year-old Robin Nedwell stars as Duncan Waring in *Doctor on the Go* on ITV ... 28-year-old Felicity Kendal and 35-year-old Penelope Keith star in *The Good Life* on BBC ... "So..." ***Love Me Love My Dog*** ("... We've lived the road too long to break up") by Peter Shelley is number three in the pop chart ... ***Take Good Care Of Yourself*** ("... I worry 'bout you") by The Three Degrees is number nine ... 33-year-old Fred West and his 21-year-old wife Rosemary murder 18-year-old Juanita Mott and bury her body beneath their house at 25 Cromwell Street in Gloucester ... 25-year-old footballer Malcolm 'Supermac' MacDonald scores all five goals (including four headers), as England thrash Cyprus 5-0 at Wembley. England's full line-up for the match is: Shilton, Madeley, Watson, Todd, Beattie, Bell, Ball, Hudson, Channon, MacDonald, Keegan, and substitute Thomas ... Dave Mackay's Derby County are Division One league champions after a nine match unbeaten run ... Colin Boulton, Peter Daniel, David Nish, Colin Todd, Ron Webster, Henry Newton, Archie Gemmill, Bruce Rioch, Franny Lee, Roger Davies and 30-year-old top scorer Kevin Hector have all been outstanding for 'The Rams' ... Billy Bingham's Everton finish three points behind Derby, in fourth position, after leading the way for much of the season ... Eddie McCreadie's Chelsea are relegated to Division Two along with Luton Town and Carlisle Utd ... Tommy 'The Doc' Docherty's Manchester Utd are promoted back to Division One ... "There once was an ugly duckling, with feathers all stubby and brown" - 35-year-old Mike Reid sings ***The Ugly Duckling*** and it peaks at number ten in the pop chart ... ***Fox On The Run*** ("... you scream and everybody comes, a running. Take a run and hide, yourself away. Foxy on the run!") by Sweet is number two ... "Rory, Rory, tell us a story" - children watch

Animal Kwackers (Boots, Bongo, Rory and Twang) on ITV ... Miss Diane teaches Benny how to read and write in the popular soap-opera *Crossroads* ... 21-year-old footballer Alan Taylor scores twice, and 19-year-old goalkeeper Mervyn Day makes crucial saves, as John Lyall's West Ham Utd beat Alec Stock's Fulham 2-0 in the FA Cup final. 28-year-old captain Billy Bonds lifts the silver trophy for the triumphant Hammers. 33-year-old Fulham captain, Alan Mullery, and his 34-year-old team-mate Bobby Moore are magnanimous in defeat. A ticket for the standing enclosure at the Empire Stadium in Wembley costs £1.50 ... Leeds Utd fans invade the pitch at the Parc des Princes in Paris when Peter Lorimer's goal is disallowed against Bayern Munich in the European Cup final. Leeds lose 2-0 to the German team which includes Sepp Maier, Gerd Muller and 29-year-old Franz Beckenbauer ... "Oh..." ***Mandy*** ("... well you came and you gave without taking") by 31-year-old Barry Manilow is number eleven in the pop chart ... ***Loving You*** ("... is easy 'cause you're beautiful") by 27-year-old Minnie Riperton is number two ... Veteran centre-forward 37-year-old Derek Dougan of Wolverhampton Wanderers announces his retirement from first-class football ... 56-year-old Joe Harvey resigns as manager of Newcastle Utd ... Schoolboys buy *Tiger and Scorcher* for 6p from the newsagent and keep up to date with the adventures of 'Johnny Cougar', 'Billy's Boots', 'Martin's Marvellous Mini', 'Nipper Lawrence', 'Skid Solo' and 'Roy of the Rovers' ... Ted and Sandra Beckham of Leytonstone are proud parents of newborn son, David ... The

England football team (Clemence, Whitworth, Beattie, Bell, Watson, Todd, Ball, Channon, Johnson, G Francis, Keegan, and substitute Thomas) thrashes Scotland 5-1 at Wembley with goals from Kevin Beattie, Colin Bell, David Johnson and 23-year-old Gerry Francis (2) ... Production at British Leyland is brought to a halt yet again, and thousands of workers are laid-off due to a strike by staff at tyre manufacturer Dunlop ... "Do, do, do the funky gibbon. (The funky gibbon). We are here to show you how. Oooh, oooh, oooh, the funky gibbon" - The Goodies perform ***Funky Gibbon*** on *Top of the Pops* ... Tight fitting tanktops (with three large star shapes on the front) are in fashion ... School children attend birthday parties - where they partake in pass-the-parcel and eat jelly and ice-cream ... The average price of a house in the UK continues to rise - it's currently at £10,700 ... A loaf of bread from the supermarket now costs 16p ... Adverts say, '*Opal Fruits* - made to make your mouth water'.

Summer 1975

Woah! I'm gonna see my girlfriend

'Yes! Britain is where she belongs... in Europe' - Prime-minister Harold Wilson and most of his Labour party colleagues campaign to remain in the European Common Market ... People go to the polls on Thursday the fifth of June and vote (by 17 million to 8 million) to stay in the European community ... Rebel Labour MPs, Tony Benn, Michael Foot and Barbara Castle, are disappointed by the outcome ... 11-year-old schoolboy Alexander Boris de Pfeffel Johnson from East Sussex makes models of buses at home ... 3-year-old Dominic Cummings enjoys a day out with his family at Barnard Castle in County Durham ... ***Stand By Your Man*** ("... and show the world you love him. Keep giving all the love you can") by Tammy Wynette is number one in the pop chart ... "Memories, like the corners of my mind. Memories, misty water colour memories of..." ***The Way We Were*** by Gladys Knight & The Pips is number four ... It's a hot summer ... Families travel to the seaside for their annual holiday ... Dads and boys build sandcastles on the beach and paddle together in the sea ... Kids enjoy

Haunted House and *Space 1999* ice-lollies from Lyons Maid ... *Casey Jones*, *Vision On* and *Robinson Crusoe* are on TV during the school holiday ... *Seaside Special* is on BBC One on Saturday evenings; 36-year-old 'Diddy' David Hamilton introduces the show from Blackpool and, a week later, 26-year-old Noel Edmonds introduces the show from Great Yarmouth ... 45-year-old Stuart Hall presents *It's A Knockout* on Friday evenings. A team from Darlington wins a closely fought contest with Berwick-upon-Tweed and Consett, and will now compete in the Jeux Sans Frontieres competition later in the year ... 43-year-old Peter Woods reads the news ... The Cambridge Rapist is caught and arrested after fleeing from the home of an intended victim ... A coach crashes at Dibbles Bridge near Hebden, killing the driver and thirty-one elderly female passengers ... Leeds Utd are banned from European football for a year because of the aggressive behaviour of their fans at the European Cup Final ... "Where are the clowns? There ought to be clowns" - ***Send In the Clowns*** by Judy Collins moves down the pop chart to number eleven ... "Do it! Do..." ***The Hustle*** by Van McCoy climbs to number four ... People enjoy a night out at the cinema ... 'In a town where anything goes, everything does in this funny bedroom farce' - 38-year-old Warren Beatty, 35-year-old Julie Christie and 29-year-old Goldie Hawn star in *Shampoo* - a smash hit at the box-office ... 'The dirty window cleaner finds out pop is just a racket!' - 24-year-old Robin Askwith stars as Timmy Lea in *Confessions of a Pop Performer* ... "Sing Lofty / Why do you whisper green grass? Why tell the trees what ain't so?" - ***Whispering Grass*** by Windsor Davis and Don Estelle is new at number one in the pop chart ... ***Sing Baby Sing*** ("... the world is getting better") by The Stylistics is number three ... 23-year-old jockey Pat Eddery rides *Grundy* to victory in the Epsom Derby ... England's cricketers lose the first Test Match of the summer against the touring Australian team. 28-year-old Tony Greig takes over from Mike Denness as England cricket captain. A male streaker runs onto the pitch and hurdles the stumps during the second Test at Lord's. 'Free George Davis' - the third Test at Headingley is abandoned, after the pitch is vandalised by protestors seeking to overturn the conviction of armed robber George Davis. England's debutant batsman, 33-year-old David Steele, performs bravely and scores runs against Australia's pace attack - but it's not enough; Ian Chappell's Aussies win the series 1-0 and retain the Ashes. England players J H Edrich, D L Amiss, B Wood, D S Steele, K W R Fletcher, M H Denness, G A Gooch, J H Hampshire, A W Greig (cpt), R A Woolmer, G R J Roope, A P E Knott (wkt), D L Underwood, P H Edmonds, C M Old, J A Snow, G G Arnold and P Lever are all downcast by an Ashes defeat ... The England cricket team also takes part in the brand new (one-day, sixty-over) Prudential Cup tournament, but loses to Australia in the semi-finals at Headingley ... "Roll over lay down and let me in..." ***Roll Over Lay Down*** by Status Quo is number nine in the pop chart ... "Our little boy is four years old and quite a little man. So we spell out the words we don't want him to understand" - ***D.I.V.O.R.C.E*** by 33-year-old Tammy Wynette is number twelve ... 31-year-old tennis star Arthur Ashe defeats 22-year-old Jimmy Conners (last year's champion) in the men's singles final at Wimbledon ... 31-year-old Billie Jean King wins the ladies' singles ... 40-year-old Gordon Lee is the new football manager of Newcastle Utd. Lee signs striker Alan Gowling from Huddersfield Town for £70,000 and sells midfielder Terry Hibbitt to Birmingham City for £100,000 ... 28-year-old centre-half Dave Watson transfers from Sunderland to Manchester City for £175,000 ... 24-year-old striker Charlie George transfers from Arsenal to Derby County for £100,000 ... 34-year-old Johnny Giles leaves Leeds Utd and joins West Bromwich Albion as player-manager ... 30-year-old Angela Rippon presents *News Extra* on BBC Two ... The trial begins of six men accused of murdering twenty-one people in last year's Birmingham pub bombings ... "Hold on there Bald Eagle. You wouldn't fire a man till he's finished his *Texan* bar would you?" - Rowntree bring out the *Texan* milk chocolate covered chew bar ... Deidre Hunt (played by 21-year-old Anne Kirkbride) marries Ray Langton (played by 32-year-old Neville Buswell) in ITV's *Coronation Street* ... ***I'm Not In Love*** ("... so don't forget it. It's just a silly phase I'm going through") by 10cc is number one in the pop chart ... "Now there, are three, steps to heaven. (Wop-wop)" - ***Three Steps To Heaven*** by Showaddywaddy is number two ... 'The antidote to panel games' - 54-year-old Humphrey Lyttelton is chairman for a new series of *I'm Sorry I Haven't A Clue* on Radio Four. 32-year-old Graeme Garden, 40-year-old Barry

Cryer, 37-year-old Willie Rushton and 35-year-old Tim Brooke-Taylor are panelists on the popular comedy show ... Harold Wilson's Labour government presides over record high inflation of 26.9% and unemployment of 1.2 million ... Motorbike stuntman Evel Knievel is rushed to hospital after being critically injured in a crash in front of a large crowd at Wembley Stadium. (The 36-year-old was attempting to jump over thirteen buses) ... "Now then, now then" - 48-year-old Jimmy Savile OBE makes children's dreams come true in his new TV show *Jim'll Fix It* ... The sun continues to shine ... People rush out to buy the latest 7-inch singles at *Woolworths* for 66p ... ***Misty*** by 36-year-old Ray Stevens is number two in the weekly pop chart ... ***If You Think You Know How To Love Me*** by Smokie is number three ... ***Jive Talkin'*** by The Bee Gees is number five ... 25-year-old boxer Joe Bugner is accused of taking a negative approach as he goes fifteen rounds with 33-year-old Muhammad Ali in Kuala Lumpur - but loses on points in a WBA/WBC heavy-weight title fight ... Wrestlers Big Daddy (44-year-old Shirley Crabtree) and Giant Haystacks (28-year-old Martin Ruane) form a formidable tag-team on ITV's *World of Sport* on Saturday afternoons ... 27-year-old racing driver James Hunt wins the Dutch Grand Prix at Zandvoort in a Hesketh-Ford. 26-year-old Niki Lauda is second in a Ferrari ... Back in England - 'P' reg cars go on sale ... A new Ford *Cortina 1300L* costs £1,649 ... A new Austin *Allegro* costs £1,159 ... The board of directors at British Leyland recommends to its shareholders that the government should be allowed to take control of the company - in return for the multi-million pound investment that's needed to keep the car manufacturer solvent ... Workers at British Leyland's Triumph factory threaten to go on strike - just as the exciting new *TR7* sports car (with state-of-the-art pop-up headlights) is about to be launched ... ***Tears On My Pillow*** ("... Pain in my heart. You on my mind") by Johnny Nash spends a week at the top of the pop chart ... More and more foreign cars are being sold in the UK ... BMW introduces the all new *3 Series* motorcar - the *316* model comes with two single-set round headlights, and the *320* comes with two dual-set round headlights ... Volkswagen launches the *Golf GTI* with a top speed of 120 mph and capable of 0-60 mph in 8.9 seconds ... "Wir fahr'n, fahr'n, fahr'n, auf der..." ***Autobahn*** by futuristic German pop group Kraftwerk is number eleven on the hit parade ... ***Listen To What The Man Said*** by Wings is number six ... 46-year-old Leonard Parkin reads the news for ITN ... Three women are injured in separate hammer attacks in Yorkshire ... The Birmingham Six are found guilty of last year's pub bombings, and each man is given twenty-one life sentences - representing the number of people murdered ... Thirty-three people are injured when an IRA bomb explodes at Caterham in Surrey ... 'Rollermania' prevails - ***Give A Little Love*** ("... take a little love, be prepared to forsake a little love") by The Bay City Rollers moves to the top of the weekly pop chart ... The new football season gets underway ... Coventry City players wear a striking new kit (manufactured by *Admiral*) - with two (dark blue and white) downward stripes on the sky-blue jersey, matching up neatly with two similar stripes on the sky-blue shorts ... 24-year-old striker David Cross scores a hat-trick as Coventry win their opening game 1-4 away at Everton ... 25-year-old Malcolm 'Supermac' MacDonald scores eight goals in the first six games for Newcastle Utd ... Manchester Utd's 32-year-old goalkeeper Alex Stepney dislocates his jaw shouting at his own defenders in a match against Birmingham City - Utd win 2-0 with both goals scored by 21-year-old Sammy McIlroy ... 21-year-old Jimmy Case scores his first goal for Liverpool in a 3-2 win over Tottenham Hotspur at Anfield ... 17-year-old David O'Leary makes his debut for Arsenal in a 0-0 draw against Burnley ... 17-year-old Chris Kamara makes his debut for Second Division Portsmouth in a 0-2 defeat against Luton Town ... "Ladies and gentlemen this is Captain Tobias Willcock welcoming you aboard Coconut Airways flight 372 to Bridgetown..." ***Barbados*** by Typically Tropical is the new number one song ... "For you are beautiful and I have loved you dearly, more dearly than the spoken word can tell" - ***The Last Farewell*** by 39-year-old Roger Whittaker is number two ... 9-year-old Denise Jane Lovell is rushed to hospital with a serious head injury, after falling from a swing in a park at Armitage in Staffordshire ... Violence has become a major problem on football terraces and in the streets outside grounds ... Seventy hooligans are arrested at a First Division match between Wolverhampton Wanderers and Manchester Utd ... There's also crowd trouble at Leicester City versus Birmingham City and Nottingham Forest versus

Plymouth Argyle ... *The Death of Reginald Perrin* - the fourth novel from 40-year-old writer David Nobbs is published ... "I... ***Can't Give You Anything (But My Love)*** by The Stylistics climbs to number one on the hit parade - and stays there for three weeks ... ***Fame*** ("... Fame, makes a man take things over") by 28-year-old David Bowie is number nineteen ... Adolescent boys find pornographic magazines in bushes near the municipal playing fields ... Eve Astor features in a recent volume of *Knave* ... The new black and gold *JPS* (special edition) Ford *Capri Mark II* motorcar turns heads on the streets of Britain ... Working-class families enjoy a chippy tea and a can of pop on Friday evenings ... Fish and chips wrapped in newspaper costs 40p ... Adverts say, '*Cresta* pop - "it's frothy man!"'

Autumn 1975

It ain't no big thing, to wait for the bell to ring

"Ooh, you are awful... but I like you." - 60-year-old Dick Emery makes millions laugh on Saturday evenings on BBC One ... The fifth series of *Upstairs Downstairs* begins on ITV, with 41-year-old Jean Marsh (as Rose), 71-year-old Angela Baddeley (as Mrs. Bridges), 51-year-old Gordon Jackson (as Hudson) and 20-year-old Lesley-Anne Down (as Georgina Worsley) ... "I am sailing, I am sailing, home again, across the sea" - ***Sailing*** by 30-year-old Rod Stewart climbs to number one in the pop chart - and stays there for four weeks ... ***It's Been So Long*** by 31-year-old George McCrae is number four ... The weather is mostly dull and breezy ... 26-year-old footballer Alan Gowling bags a hat-trick as Gordon Lee's Newcastle Utd thrash Bill McGarry's Wolverhampton Wanderers 5-1 in Division One ... "Need. Need. Got. Need. Got. Need. Got." - schoolboys swap *Soccer Stars '75-'76* football stickers on the playground ... Schoolgirls flick through *Look-In* magazine - searching for pictures of The Bay City Rollers ... The fifth series of popular sit-com *Man About the House* is on ITV - starring 25-year-old Paula

Wilcox, 25-year-old Sally Thomsett and 31-year-old Richard O'Sullivan ... A new series of *The Liver Birds* is on BBC One, starring 26-year-old Elizabeth Estensen as Carol and 33-year-old Nerys Hughes as Sandra ... ***Moonlighting*** ("... they're leaving everything. Moonlighting, they're losing all their friends") by 27-year-old Leo Sayer is number two in the pop chart ... ***Heartbeat*** by Showaddywaddy is number seven ... 58-year-old Chancellor of the Exchequer Denis Healey is under pressure - the economy has moved into recession ... Industrial disputes continue - with unions making big demands on the Labour government ... Production of British Leyland's new Austin *18/22 (Princess)* motorcar is affected by on-going strike action. Production of Morris *Marinas* and Austin *Allegros* also slows down ... "When I get me moped out on the road, I'm gonna ride, ride, ride" - 30-year-old Brummy comedian Jasper Carrott is number five in the pop chart with ***Funky Moped*** ... "Run around now!" - 35-year-old Cockney comedian Mike Reid hosts *Runaround* - a TV game show for children ... 45-year-old Brian Redhead is a new presenter on BBC Radio Four's *Today* program on weekday mornings ... Iceland extends its territorial fishing waters around its shoreline to two-hundred nautical miles. Previously, it was fifty. British trawlers continue to operate in the disputed zone and political tensions rise between Harold Wilson and Kristjan Eldjarn the president of Iceland ... "If you want a sweet, sweet love tonight, call me and I'll make you feel alright" - ***I'm On Fire*** by 5000 Volts is number four in the pop chart ...***Una Paloma Blanca*** ("... I'm just a bird in the sky") by 30-year-old Jonathan King is number ten (and will climb to number five) ... 50-year-old Richard Baker and 41-year-old Richard Whitmore present the *9 O'Clock News* on BBC One ... 59-year-old prime-minister Harold Wilson and 49-year-old Queen Elizabeth II attend the opening of the new North Sea oil pipeline ... Evil 47-year-old Peter Cook (aka The Cambridge Rapist) is sentenced to life in prison and Judge Melford Stevenson concludes, "In your case, I am recommending that life in prison means exactly that." ... The IRA steps up its bombing campaign. An explosion at the Hilton Hotel in London kills two and injures sixty-three people. An explosion at Green Park tube station kills one person. An explosion at a London restaurant kills two and injures twenty-three people ... Elsewhere in the country - life continues as normal ... Children return home at the end of a school day to watch *Play School*, *Deputy Dawg*, *Jackanory*, *Animal Magic*, *John Craven's Newsround*, *The Record Breakers* and *The Magic Roundabout* - before the news begins on BBC One ... 43-year-old Elizabeth Taylor and 49-year-old Richard Burton re-marry, after divorcing just sixteen months ago ... ***There Goes My First Love*** ("... with the guy I used to call my friend") by The Drifters is number three in the pop chart ... ***Motor Bikin'*** ("... movin on the Queen's highway lookin' like a streak of lightnin')" by Chris Spedding is number fourteen ... The latest Honda *PC50* moped has a top speed of 31 mph ... 'Thrilla in Manila' - 33-year-old boxer Muhammad Ali retains his world heavy-weight title - beating 31-year-old Smokin' Joe Frazier by a

Technical Knock Out in the fifteenth round in the Philippines ... Back in England - football hooligans invade the pitch in an attempt to get the match abandoned as Chelsea lose 0-3 to Luton Town in Division Two ... British Rail cancel their 'football specials' due to rowdy behaviour and widespread vandalism on trains ... England manager Don Revie calls for birching to be re-introduced as a punishment for football thuggery ... "It ain't no big thing, to wait for the bell to ring. It ain't no big thing, the toll of the bell" - ***Love Is The Drug*** by Roxy Music climbs to number two in the pop chart ... "Hey!.." ***Fattie Bum Bum*** ("... You sweet sugar dumpling") by Carl Malcolm is number eight ... Hundreds of thousands of people enjoy a day out at the 1975 Motor Show at Earls Court ... 'The car everyone dreams of. But very, very few can ever own' - Jaguar launches the *XJ-S* as a replacement for the ageing *E-Type*. The new V12 model has a top speed of 150 mph and accelerates from 0-60 mph in 6.8 seconds ... 'For a Fortunate Few' - Lotus launches the futuristic, wedge shaped *Esprit* sports car - top speed is 138 mph and 0-60 mph comes in 6.7 seconds ... 'Cavalier is here. Where family and sporty motoring come together' - Vauxhall launches the *Cavalier* (a four door saloon) as a replacement for the ageing *Victor* ... 'The new Chrysler Alpine is here' - Chrysler launches the *Alpine* (a 5-door hatchback) as a replacement for the ageing Hillman *Hunter* ... A light-blue, three-wheeled *Invacar* is parked at the side of the football pitch at Turf Moor as Burnley draw 4-4 with Norwich City ... Tommy 'The Doc' Docherty's newly promoted Manchester Utd are top of

Division One with Lou Macari, Stuart Pearson and 21-year-old Sammy McIlroy in tremendous form ... Working-class lads wear donkey jackets and Dr. Marten boots ... 16-year-old Lenny Henry from Dudley is the latest winner on TV talent show *New Faces* ... "You're nicked!" - 33-year-old John Thaw and 27-year-old Dennis Waterman star as Reagan and Carter in a new series of *The Sweeney* on Thursday nights at 9 p.m. ... 25-year-old footballer Malcolm 'Supermac' MacDonald (of Newcastle Utd and England) sprints 100m in under eleven seconds on BBC One's *Superstars* ... "Don't mention the war!" - 36-year-old John Cleese stars in *Fawlty Towers* on BBC Two ... 29-year-old Diane Keen appears in *The Cuckoo Waltz* on ITV ... 38-year-old Willie Bell is the new football manager of Birmingham City ... 30-year-old Dave Lee Travis is the new presenter of Radio One's tea-time show ... ***Hold Me Close*** ("... don't let me go, oh no") by 28-year-old David Essex is new at number one in the pop chart ... "I believe in miracles. Where you from?..." ***You Sexy Thing*** by Hot Chocolate reaches number two ... Punk rockers Steve Jones, Paul Cook, Glen Matlock and Johnny Rotten form The Sex Pistols ... 38-year-old Michael Nicholson reads the lunchtime news for ITN ... A woman is found murdered in Yorkshire ... 50-year-old Ross McWhirter is shot dead on his doorstep in London by the Provisional IRA ... 42-year-old Barry Norman presents the late night movie review program *Film 75* on BBC One ... 'The Adventure You Will Never Forget!' - *The Land That Time Forgot* is now showing at cinemas across the country ... Popular fictional detective

Hercule Poirot takes a final bow in *Curtain* - the latest 'whodunit' novel from 85-year-old crime-writer Agatha Christie ... 10 "Are the stars out tonight? I don't know if it's cloudy or bright..." ***I Only Have Eyes For You*** by 34-year-old Art Garfunkel spends two weeks at number one ... Don Revie's England football team draws 1-1 with Portugal in Lisbon and fails to qualify for next year's European Championships. Goalkeeper Ray Clemence; defenders Steve Whitworth, Dave Watson, Paul Madeley and Kevin Beattie; midfielders Colin Todd, Trevor Brooking and Gerry Francis; forwards Mike Channon, Kevin Keegan and Malcolm 'Supermac' MacDonald; and substitutes Allan 'sniffer' Clarke and Dave Thomas all return home disappointed ... Back in England - 42-year-old Dickie Davies introduces *World Of Sport* on ITV on Saturday afternoons ... 43-year-old Brian Moore presents *On The Ball* ... 31-year-old Franny Lee of Derby County and 32-year-old Norman Hunter of Leeds Utd have a punch-up during a First Division match at the Baseball Ground. Both players are sent off - and continue fighting as they leave the pitch ... 23-year-old Gerry Francis scores twice as Dave Sexton's Queens Park Rangers thrash Everton 5-0 ... 22-year-old Paul Mariner scores twice as Plymouth Argyle beat Oxford Utd 2-1 in Division Two ... 19-year-old Laurie Cunningham scores a goal for Orient in a 1-1 draw against Fulham ... 19-year-old Andy Gray transfers from Dundee United to Aston Villa for £110,000 - and scores his first League goal in a 1-1 draw against Tottenham Hotspur at Villa Park ... "Like a..." ***Rhinestone Cowboy***

("... riding out on a horse in a star spangled rodeo") by Glen Campbell is number four in the pop chart ... "So when you're near me, darling can't you hear me..." ***S. O. S.*** by Abba is number six ... "Ground control to Major Tom. Take your protein pills and put your helmet on" - ***Space Oddity*** by 28-year-old David Bowie climbs to number one... Hundreds of thousands of viewers tune-in to see wrestlers (and former tag-team partners) 45-year-old Big Daddy and 29-year-old Giant Haystacks face each other in a televised bout on ITV's *World Of Sport* ... Over on BBC One, a new series of *The Wombles* begins with Bungo getting stuck up a tree ... A new series of *Dad's Army* also begins, with Captain Mainwaring's platoon being mistaken for Nazis ... BBC One TV programs on a Saturday night include: *The Basil Brush Show* - with Roy North and Basil Brush; *Dr. Who* - starring 41-year-old Tom Baker as the Doctor and 29-year-old Elisabeth Sladen as his assistant Sarah Jane; *Bruce Forsyth and The Generation Game* - with 47-year-old Bruce and his assistant Anthea Redfern; *Kojak* - with Telly Savalas; and *Match of the Day* - introduced by 47-year-old Jimmy Hill ... 27-year-old Steve Heighway, 26-year-old John Toshack and 24-year-old Kevin Keegan score the goals as Bob Paisley's Liverpool beat Tommy 'The Doc' Docherty's newly promoted Manchester Utd 3-1 in front of 49,136 spectators at Anfield. (20-year-old Steve Coppell scores Utd's consolation goal) ... ***What A Diff'rence A Day Makes*** by 39-year-old Esther Phillips reaches number six in the pop chart ... "And I'm going down to the town tonight to get a new B. I. R. D" - ***D.I.V.O.R.C.E*** (a comedy song) by 33-year-old Billy Connolly from Glasgow spends a week at number one ... Motoring technology moves on apace ... The futuristic ‘wedge’ shaped *Austin Princess* motorcar has state-of-the-art quartz halogen headlamps. The *2200HL* has a top speed of 104 mph and can accelerate from 0-60 mph in 13.5 seconds ... The weather turns cold ... Children (with woollen gloves sewn into the sleeves of their coats) rush home from school ... Mum bakes a *Fray Bentos* pie for dinner.

Winter 1975 - 1976

Mamma, just killed a man

Heavy rain and blustery gales give way to mild and dry weather ... 'George Davis is Innocent' - the campaign to free convicted armed robber George Davis gathers momentum ... "I see a little silhouette of a man. Scaramouche. Scaramouche. Will you do the Fandango? Thunderbolt and lightning, very, very frightening me. Gallileo (Gallileo). Gallileo (Gallileo). Gallileo (Gallileo). Figaro. Magnifico" - ***Bohemian Rhapsody*** by Queen moves up to number one in the pop chart - and stays there for nine weeks! ... The latest 'Cod Wars' continue in the seas off the coast of Iceland ... An Icelandic gun boat opens fire on British trawlers, after being rammed, and Royal Navy frigates are sent to the area ... Back in England - 34-year-old cricketer David Steele is voted BBC's 'Sports Personality of the Year' - after his heroic performance in this year's Ashes series ... Dave Sexton's Queens Park Rangers lead the way in football's League Division One after an unbeaten run of eight games ... Liverpool, Derby County and Manchester Utd are all close behind ... 21-year-old Gordon Hill scores his first goal for

Manchester Utd - in a 1-4 away win against Sheffield Utd ... Fashion conscious teenagers wear Oxford 'bags' with side pockets and three-button high waist bands ... Collars on shirts measure around five-inches ... 'Platforms' on shoes and boots measure around six-inches ... 19-year-old Richard Madeley reports the local news for BBC Radio Carlisle ... 28-year-old disc jockey Simon Bates sits in for 'Diddy' David Hamilton on Radio One's afternoon show ... "Sitting in the sun waiting for a senorita to show" - ***Happy To Be On An Island In The Sun*** by 29-year-old Demis Roussos climbs from number thirteen to number five in the pop chart... ***Love Hurts*** ("... Love scars, love wounds and mars") by 31-year-old Jim Capaldi falls from number twelve to number sixteen ... Hallmark Records release *The Best of Top of the Pops '75* - a budget priced cover-version pop compilation LP with an energetic blonde girl on the sleeve ... "The RAF's knocked two years off your life, now isn't that a sin? There's only one way to get out, and that's to get some in. GET SOME IN!" *Get Some In!* - a new sit-com set in the time of National Service (with 37-year-old Tony Selby and 25-year-old Robert Lindsay) is on ITV ... 'Mah-na, mah-na. Doo-doo, doo-doo-doo' - 51-year-old Benny Hill stars in a new edition of *The Benny Hill Show* ... 31-year-old Angela Rippon presents BBC One's *Nine O'Clock News* ... 39-year-old Donald Nielson (aka the Black Panther) is arrested after a fight with two police officers in Mansfield. A few days later, Nielson is charged with the kidnap and murder of Lesley Whittle ... 46-year-old champion motor-racing driver Graham Hill and five others die in a plane crash in Hertfordshire ... Four members of an IRA unit take two people hostage and occupy a flat on Balcombe Street in Marylebone. The men give themselves up after six days and are taken into custody ... The Ulster Defence Association claims responsibility for a bomb which explodes injuring five people at a pub on the Kilburn High Road in London ... The weather turns wintery with freezing rain falling across the Midlands and the North ... ***All Around My Hat*** ("... I will wear the green willow, and all around my hat for a twelve month and a day") by Steeleye Span is number five ... "You're gonna need a bigger boat" - *Jaws*, starring 43-year-old Roy Scheider, is a huge hit at cinemas ... 'The Carry On team: Looking a Site for Sore Thighs!' - *Carry On Behind* (with 49-year-old Kenneth Williams as Professor Crump, 41-year-old Bernard Bresslaw as Arthur Upmore and 57-year-old Kenneth Connor as Major Leap) is also now showing ... More than 100,000 Ford *Cortinas* have been sold in Britain this year. 85,000 *Minis*, 78,000 *Marinas* and 63,000 *Allegros* have also been sold ... Families gather around ITT *CVC9* 26-inch colour television sets with wood effect ... 66-year-old Fanny Cradock shows the nation how to stuff a turkey in *Fanny Cradock Cooks for Christmas* on BBC One in the afternoons ... Approximately eleven million people watch the final episode of Upstairs Downstairs on ITV on the evening of Sunday the twenty-first of December ... "I remember one Christmas morning, a winter's light and a distant choir. And the peal of a bell, and that Christmas tree smell, and their eyes full of tinsel and fire" - ***I Believe***

In Father Christmas by Greg Lake is number two on the hit parade ... The novelty record ***Renta Santa*** by Chris Hill is number ten ... Husbands buy their wives a bottle of *Tweed* perfume (by Lentheric) for Christmas ... Families wrap presents and place them beneath silver/white imitation Christmas trees in the living room ... Tinsel and sparkling baubles hang from the branches ... Lucky young boys play with their push-along Evel Knievel stunt motorcycles on Christmas morning ... A *Kasuga* tape-recorder with microphone is £14.95 from *Argos* ... A Mighty *Tonka* Dump Truck is £8.45 ... The *Play-Doh 'Fun Factory'* set from Palitoy is 99p ... BBC One broadcasts *The Wizard of Oz* (starring Judy Garland) and the TV premiere of *Butch Cassidy and the Sundance Kid* (starring Paul Newman and Robert Redford) ... Frank Spencer learns to drive in the Christmas special of *Some Mothers Do 'Ave 'Em* ... Captain Mainwaring's drunken brother, Barry, turns up in *Dad's Army* on Boxing Day. 60-year-old Arthur Lowe plays both parts ... "In the Blue Ridge Mountains of Virginia, on..." ***The Trail Of The Lonesome Pine*** by Hollywood comedy icons Laurel and Hardy with the Avalon Boys climbs to number two in the pop chart ... "Don't let me hear you say life's taking you nowhere, Angel" - ***Golden Years*** by 28-year-old David Bowie is number eight ... 58-year-old Googie Withers makes her final appearance as the prison governor in *Within These Walls* ... 42-year-old Michael Caine and 45-year-old Sean Connery star in *The Man Who Would Be King* at cinemas ... Footballers John Toshack and Phil Neal score the goals as

Bob Paisley's Liverpool move to the top of Division One, by beating Dave Sexton's Queens Park Rangers 2-0 in front of 39,182 at Anfield ... Bob Latchford scores for Billy Bingham's Everton, and Lou Macari scores for Tommy 'The Doc' Docherty's Manchester Utd, in a 1-1 draw in front of 41,732 at Goodison Park ... 22-year-old Ronnie Moore scores four goals as Tranmere Rovers thrash Stockport County 5-0 in Division Four ... 47-year-old comedian Bob Monkhouse hosts the game show *Celebrity Squares* on TV. Charlie Drake, Des O'Connor, Noele Gordon, John Inman, Pat Coombs, Diana Dors, Alfred Marks, Arthur Mullard, Keith Harris and Cuddles the Monkey are the guest stars ... ***Bohemian Rhapsody*** by Queen (with 24-year-old John Deacon, 26-year-old Roger Taylor, 28-year-old Brian May and 29-year-old Freddie Mercury) remains at number one in the pop chart ... ***It's Gonna Be A Cold Cold Christmas*** ("... without you") by 24-year-old Dana reaches number four ... The progressive instincts of Labour's 55-year-old Home Secretary Roy Jenkins delivers two major pieces of legislation ... The Sex Discrimination Act and the Equal Pay Act become law ... The economy remains in recession ... 129 million tonnes of coal have been mined this year ... Inflation remains high - it's currently at 25%! ... A pint of milk has gone up from 6p to 8½p ... A loaf of bread has risen from 16p to 17p ... A pint of *Carlsberg* in the Red Lion costs 31p... A pint of Watney's *Special Bitter* is 25p ... A packet of twenty cigarettes is 42p ... Labour prime-minister Harold Wilson smokes his pipe, and ponders the new year ahead ..."Who'll have a fish-ee, on a little dish-ee" - the nation is gripped on Thursday evenings by new TV drama *When The Boat Comes In* starring 50-year-old James Garbutt as Bill Seaton, 34-year-old Susan Jameson as Jessie Seaton and 40-year-old James Bolam as Jack Ford ... 44-year-old Jimmy Ellis plays Inspector Lynch in a new series of *Z Cars* - shown at 7.20 p.m. on Monday evenings (straight after *Ask The Family*) ... Lyn Marshall presents *Wake Up To Yoga* on Sunday mornings on ITV - and people learn how to do the 'bridge' and the 'downward dog' ... Children devour *Fizzy Cola* flavoured *Spangles* ... 52-year-old Richard 'Dicky' Attenborough becomes a Sir in the New Year's Honours list ... Hurricane force winds cause widespread damage to trees and power lines ... A shortage of potatoes sees prices soar in shops. Five pounds of King Edwards now cost four times more than they did twelve months ago ... The latest 'Cod Wars' continue in the seas off the coast of Iceland with British trawlers still operating in the disputed waters. Royal Navy frigate HMS *Andromeda* collides with an Icelandic patrol ship - and both captains blame the other. Iceland cuts off diplomatic relations with Britain ... Back in England - there's growing speculation that Liberal party leader Jeremy Thorpe MP was involved in a case of attempted murder. Rumours imply Thorpe was acting to silence a former lover who'd threatened to expose their homosexual love affair ... "Ooooh..." ***Love To Love You Baby*** by 27-year-old Donna Summer is number four in the pop chart ... ***No Regrets*** by The Walker Brothers is number seven ... "Magic, our Morris!" - *Oh No, It's Selwyn Frogitt* is on ITV with 47-year-old Bill Maynard in the title role ... "Your letter was only the start of it. One letter and now you're a part of it. Now you've done it, Jim has fixed it for you, and you, and you" - a second series of *Jim'll Fix It* (hosted by 49-year-old Jimmy Savile OBE) keeps the kids entertained on BBC One ... "I've been cheated by you since I don't know when. So, I made up my mind it must come to an end. Look at me now. Will I ever learn?" - ***Mamma Mia*** by Abba reaches number one in the pop chart ... "I've got the money, I've got the place. You've got the figure, you've got the face. Let's get together, the two of us over a..." ***Glass Of Champagne*** by Sailor peaks at number two ... After spending nine weeks at number one, ***Bohemian Rhapsody*** by Queen moves down to number three ... A cold front moves in from the North - bringing sleet and snow ... "Come along Candice Marie / Slow down Keith" - 28-year-old Alison Steadman is Candice Marie and 29-year-old Roger Sloman is Keith in Mike Leigh's *Nuts In May* - a dark comedy, broadcast as part of BBC's *Play for Today* series ... Veteran crime-writer Dame Agatha Christie dies aged 85 in Wallingford ... A 42-year-old women is stabbed to death in Leeds ... IRA terrorist cells are planning more atrocities in London. Twelve small devices explode in the West End injuring one person ... 49-year-old Queen Elizabeth II opens the new National Exhibition Centre near Birmingham ... 35-year-old footballer Jimmy Greaves plays for non-league Brentwood and fights alcoholism ... Non league Wimbledon draw 0-0 against Yeovil Town at Plough Lane ... 11-year-old

Vinnie Jones from Watford fights boys on the playground at school ... 26-year-old ice-skater John Curry wins a gold medal at the Winter Olympics in Innsbruck ... "I'm just a..." ***Love Machine*** ("... and I won't work for nobody but you") by The Miracles is number three on the hit parade ... ***We Do It*** ("... every night, every day, in any possible way, but we do it") by R & J Stone is number five ... Denise Perry (36D) from Pinner makes her first appearance on page three of *The Sun* ... Supersonic airplane Concorde takes off on its first commercial flight - the *British Airways* jet flies from Heathrow to Bahrain with a cruising speed of 1,350 mph ... The new Porsche *911 Turbo* sports car has a top speed of 153 mph and can accelerate from 0-60 mph in 6.1 seconds ... The last Hillman *Imp* motorcar rolls off the production line at Linwood in Scotland ... 31-year-old ventriloquist Roger De Courcey and his puppet, Nookie Bear, are making names for themselves on ITV's talent show *New Faces* ... A crop of young footballers are making names for themselves on the back pages of the daily newspapers ... 21-year-old Birmingham City striker Trevor Francis scores his eleventh goal of the season in a 2-1 defeat against high-flying Queens Park Rangers ... 19-year-old 'super sub' David Fairclough comes on (for Steve Heighway) and scores twice as Liverpool beat Burnley 2-0. (Liverpool are now fourth in Division One - two points behind leaders Queens Park Rangers and one point behind Manchester Utd and Derby County) ... 18-year-old Glenn Hoddle makes his debut for Tottenham Hotspur and scores the winning goal for Terry Neill's team in a 1-2 away win at Stoke City ... 23-year-old Martin O'Neill scores twice as Brian Clough's Nottingham Forest beat Jimmy Frizzell's Oldham Athletic 4-3 in Division Two ... 18-year-old Peter Barnes and 26-year-old Dennis Tueart score the goals as Tony Book's Manchester City beat Gordon Lee's Newcastle Utd 2-1 in the League Cup final at Wembley - and the players receive tankards as a memento of the occasion ... "I'll dedicate to you, all my love my whole life through. I'll love you..." ***Forever And Ever*** by Slik, a pop group from Glasgow, with 22-year-old lead singer, Midge Ure, is number one on the hit parade ... "Aye 'n' I'll feel safer if we change the subject and call it..." ***Dat*** by 25-year-old Pluto Shervington is number six ... The nation's finances are in a poor state ... Labour prime-minister Harold Wilson and Chancellor of the Exchequer Denis Healey stick to their socialist ideals, despite growing criticism over the faltering economy and the low value of the pound - it's now worth just $2.08 ... 50-year-old Leader of the Opposition Margaret Thatcher makes a speech warning against the threats of communism - and a Russian newspaper describes her as the 'Iron Lady' ... "E..." ***Evil Woman*** by the Electric Light Orchestra is number ten in the pop chart ... "Oh what a night. Late December back in '63" - ***December '63 (Oh What A Night)*** by The Four Seasons is new at number one ... Crowds flock to the cinema to see 38-year-old Jack Nicholson (as Randle P. McMurphy) and 41-year-old Louise Fletcher (as Nurse Ratched) in the hit movie *One Flew Over the Cuckoo's Nest* ... 65-year-old Arthur Mullard and 52-year-old Queenie Watts star in *Yus My Dear* on ITV

... 33-year-old Bob Hoskins and 31-year-old Martin Shaw feature in *On The Move* on BBC One ... 26-year-old footballer Malcolm 'Supermac' MacDonald scores the winning goal as Newcastle Utd beat Derby County 4-3 in front of 44,488 spectators at St. James' Park ... Asa Hartford, Dennis Tueart and Joe Royle score the goals as Manchester City beat Everton 3-0 in front of 33,148 spectators at Maine Road ... Artist (and Manchester City supporter) L. S. Lowry dies aged 88 in Glossop ... 14-year-old Nicholas Lyndhurst stars in BBC One's *The Prince and the Pauper* on Sunday evenings ... *Rise & Shine* - a new cereal from Kellogg's gets you going in the morning.

Spring 1976

Though it hurts to go away, it's impossible to stay

The value of the pound falls below two-dollars for the first time - it's now worth just $1.90 ... Out of the blue, 60-year-old prime-minister Harold Wilson resigns and 64-year-old Jim Callaghan takes over at Number 10 ... "Baby..." ***Love Really Hurts Without You*** by 26-year-old Billy Ocean reaches number two on the hit parade ... ***Miss You Nights*** by 35-year-old Cliff Richard stalls at number fifteen ... 47-year-old Jeremy Thorpe is forced to resign as leader of the Liberal party - amidst continuing allegations of his involvement in a plot to commit murder. 62-year-old former leader Jo Grimond takes over from Thorpe on a temporary basis ... 38-year-old Jill Gascoine appears in the latest series of *The Onedin Line* on BBC One ... 26-year-old Paula Wilcox, 25-year-old Sally Thomsett and 31-year-old Richard O'Sullivan star in the sixth and final series of popular sit-com *Man About the House* on ITV ... Eamonn Andrews surprises 80-year-old Arnold Ridley (who plays Private Godfrey in *Dad's Army*) on *This is Your Life* ... Brotherhood of Man win the Eurovision song contest in the

Netherlands singing ***Kisses For Me*** ("... bye-bye, baby. Bye-bye") ... 45-year-old Princess Margaret and 46-year-old Lord Snowdon split up after fifteen years of marriage ... "Oh, I love to love, but my baby just loves to dance" - ***I Love To Love (But My Baby Loves To Dance)*** by 22-year-old Tina Charles is number one in the pop chart ... School children return home each day to watch *Play School*, *Crystal Tipps*, *Jackanory*, *Goober and the Ghost Chasers*, *John Craven's Newsround*, *Vision On* and *Ivor the Engine* - before the news begins on BBC One ... An IRA bomber explodes a device at West Ham railway station - then shoots and kills a train driver. Twelve days later - a bomb is detonated at the Ideal Home Exhibition at Olympia - killing one person and injuring more than eighty ... Elsewhere in the country - life continues as normal ... Central London has its warmest Easter for twenty-four years ... 20-year-old Stephen Simmons is tried and convicted of robbery after being 'fitted-up' by bent copper DS Derek Ridgewell ... 11-year-old catholic schoolboy Piers Stefan O'Meara from East Sussex confesses his sins to a priest, and storms off from the confessional booth, in a huff, when he's given ten Hail Marys as penance ... Britain's winning song from Eurovision, ***Kisses For Me*** by Brotherhood of Man, reaches number one in the pop chart - and stays there for six weeks! ... "Ah, breaker one-nine. This here's the Rubber Duck. You gotta copy on me?" - ***Convoy*** by CW McCall reaches number two ... 27-year-old disc jockey Les Ross joins BRMB radio station in Birmingham ... The town centre of Rugeley in Staffordshire is pedestrianised ... A six-wheeled Tyrrell racing car, driven by Jody Scheckter, makes its Formula One debut at the Spanish Grand Prix. The race is won by Britain's James Hunt in a conventional four-wheeled McLaren ... 'Tomorrow. Today. The new Rover 3500' - the stunning Rover *SD1* is launched at the Geneva Motor Show. The stylish and luxurious car will go on sale shortly in the UK, with a base level price of £4,750 ... The new management team at British Leyland is trying desperately to keep pace with rival European and Japanese car manufacturers. The latest *Dolomite Sprint* now has headrests, radio and a laminated wind-screen as standard. The all new Triumph *TR7* sports car has a top speed of 109mph and can accelerate from 0-60 mph in 9.8 seconds ... 29-year-old footballer Chris Nicholl scores all four goals (including two own goals) as his team Aston Villa draws 2-2 with Leicester City in Division One ... 26-year-old Stuart Pearson scores twice for Manchester Utd in a 3-4 victory over Gordon Lee's Newcastle Utd ... 19-year-old 'super sub' David Fairclough comes on (for John Toshack) and scores a brilliant individual goal in the 87th minute, as Liverpool beat Everton 1-0 at Anfield ... 23-year-old eccentric centre-forward Robin Friday scores twice as Reading beat Darlington 4-1 in Division Four ... "He's a..." ***Pinball Wizard*** ("... there has got to be a twist") by 29-year-old Elton John is number seven in the pop chart ... ***Take It To The Limit*** by The Eagles is number twelve ... Families sit together and watch TV ... Elsie Howard (formerly Elsie Tanner) returns to *Coronation Street* after splitting up with her husband. Fred

Gee is the new 'pot man' at 'The Rovers Return' pub. Minnie Caldwell leaves Weatherfield to live in Whaley Bridge ... "Goodnight all" - the final episode of *Dixon of Dock Green* is broadcast on BBC One, with 80-year-old Jack Warner in the title role ... Pan's People appear on *Top of the Pops* for the last time ... "Shy girl, sexy girl. They all like that fancy world" - ***Girls Girls Girls*** by Sailor is number seven in the pop chart ... ***S-S-S-Single Bed*** by Fox (with 31-year-old singer Susan Traynor - aka Noosha Fox) is number four ... The ever popular 62-year-old comedy actor Sid 'cor blimey' James suffers a heart attack and dies while performing on stage in Sunderland ... 43-year-old Ray 'Dracula' Reardon beats 27-year-old Alex 'Hurricane' Higgins in the world snooker final at Middlesbrough ... *Rag Trade* wins the Grand National at Aintree. *Red Rum* is second ... "I was walking through the jungle just the other night. Ah, well I heard a big a rumble and I thought it was a fight" - ***Jungle Rock*** by 52-year-old Hank Mizell is number three in the pop chart ... "Can you hear the drums Fernando? I remember long ago another starry night like this" - ***Fernando*** by Abba (with 26-year-old blonde Agnetha Faltskog and 30-year-old brunette Anni-Frid Lyngstad) is number one ... The sun shines ... Temperatures rise ... 39-year-old Lawrie McMenemy's Second Division Southampton football team causes a major shock in the FA Cup final - by beating Tommy 'The Doc' Docherty's Manchester Utd 1-0. 25-year-old Bobby Stokes scores the winning goal in the eighty-third minute. 32-year-old Peter Rodrigues (captain of 'The Saints') climbs the

Wembley steps and lifts the famous silver trophy. A ticket for the standing enclosure at the Empire Stadium costs £2.50 ... "Comes up peanuts, slice after slice" - *Marathon* chocolate bars are advertised on ITV ... 31-year-old Angela Rippon reads the news on BBC One ... 50-year-old Leader of the Opposition Margaret Thatcher visits Coventry to support the local Conservative candidate at a by-election ... "She's just a devil woman, with evil on her mind. Beware the devil women, she's gonna get you" - ***Devil Woman*** by Cliff Richard is number nine in the pop chart ... "Thus began the saga on the M1 motorway, of the biggest bloomin' convoy outside the USA" - ***Convoy GB*** by Laurie Lingo and the Dipsticks is number four ... The 1975/76 football season is coming to an end ... 19-year-old Liverpool 'super sub' David Fairclough comes on (for Jimmy Case) and scores a late goal as 'The Reds' beat Stoke City 5-3. Bob Paisley's team also gains victories over Manchester City (3-0) and Wolverhampton Wanderers (3-1) to become the new champions of Division One. 28-year-old goalkeeper Ray Clemence and 25-year-old full-back Phil Neal have played in every match. 27-year-old John Toshack and 25-year-old Kevin Keegan have scored twenty-eight goals between them. Tommy Smith, Ian Callaghan, Joey Jones, Emlyn Hughes, Phil Thompson, Brian Hall, Peter Cormack, Ray Kennedy, Jimmy Case, Steve Heighway and 'super sub' David Fairclough have also been in fine form ... Dave Sexton's Queens Park Rangers (with Phil Parkes, Dave Clement, Ian Gillard, Frank McLintock, Dave Webb, Gerry Francis, John Hollins, Mick

Leach, Don Masson, Don Givens, Dave Thomas and 27-year-old Stan Bowles) are runners-up ... Tommy 'The Doc' Docherty's Manchester Utd (with Alex Stepney, Alex Forsyth, Stewart Houston, Gerry Daly, Brian Greenhoff, Martin Buchan, Steve Coppell, Sammy McIlroy, Stuart Pearson, Lou Macari and 22-year-old Gordon Hill) are third ... Willie Bell's Birmingham City avoid relegation with a 3-1 victory over Tottenham Hotspur ... Wolverhampton Wanderers are relegated and sack manager Bill McGarry - 43-year-old Sammy Chung takes over at the Molineux ... Bob Stokoe's Sunderland, Alan Dicks' Bristol City and Johnny Giles' West Bromwich Albion all gain promotion from Division Two ... 57-year-old Bertie Mee steps down as manager of Arsenal after ten years in charge at Highbury ... Liverpool beat Club Bruges 4-3 on aggregate (over two legs) to win the UEFA Cup, with 25-year-old Kevin Keegan (2), 21-year-old Jimmy Case and 24-year-old Ray Kennedy scoring the goals ... "For the nine months I carried you, growing inside me…" ***No Charge*** by JJ Barrie climbs to number one in the pop chart ... "Some people want to fill the world with…" ***Silly Love Songs*** by Wings reaches number two ... 50-year-old Richard Baker reads the news on BBC One ... A 20-year-old woman is injured in a hammer attack in Leeds ... 55-year-old Home Secretary Roy Jenkins authorises the release of George Davis from prison - saying last year's conviction for armed robbery is, "unsafe." ... The latest 'Cod Wars' continue in the seas off the coast of Iceland. HMS *Falmouth* rams into an Icelandic patrol ship to prevent it from cutting the fishing lines of a British trawler ... Back in England - it's warm and sunny in late May with a long summer heatwave being forecast ... 27-year-old England goalkeeper Ray Clemence makes a howler at Hampden Park, and allows Kenny Dalglish to score an easy winning goal for Scotland in a 2-1 victory. England's full line-up for the match is: Clemence, Todd, Mills, Thompson, McFarland, Kennedy, Keegan, G Francis, Pearson, Channon, Taylor and substitutes Doyle and Cherry ... ***More, More, More*** ("... how d'ya like it? how d'ya like it?) by The Andrea True Connection is number five in the pop chart ... "Come closer, come closer, my darling, come closer" - ***My Resistance Is Low*** by 32-year-old Robin Sarstedt is number three ... Boys speed down steep hills on Dawes *Galaxy* racing bicycles ... 25-year-old Barry Sheene wins the opening three Grand Prix races in France, Austria and Italy in the 500cc world motorcycle championship ... A public information film aimed at car drivers says, "Think Once! Think Twice! Think Bike!"

Summer 1976

When I was down, I was your clown

A scorchingly hot summer leads to a nationwide drought ... Frozen orange *Jubblys* are in demand ... Swarms of ladybirds annoy holiday-makers ... Raleigh launches the *Grifter* bicycle with *Sturmey-Archer* 3-speed twist grip control gears. The smaller *Strika* and *Boxer* models are also introduced as part of Raleigh's exciting new range ... 'Good, rich and thick. A milk-chocolate brick" - Rowntree's *Yorkie* chocolate bar is new ... Children enjoy their six-week holiday from school - playing out all day, only returning home occasionally to gulp down orange squash ... The Handsacre estate gang throw stones at the Ford Way gang in the field beside the brook in Old Road, Armitage near Rugeley ... *Belle and Sebastian* is on BBC One on weekday mornings ... *It's A Knockout* is on BBC One on Friday evenings. A team from Newbury wins a closely fought contest with Winchcombe and Cirencester, and will now compete in the Jeux Sans Frontieres competition later in the year ... 40-year-old jockey Lester Piggott rides *Empery* to victory in the Epsom Derby ... The sun continues to shine ... Women wear hotpants and bikini tops ... Men wear 'cut-off' denim jeans and T shirts ... 'They came in search of Paradise' - *Bounty* chocolate bars are advertised on TV ... 'The happy sound of Radio One' - 31-year-old DJ Dave Lee Travis presents the afternoon show on Radio One ... "I drove my tractor through your haystack last night. Oooh arr! Oooh arr!" - ***Combine Harvester (Brand New Key)*** by The Wurzels is top of the pop chart ... ***The Boys Are Back In Town*** by Thin Lizzy is number eight ... 44-year-old Reginald Bosanquet and 48-year-old Sandy Gall present ITN's *News at Ten* program ... An agreement over fishing rights is reached between Iceland and the UK and the latest 'Cod Wars' come to an end. A zone of two-hundred nautical miles from the coastline of Iceland is established, with British trawlers being granted limited rights to fish within the newly defined area ... 38-year-old David Steel is the new leader of the Liberal party - replacing interim leader Jo Grimond ... *British Airways'* Concorde supersonic jet flies on a new commercial route to the USA - from Heathrow to Washington ... The value of the pound tumbles further - it's now worth just $1.70 ... Pressure grows on 64-year-old prime-minister Jim Callaghan and 59-year-old Chancellor of the Exchequer Denis Healey ... Margaret Thatcher's opposition Conservative party moves ahead of Labour in the opinion polls ... ***You To Me Are Everything*** ("... the sweetest song that I could sing. Oh, baby. Oh baby") by The Real Thing is new at number one in the pop chart ... ***Young Hearts Run Free*** by Candi Staton is number two ... The summer heatwave continues ... Thermometers record temperatures of 100 degrees Fahrenheit - in the shade! ... The hot sunshine is relentless ... Calamine lotion soothes the skin of sunburnt children ... 29-year-old popstar Elton John is the new football chairman at Fourth Division Watford FC. Elton teams up with 36-year-old manager Mike Keen, and the two men begin working on an ambitious plan to get 'The Hornets' into Division One ... Footballers 26-year-old Stuart Pearson, 25-year-old Kevin Keegan and 27-year-old Mick Channon score the goals for Don Revie's England team (Clemence, Todd, Mills, Thompson, Madeley, Cherry, Keegan, Channon, Pearson, Brooking, G Francis) in a 1-4 victory over Finland in Helsinki ... 29-year-old Tony Greig is England's cricket captain for the summer Test series against Clive Lloyd's West Indians. Lightning fast bowlers Michael Holding and Andy Roberts rip through the English batsmen - and the West Indies win the series 3-0, with victories at Old Trafford, Headingley and the Oval ... "Stay away from my window. Stay away from my back door too" - ***Tonight's The Night*** by 31-year-old Rod Stewart reaches number five in the pop chart ... "I wear my..." ***Heart On My Sleeve*** by Gallagher and Lyle peaks at number six ... Punk rock is becoming popular with some unruly young people ... The Sex Pistols play a gig at the Lesser Free Trade Hall in Manchester. 20-year-old Peter Hook, 20-year-old Bernard Sumner and 17-year-old Steven Patrick Morrissey are amongst the audience - each paying 50p to attend ... 'You have been warned. The Omen is here' - *The Omen*, starring 60-year-old Gregory Peck and 40-year-old Lee Remick, is now showing at cinemas ... 'Girls drive him wild ... and he loves it!' - 25-year-old Robin Askwith stars as Timmy Lea in *Confessions of a Driving Instructor* ... 44-year-old Elizabeth Taylor and

50-year-old Richard Burton divorce for a second time - just nine months after re-marrying ... "Come on, come on..." ***Lets Stick Together*** by 30-year-old Bryan Ferry reaches number four in the pop chart ... "Jolene, Jolene, Jolene..." ***Jolene*** ("... I'm beggin' of you, please don't take my man") by 30-year-old Dolly Parton reaches number seven ... 25-year-old Barry Sheene rides his Suzuki to victory in the Dutch and Swedish 500cc motor cycle Grands Prix and becomes world champion ... Formula One driver Jody Scheckter wins the Swedish motor racing Grand Prix at Anderstorp in a six-wheeled Tyrrell car. Britain's James Hunt finishes in fifth position in a conventional four-wheeled McLaren ... Back in England - the summer heatwave continues ... The hot sunshine beats down ... Parched stray dogs roam the streets seeking water and shade ... "Ever and ever. Forever and ever. You'll be the one, that shines in me, like the morning sun" - ***Forever And Ever*** by 30-year-old Demis Roussos is number one for a week in July ... 33-year-old tennis player Mark Cox from Leicester loses to Vitas Gerulaitis in the second round of the men's singles at Wimbledon. 20-year-old Bjorn Borg from Sweden becomes the new champion after beating 29-year-old Ilie Nastase (6-4, 6-2, 9-7) in the final ... "Don't go breaking my heart. I couldn't if I tried." - ***Don't Go Breaking My Heart*** by 29-year-old Elton John and 29-year-old Kiki Dee is number one for six weeks in July and August ... 'Save Water. It's Scarce' - the hot weather continues and water is in short supply. Stand-pipes appear on street corners - and people queue to fill their pots and pans ... 52-year-old Minister for

Drought Dennis Howell and his wife share their bath water - Howell goes on television and encourages other people to do the same ... At Oxford Crown Court, 39-year-old Donald Nielson (aka the Black Panther) is found guilty of the kidnap and murder of Lesley Whittle and sentenced to life imprisonment ... 51-year-old former Labour MP John Stonehouse (who attempted to fake his own death) is found guilty of fraud, theft and deception and sentenced to seven years ... Devshi Bhudia is sacked for working too slowly at the Grunwick photographic processing factory in Willesden - a number of fellow workers walk-out in protest ... "When your body's had enough of me and I'm layin' flat out on the floor. When you think I've loved you all I can, I'm gonna love you..." ***A Little Bit More*** by Dr. Hook is number two in the pop chart ... ***Heaven Must Be Missing An Angel*** ("... Missing an angel, child, 'cause you're here with me right now") by Tavares climbs to number four ... The chimes of Big Ben - the Great Clock of Westminster - fall silent when metal fatigue damages the mechanism ... 'The following information is classified: TOP SECRET' - *The Bionic Woman* is new on TV - with 27-year-old Lindsay Wagner in the title role ... Hilda and Stan Ogden (played by 49-year-old Jean Alexander and 61-year-old Bernard Youens) are proud owners of a new mural, depicting three flying ducks, in the living-room at number 13 *Coronation Street* ... Trendy young men with moustaches, tight white trousers and Ford *Capris* take their girlfriends for a night out at the disco ... ***You Should Be Dancing*** ("... Yeah!") by The Bee Gees (a group comprising of the three brothers Gibb: 29-year-old Barry and 26-year-old twins Robin and Maurice) is new at number five in the pop chart ... "I pull my blue..." ***Jeans On*** ("... I pull my old, blue jeans on") by 31-year-old David Dundas is number three ... Keith Best presents the weather forecast on BBC One ... The heatwave continues ... Parks, lawns and grass verges are bleached white in the hot sun ... 28-year-old racing driver James Hunt wins the British Grand Prix in his McLaren - but is later disqualified ... 27-year-old Niki Lauda crashes and is badly burned in his Ferrari at the German Grand Prix ... 'R' reg cars go on sale ... 'Ford's new baby. Never has so much advanced engineering gone into a small car' - Ford launches the *Fiesta* - a small hatch-back motor car designed to give 86% all-round vision. The *1.0 Popular* base model costs £1,856 ... Four star leaded petrol rises in price to 77p a gallon ... 32-year-old Tony Gubba presents *Grandstand* on BBC One television ... 22-year-old swimmer David Wilkie wins gold for Britain in the 200 metre breaststroke at the Montreal Olympics ... 28-year-old Brendan Foster wins bronze on the track in the 10,000 metres ... 25-year-old Princess Anne is part of the British equestrian team ... "Sky rockets in flight..." ***Afternoon Delight*** by The Starland Vocal Band peaks at number eighteen in the pop chart ... "The last time I saw George alive, was in the summer of seventy-five, he said he was in love, I said 'I'm pleased'" - ***The Killing Of Georgie (Parts One And Two)*** by Rod Stewart reaches number two ... The second series of sit-com *Get Some In!* is on ITV - starring 38-year-old Tony Selby as

Corporal Marsh and 26-year-old Robert Lindsay as Jakey Smith ("with three 'f's") ... ***Don't Go Breaking My Heart*** by Elton John and 29-year-old Kiki Dee remains at number one in the pop chart ... Terry Neill succeeds Bertie Mee as manager of Arsenal and signs 26-year-old striker Malcolm 'Supermac' MacDonald from Newcastle Utd for £333,333 ... 18-year-old Cyrille Regis from Harlesden joins non-league team Hayes FC ... The new football season gets underway ... Bob Paisley's Liverpool beat Lawrie McMenemy's Southampton 1-0 in the Charity Shield at Wembley - 27-year-old John Toshack scores the winning goal. A week later hundreds of hooligans fight each other at matches up and down the country ... Fans invade the pitch at Derby County versus Manchester Utd - where dozens of supporters are injured and three policeman are taken to hospital ... Violence also breaks out at Nottingham Forest versus Wolverhampton Wanderers ... Segregation of rival supporters becomes a key issue. The FA considers erecting fences to separate terraced areas ... "All those people gathered there (in Zai - in Zaire), to see the rumble in the jungle - there, there, there..." ***In Zaire*** by Johnnie Wakelin is number four in the pop chart ... "Someone's knockin' at the door, somebody's ringin' the bell. Do me a favour, open the door and..." ***Let 'Em In*** by Wings is number two ... The average price of a house in the UK has risen by over £1,000 in the past twelve months - it now stands at £11,700 ... A pint of lager in the Red Lion has risen to 38p ... '*Heineken* - refreshes the parts other beers cannot reach'.

Autumn 1976

Friday night and the lights are low

38-year-old Barbara Edwards presents the weather forecast on BBC One ... Thunderstorms arrive and the great summer heatwave comes to an end ... Bosses at the Grunwick photographic processing factory in Willesden sack 137 workers for going on strike in support of a colleague who was dismissed in August ... 11-year-old schoolboy Robert Brydon from Port Talbot in South Wales sits at home watching TV ... A new series of *The Two Ronnies* begins on BBC One on Saturday nights, with 46-year-old Ronnie Barker and 45-year-old Ronnie Corbett, and featuring a short comedy drama called 'The Phantom Rasberry Blower of Old London Town' (written by Spike Milligan) ... 10-year-old schoolboy Stephen Coogan from Middleton in Manchester sits at home watching TV ... *The Muppet Show* begins on ITV on Sunday evenings, with puppets Fozzie, Kermit and Miss Piggy providing a wide variety of entertainment. Statler and Waldorf look on from the balcony of a theatre box - unimpressed ... "What's got four legs, walks peculiar, talks with all the choicest words? What's got four arms, loves to grab you? Answer is, two Liver Birds" - A new series of *The Liver Birds* is on BBC One on Sunday evenings, starring 27-year-old Elizabeth Estensen as Carol and 34-year-old

Nerys Hughes as Sandra ... "You can dance, you can jive, having the time of your life. See that girl, watch that scene, digging the..." ***Dancing Queen*** by Abba moves up to number one in the pop chart - and stays there for six weeks! ... "When the moon shines on the cow shed and we're rollin' in the hay. All the cows are out there grazing and the milk is on it's way." - ***I Am A Cider Drinker (Paloma Blanca)*** by The Wurzels reaches number three ... 20-year-old centre-forward Andy Gray scores a hat-trick as Aston Villa thrash Ipswich Town 5-2 in front of 39,916 spectators at Villa Park ... 26-year-old Malcolm 'Supermac' MacDonald scores for Arsenal in a 3-1 win over Everton in front of 34,076 at Highbury ... *Striker* - a five-part footballing serial for children begins on BBC One on Wednesday evenings ... *The New Avengers* begins on ITV with Patrick Macnee as Steed, Gareth Hunt as Gambit and 30-year-old Joanna Lumley as Purdey (a hot chick driving a yellow *TR7* sports car) ... "And I..." ***Can't Get By Without You*** ("... no way") by The Real Thing is number two in the pop chart ... ***I Only Wanna Be With You*** by The Bay City Rollers is number four ... "Sunday, Monday, happy days! Tuesday, Wednesday, happy days! Thursday, Friday, happy days! The weekend comes, my cycle hums, ready to race to you. These days are ours, happy and free!" - 'Cool' and 'Ace-a-mundo' are new catch phrases as 30-year-old Henry Winkler stars as The Fonz in *Happy Days* ... 33-year-old John Major is selected as the Conservative parliamentary candidate for Huntingdonshire ... *Roy of the Rovers* is a brand new paper for boys - as the footballing saga of Roy Race and his Melchester Rovers team-mates transfers from *Tiger and Scorcher* to its own publication ... 25-year-old footballer Kevin Keegan falls off his bike on *Superstars* and is badly injured ... ***Dance Little Lady, Dance*** ("... You know you've only got one chance") by 22-year-old Tina Charles peaks at number six in the pop chart ... ***Blinded By The Light*** ("... Revved up like a deuce, another runner in the night") by Manfred Mann's Earth Band also reaches number six ... "Four candles. No, fork handles! Handles for forks!" - Millions of BBC One viewers are in tears of laughter when The Two Ronnies perform an hilarious new comedy sketch set in an iron mongers ... "Eleven minutes late. Staff difficulties at Hampton Wick" - 49-year-old Leonard Rossiter stars in *The Fall and Rise of Reginald Perrin* (a new TV comedy based on a novel written by 41-year-old David Nobbs from Orpington) ... "I must get it all down, quickly. Before they finish me off" - 38-year-old Derek Jacobi stars in *I Claudius* on BBC Two - along with 43-year-old Sian Phillips, 40-year-old Brian Blessed, 36-year-old Patrick Stewart and 36-year-old John Hurt ... "Please, could Posh Paws roar down the phone to me?" - 27-year-old Noel Edmonds presents *Multi-Coloured Swap Shop* on Saturday mornings - and Nigel from Stroud would like to exchange *Cluedo* for *Ker-Plunk* ... "Mii-iss-issippi, you've been on my mind" - ***Mississippi*** by Pussycat climbs to number one in the pop chart - and stays there for four weeks ... ***When Forever Has Gone*** by 30-year-old Demis Roussos is number five ... 43-year-old Dickie Davies presents *World Of Sport* on ITV on Saturday afternoons ... 43-year-old Frank Bough presents *Grandstand* on BBC One ... 'Mackay Sacked' is the back-page newspaper headline as 42-year-old football manager Dave Mackay takes his leave of Derby County - and is replaced by Colin Murphy at the Baseball Ground ... Jack Charlton's Middlesbrough beat John Bond's Norwich City 1-0 (with a goal from 23-year-old Graeme Souness) and move to the top of Division One ... Fighting breaks out at Elland Road as Jimmy Armfield's Leeds Utd lose 0-2 to Tommy 'The Doc' Docherty's Manchester Utd ... Even worse crowd trouble breaks out when supporters invade the pitch at Villa Park during a 'friendly' between Aston Villa and Rangers ... 46-year-old Bob Stokoe leaves Sunderland after serving for four years as manager - 47-year-old Jimmy Adamson takes over at Roker Park ... 26-year-old boxer Joe Bugner beats Richard Dunn by a first round knock-out at Wembley to retain his European heavy-weight title ... 43-year-old Barry Norman presents the late night movie review program *Film 76* on BBC One ... 'It's the Biggest Bang since the War!' - *Carry On England* is at cinemas, starring 58-year-old Kenneth Connor, 46-year-old Windsor Davies and 46-year-old Joan Sims ... 33-year-old Robert de Niro stars in *Taxi Driver* ... Dads watch *Top of the Pops* on BBC One on Thursday evenings as Legs and Co. make their debut ... ***You Make Me Feel Like Dancing*** ("... I'm gonna dance the night away") by 28-year-old Leo Sayer is number two in the pop chart ... "Haah-aah, howzat! You messed about, I caught you out..." ***Howzat*** by Sherbet is number three ... The punk rock 'scene' spreads across the land ... Youngsters do creative things with safety pins ... The Sex Pistols sign to EMI records ... The new super-sleek *Inter-City 125* train runs between London and Bristol ... 50-year-old Jimmy Savile OBE says, "This is the age of the train." ... School children drink water from *Duralex* glasses at lunch-time - before playing British-Bulldog on the playground ... 29-year-old racing driver James Hunt finishes third in the Japanese Grand-Prix to become the new world motor racing champion - pipping his fierce rival Niki Lauda to the title by just one point ... Back in England - 30-year-old footballer 'super' Georgie Best makes his debut for Fulham and scores after just seventy-one seconds in a 1-0 win against Bristol Rovers in Division Two ... 23-year-old striker Paul Mariner transfers from Second Division Plymouth Argyle to First Division Ipswich Town ... Referees use red and yellow cards for the first time ... Dave Wagstaffe of Blackburn Rovers sees red after being sent-off just thirty-six minutes into a match against Orient ... "Disco..." ***Disco Duck*** ("... Alright!") by Rick Dees and his Cast of Idiots reaches number six on the hit parade ... ***I'll Meet You At Midnight*** ("... under the moonlight") by Smokie is number eleven ... Ford launches the box shaped *Cortina MkIV* motorcar. The 1.6 litre version has a top speed of 93 mph and can reach 60 mph in 13 seconds ... 'Make someone happy with a phone-call' - a yellow cartoon bird called 'Buzby' advertises three-minute, off-peak telephone calls for just 10p ... 'The Workers United Will Never Be Defeated' - 43-year-old Jayaben Desai leads the protests of sacked workers from the Grunwick photographic processing factory. 54-year-old Len Murray (General Secretary of the TUC) urges all trade unions to lend their support ... The economy is performing badly under 64-year-old Jim Callaghan's Labour government. The unemployment figure is high - standing at 1.3 million. Inflation is also high - at 17%. The balance of payment deficit is almost £1 billion and interest rates are at 15%. The pound falls in value against the dollar to an all-time record low of $1.54 ... Chancellor of the Exchequer Denis Healey requests a loan of $3.9 billion from the IMF. The 59-year-old then cancels a foreign trip and arrives back at Labour's party conference in Blackpool to explain why the loan is necessary ... Foggy, Compo and Clegg get up to no good in *Last of the Summer Wine* on BBC One ... Grumpy Albert Tatlock (played by 80-year-old Jack Howarth) and miserable Ena Sharples (played by 78-year-old Violet Carson) get drunk together in the bar of 'The Rovers Return' in *Coronation Street* on ITV ... *Sleeping Murder: Miss Marple's Last Case* - by recently deceased crime-writer Dame Agatha Christie is on sale now in bookshops for £3.50 ... ***If You Leave Me Now*** ("… you'll take away the biggest part of me") by Chicago is the new number one pop song ... "I was lost in France, in the fields the birds were singing. I was lost in France and the day was just beginning" - ***Lost In France*** by Bonnie Tyler is number nine ... "What a…" ***Beautiful Noise*** ("… coming up from the street") by Neil Diamond is number thirteen ... 26-year-old footballer Trevor Whymark scores four goals as Bobby

Robson's Ipswich Town move up to second position in Division One, with a 7-0 thrashing of West Bromwich Albion. (John Wark, Kevin Beattie and Paul Mariner are also on the score-sheet for the 'Tractor Boys') ... Kevin Keegan and Joey Jones score the goals as league leaders Liverpool beat Bristol City 2-1 at Anfield ... Television technology moves on apace - sets with cordless remote controls are now available from *Radio Rentals* ... 66-year-old Arthur Mullard and 53-year-old Queenie Watts star in *Yus My Dear* on ITV ... 46-year-old Windsor Davies, 43-year-old Don Estelle and 41-year-old Melvyn Hayes star in *It Ain't Half Hot Mum* on BBC One ... 33-year-old fascist Martin Webster addresses a group of National Front supporters in Walsall ... "Nuts, whole hazel nuts. Urgh! Cadbury's take 'em and they cover them in chocolate" - Cadbury's *Wholenut* bars are advertised on television ... The *Bargain Madness* discount store opens in Blackpool - it will eventually become *B&M Bargains* ... 31-year-old ventriloquist Roger De Courcey and his puppet, Nookie the Bear, steal the show at the Royal Variety Performance, appearing in front of 76-year-old Queen Elizabeth the Queen Mother at the London Palladium ... 41-year-old entertainer Rod Hull and his puppet, Emu, attack chat-show host Michael Parkinson on late night BBC One television ... "I am an anti-Christ! I am an anarchist!" - ***Anarchy In The UK*** by The Sex Pistols enters the pop chart at number forty-three.

Winter 1976 - 1977

Little darling, let's walk, let's talk

"You dirty barstard!" - The Sex Pistols shock millions by swearing on TV ... Punk rock divides the nation ... Mohair jumpers and PVC trousers are in demand ... 12-year-old schoolboy Steve Lamacq from Colne Engaine in Essex plays records in his bedroom ... Colchester Utd beat Darlington 4-0 in Division Four, with Bobby Gough, Steve Dowman (2) and Lindsay Smith on the score-sheet ... 23-year-old Paul Mariner scores the only goal of the match as Bobby Robson's Ipswich Town defeat Bob Paisley's Liverpool 1-0 in a top-of-the-table clash in Division One ... The UK economy remains in dire straits ... Chancellor of the Exchequer Denis Healey is forced to make cuts in public spending under the terms of the $3.9 billion loan from the IMF ... Times are hard for families living in 'run-down' industrial areas of the country ... Just 124 million tonnes of coal have been mined in Britain this year ... Inflation has fallen slightly to 16.5%, but property prices continue to rise - the average cost of a house is now over £12,000 ... Jim Callaghan's Labour government has slipped behind Margaret Thatcher's opposition Tory party in the polls ... ***Money Money Money*** ("... must be funny, in the rich man's world") by Abba is number three in the pop chart ... "Let's go for a little walk. Under the moon of love. Let's sit right down and talk..." ***Under The Moon Of Love*** by Showaddywaddy is new at number one ... 42-year-old John Noakes, 37-year-old Peter Purves and 29-year-old Lesley Judd present *Blue Peter* on BBC One. The Christmas Appeal is underway with thousands of children sending in old postage stamps and postcards to help raise money for those affected by civil war in Lebanon ... ***Portsmouth*** by 23-year-old Mike Oldfield is number three in the pop chart ... Christmas approaches ... TV adverts declare, 'That's the Wonder of *Woolworths*' ... Schoolboys make their lists for Santa Claus ... *Up Periscope* costs £5.49 ... *Super Flight Deck* is £4.50 ... *Buck-a-Roo* is £2.75 ... The latest *All Star Super Striker* table-top football game (from *Palitoy*) now comes with a 'super texture pitch' ... *Matey* bubble bath is a popular stocking filler ... Dads know what to expect ... The *Ronco* Record Vacuum is £5.99 ... A gift set of *Old Spice* aftershave and talc for men is £1.69 ... "And it went, la-la-la-la-la-la-la-la-la-lah, la-la-la-la-la-la-lah. Peace and goodwill to all men, and love for the child" - ***A Spaceman Came Travelling*** by Chris de Burgh plays on a transistor ... 29-year-old entrepreneur Alan Sugar sells imported car radios and music cassette players to independent electrical retailers in London ... 41-year-old actor Johnny Briggs plays Mike Baldwin - a new character on ITV's ever popular soap-opera *Coronation Street* ... "Leave it out, guv'nor!" - the third series of hard-hitting cop drama *The Sweeney* (starring 34-year-old John Thaw as Jack Reagan and 28-year-old Dennis Waterman as George Carter) comes to an end ... "Can anybody find me..." ***Somebody To Love*** by Queen is number two in the singles chart ... ***Sorry Seems To Be The Hardest Word*** by Elton John is number eleven ... Hallmark Records release *The Best of Top of the Pops '76* - a budget priced cover-version pop compilation LP with blonde Jilly Johnson in a sultry pose on the sleeve ... "What do you hear on the street these days, Huggy?" - *Starsky & Hutch* (starring Paul Michael Glaser, David Soul and with 30-year-old Antonio Fargas as Huggy Bear) is a popular new TV program for Saturday nights ... Millions tune in to ITV's *Muppet Show* on Sunday evenings - where the outrageous Miss Piggy attempts to make Kermit jealous by flirting with the male guest stars ... The second series of *When the Boat Comes In* is on BBC One on Friday nights ... Housewives keep jars of spices on a wooden rack, mounted on the wall of the kitchen ... Food is served on a push-a-long, three-tiered dinner trolley ... 'Splash it all over' - Henry Cooper, Barry Sheene and Kevin Keegan promote *Brut* aftershave ... 27-year-old Olympic ice-skating champion John Curry is BBC's 'Sports Personality of the Year' ... 30-year-old footballer Fabio Capello plays in the Italian team which beats Don Revie's England 2-0. England's line-up for the match is: Clemence, Clement, Mills, B Greenhoff, McFarland, Hughes, Keegan, Channon, Bowles, Cherry, Brooking and substitute Beattie ... Last season's Division One champions and current league leaders,

Liverpool, are thrashed 5-1 by Ron Saunders' Aston Villa, with 21-year-old Andy Gray and 19-year-old John Deehan both scoring twice for the Midlands' club ... "It's a..." ***Living Thing*** ("... it's a terrible thing to lose") by Electric Light Orchestra climbs to number four on the hit parade ... ***Lean On Me*** by Mud is number seven ... 26-year-old footballer Malcolm 'Supermac' MacDonald scores a hat-trick as Terry Neill's Arsenal beat Gordon Lee's Newcastle Utd 5-3 at Highbury ... 30-year-old 'super' Georgie Best makes a rude gesture and swears at the referee in a match between Fulham and Chelsea ... There's a flurry of activity on football's transfer market ... 28-year-old Larry Lloyd leaves Coventry City and joins Brian Clough's Nottingham Forest ... 28-year-old Bruce Rioch leaves Derby County and joins Billy Bingham's Everton ... 31-year-old Alan Ball leaves Arsenal and signs for Southampton for £60,000 ... 44-year-old movie star Elizabeth Taylor marries her sixth husband - 49-year-old US politician John Warner at Richmond in Virginia ... Back in Britain - the economy is struggling and prices are rising ... Prime-minister Jim Callaghan and his Labour government are criticised for their poor handling of the country's finances ... People escape the grim pressures of life with a night out at the pictures ... 51-year-old Peter Sellers stars in *The Pink Panther Strikes Again* ... 34-year-old Michael York and 23-year-old Jenny Agutter star in *Logan's Run* ... 37-year-old Bill Giles presents the weather forecast on BBC One ... There's widespread heavy snow in the week before Christmas ... "A ray of hope flickers in the sky. A tiny star lights up way up high. All across the land, dawns a brand new morn. This comes to pass..." ***When A Child Is Born*** by 41-year-old Johnny Mathis is number one in the pop chart ... Digital watches are all the rage ... A gold *Seiko* with red digital display (which illuminates at the press of a button) is £78.95 ... A silver *Imado* with red digital display costs £53.50 ... A five-function digital watch from *Metac* is £39.95 ... A *Trafalgar 61036* is £21.95 ... On Christmas morning, excitable kids play out on their new bikes ... A Silver Jubilee special edition of the Raleigh *Chopper* bicycle has a silver coloured frame and 10-spoke alloy wheels ... A Bantel *Hugh Porter* racer has dropped handlebars, 5-speed Derailleur gears and sports mudguards ... "Don't forget the cuddly toy" - 48-year-old TV presenter Bruce Forsyth hosts the ever popular *Generation Game* on BBC One in the evening ... 32-year-old newsreader Angela Rippon shows her legs on *Morecambe and Wise* in front of 28 million viewers ... The musical, *Oliver!*, is broadcast in the afternoon on Christmas Day. The film, *Airport*, starring Burt Lancaster, is broadcast in the evening. *The Wizard of Oz* is shown on Boxing Day ... "Oh, I don't know why she's leaving, or where she's gonna go. I guess she's got her reasons but I just don't want to know, 'cause for twenty-four years I've been..." ***Living Next Door To Alice*** by Smokie is number five in the pop chart ... "The stars are shining bright, and I'm feelin' just right for..." ***Grandma's Party*** ("... tonight") by 31-year-old Paul Nicholas is number nine ... A new eight part drama for children called *The Phoenix and the Carpet* airs on BBC

One on Wednesday evenings at ten past five (after *Goober and the Ghost Chasers*) ... Southampton footballer Mick Channon scores twice in a 2-1 victory over Bristol Rovers and celebrates his goals by making a windmill action with one arm ... 24-year-old eccentric centre-forward Robin Friday transfers from Third Division Reading to Second Division Cardiff City for £28,000 ... Trendy courting couples enjoy a night out at a *Berni Inn* ... Steak (well-done) and chips is a popular choice from the menu, followed by Black Forest gateau ... Adverts say, 'Martini Rosso - Anytime, any place, anywhere' ... 1977 is underway ... Punk rock continues to thrill and shock in equal measure ... Spiky haired teenagers pogo, spit and throw beer at raucous gigs all around the country ... 22-year-old Stuart Goddard from London changes his name to Adam Ant ... Troublesome band The Sex Pistols are sacked by record company *EMI*. The 'Pistols sign with *A&M* - have another fall out - and eventually sign for 26-year-old Richard Branson's *Virgin* label ... 31-year-old Malcolm McLaren sits at home, counting his money ... The football season continues ... 24-year-old eccentric centre-forward Robin Friday scores two goals on his debut for Cardiff City in a 3-0 victory over Fulham in front of 20,268 spectators at Ninian Park ... Heavy snow in mid January causes chaos on the roads with many motorists forced to abandon their cars ... Schoolboys make 'slides' on the pavement - and take turns to see who can glide the furthest over the compacted snow ... "So let the..." ***Sideshow*** ("... begin. Hurry, hurry. Step right on in") by Barry Biggs is number three in the pop chart ...

"You gave up the only one that ever loved you, and went back to that..." ***Wild Side Of Life*** by Status Quo is number nine ... 30-year-old David Bowie releases the *Low* album, with tracks *Breaking Glass* and *Sound And Vision* on side one, and with *Subterraneans* as the closing track on side two ... 48-year-old Bruce Forsyth is the guest star (appearing alongside Fozzie, Kermit, Animal and Miss Piggy) on ITV's hugely popular Sunday evening program *The Muppet Show* ... 32-year-old Michael Fish presents the weather forecast on BBC One ... The snow thaws, leading to widespread flooding ... 44-year-old Andrew Gardner and 44-year-old Reginald Bosanquet present the news for ITN ... 50-year-old Queen Elizabeth II travels to Tonga to begin her Silver Jubilee tour, before moving onto Fiji and New Zealand ... 64-year-old Labour prime-minister Jim Callaghan is becoming more and more unpopular ... Inflation is rising and unemployment now stands at 1.4 million ... Sacked workers continue to picket the Grunwick photographic processing factory in Willesden ... A homeless woman is murdered in Leeds ... Police confirm that the recent murders of women in Yorkshire could be linked ... The IRA sets off seven bombs around London's West End - thankfully there are no fatalities ... "Don't give up on us, baby. Don't make the wrong seem right. The future isn't just one night. It's written in the moonlight" - ***Don't Give Up On Us*** by 33-year-old David Soul climbs to number one in the pop chart - and stays there for four weeks ... ***The Things We Do For Love*** by 10cc is number six ... 40-year-old Gordon Honeycombe reads the news for ITN ...

38-year-old David Owen is the new Foreign Secretary in Jim Callaghan's Labour government ... 36-year-old convicted murderer Gary Gilmore says, "Let's do it!" - and is executed by firing squad in Utah ... 52-year-old Jimmy Carter is inaugurated as US president in Washington ... Back in England - around 18 million TV viewers watch *Coronation Street* twice a week (on Mondays and Wednesdays at 7.30 p.m.). Ray and Deidre Langton (played by 34-year-old Neville Buswell and 22-year-old Anne Kirkbride) are proud parents of a newborn baby girl called Tracy. 25-year-old Cheryl Murray makes her first appearance as Suzie Birchall ... "She's crazy like a fool. What about..." ***Daddy Cool*** by Boney M climbs to number six in the pop chart ... "Working at the..." ***Car Wash*** by Rose Royce reaches number nine ... "Beep-beep, beep-beep, yeah! Traffic news on Radio One" - the latest traffic updates are transmitted on Radio One ... A new twelve-mile stretch of M11 motorway opens between Redbridge and Harlow ... More and more foreign cars are being sold in the UK ... The new Alfa Romeo *Alfasud Sprint* (with disc-brakes and a top speed of 103 mph) is now in showrooms ... The new Fiat *127 Sport* (with cloth upholstered seats and a top speed of 100 mph) is also available ... There's heavy rain in mid February ... Footballers play 'the beautiful game' on muddy pitches ... 27-year-old Brian Kidd scores four goals as Tony Book's Manchester City thrash Leicester City 5-0 at Maine Road ... Kevin Keegan, John Toshack and Joey Jones score the goals as Bob Paisley's Liverpool beat Derby County 3-1 at Anfield ... Brian Talbot, John Wark,

Keith Bertschin and Paul Mariner score the goals as Bobby Robson's Ipswich Town beat Arsenal 1-4 at Highbury ... Aston Villa's 21-year-old centre-forward Andy Gray is fined £75 for making a 'V' sign at Manchester Utd fans ... ***Dr. Love*** ("... please come running can't you see I'm in pain") by 22-year-old Tina Charles climbs to number four in the pop chart ... ***Isn't She Lovely*** ("... isn't she wonderful") by 28-year-old David Parton also reaches number four ... Sammy Chung's Wolverhampton Wanderers are top of Division Two ... Peter Morris' Mansfield Town are top of Division Three ... Big Ron Atkinson's Cambridge Utd are top of Division Four ... Everton sack manager Billy Bingham and appoint 42-year-old Gordon Lee ... 22-year-old Trevor Francis (of Birmingham City) makes his debut for England in a 0-2 defeat against Holland at Wembley. England's full line-up for the match is: Clemence, Clement, Beattie, Doyle, Watson, Madeley, Keegan, Greenhoff, T Francis, Bowles, Brooking, and substitutes Pearson and Todd ... 30-year-old 'super' Georgie Best spends a few days in hospital after crashing his car in the early hours in Knightsbridge ... ***You're More Than A Number In My Little Red Book*** ("... you're more than a one night date") by The Drifters is number five in the pop chart ... "Just got back from the downtown Palais where the music was so sweet it knocked me right back in the alley. I'm ready. Yeah, yeah, yeah I'm ready" - ***Rockaria!*** by Electric Light Orchestra is number nine ... Hi-fi audio technology moves on apace ... 29-year-old entrepreneur Alan Sugar promotes his new *Amstrad 8000* stereo amplifier to independent electrical retailers in London ... Television technology moves on apace ... 36-year-old inventor Clive Sinclair markets a new two-inch TV set for £175.95 ... *Robin's Nest*, with 32-year-old Richard O'Sullivan and 28-year-old Tessa Wyatt, is on TV ... "Once upon a time there were three little girls who went to the police academy" - Men watch spellbound as *Charlie's Angels*, with Kate Jackson as Sabrina, Jaclyn Smith as Kelly and 29-year-old Farrah Fawcett-Majors as Jill, is shown on British TV for the first time ... 27-year-old Sissy Spacek stars in *Carrie* at cinemas ... Footballers Alan Gowling and Micky Burns score the goals for Newcastle Utd in a 2-0 victory over Tottenham Hotspur - Spurs are now bottom of Division One and in real danger of being relegated to Division Two ... ***Don't Cry For Me Argentina*** ("... the truth is, I never left you") by 30-year-old Julie Covington spends a week at number one in the pop chart ... ***Boogie Nights*** ("... ain't no doubt, we are here to party") by Heatwave climbs to number two ... Boys play out - racing against each other on bicycles ... 10-year-old Andrew Lovell, 9-year-old Neil Roper and 9-year-old Anthony Sutton speed around 'the block' on their bikes at Ford Way in Armitage ... A red Raleigh BSA *Tour-de-France* with dropped handle bars, 10-speed Derailleur gears, water bottle and toe-clips costs £96.95 (or £2.56 for 38 weeks from mum's catalogue) ... 11-year-old schoolboy Rick Astley from Newton-le-Willows in Lancashire listens to records in his bedroom ... ***When I Need You*** ("... I just close my eyes and I'm with you") by 28-year-old Leo Sayer spends three weeks at number one in the pop chart ... "Step back in time, me Ro-me-oh. My Juliet and take me home" - ***Romeo*** by Mr. Big is number four ... "Now is the time to send us a line, for your Hoseason's boating brochure. We've got all kinds of craft that'll suit you just for fine for messing about on the water" - Middle-class families peruse glossy holiday pamphlets, before booking a two week summer break ... Housewives go shopping at *Fine Fare* or *Gateway* supermarkets ... A loaf of bread costs 20p ... A jar of lemon curd is 14p ... A pint of milk is 11½p ... A pack of twenty cigarettes is 55p ... The new *Double Decker* chocolate bar from Cadbury's tastes good ... "Tell 'em about the honey, mummy!" - the Honey Monster advertises *Sugar Puffs* on TV.

Spring 1977

Pearl's a singer

Jim Callaghan's under-fire Labour party loses a crucial by-election at Ashfield (usually a safe seat). A political pact is set up between the Labour government and David Steel's Liberals ... Prime-minister Callaghan zooms across the Atlantic on Concorde to meet president Carter in the US ... Queen Elizabeth II's Silver Jubilee tour moves onto Australia - the 50-year-old monarch visits Canberra for the State Opening of Parliament and then travels to Newcastle, Sydney, Nuriootpa and Perth ... Back in Britain - 59-year-old Chancellor of the Exchequer Denis Healey delivers his fifth Budget and announces a cut in the basic rate of income tax ... 'The antidote to panel games' - 55-year-old Humphrey Lyttelton is chairman for a new series of *I'm Sorry I Haven't A Clue* on Radio Four. 34-year-old Graeme Garden, 41-year-old Barry Cryer, 39-year-old Willie Rushton and 36-year-old Tim Brooke-Taylor are panelists on the popular comedy show ... People buy the latest 7-inch pop singles at *Our Price* for 75p ... "Chanson d'amour. (Ra-da-da-da-da). Je t'adore" - ***Chanson D'Amour*** by Manhattan Transfer spends three weeks at number one on the hit parade ... "Oh, Moody Blue, tell me am I getting' through" - ***Moody Blue*** by 42-year-old Elvis Presley reaches number six ... Footballers Kevin

Keegan and Steve Heighway score the goals for Liverpool as Bob Paisley's team beats Tony Book's Manchester City 2-1 in a top-of-the-table clash in Division One. (Brian Kidd scores City's goal) ... 25-year-old Steve Perryman makes his three-hundreth appearance for Tottenham Hotspur in a 3-0 victory over Queens Park Rangers - the win gives Spurs two vital points in their fight against relegation ... Families gather around Ferguson *Colourstar TX* television sets ... BBC One broadcasts a six-part mini-series called *Roots* (with Kunta Kinte, Kizzy and Chicken George) ... "Behold, the lamb of God who takes unto himself the sins of the world" - 32-year-old Robert Powell stars as Jesus in *Jesus of Nazareth* in ITV's blockbuster mini-series ... "Magic, our Morris!" - 48-year-old Bill Maynard stars as Selwyn Frogitt in series two of *Oh No, It's Selwyn Frogitt* ... Approximately 20 million viewers tune-in to see Len Fairclough (played by 47-year-old Peter Adamson) marry Rita Littlewood (played by 43-year-old Barbara Knox) in the ever popular soap-opera *Coronation Street* ... "When, when you smile, when you smile at me. Well, well I know our love will always be" - ***When*** by Showaddywaddy is number four in the pop chart ... ***Red Light Spells Danger*** ("... Can't hold out much longer") by 27-year-old Billy Ocean is number two ... 32-year-old Angela Rippon reads the news on BBC ... Two Boeing *747* jumbo jets collide on the ground in Tenerife killing 583 people - it's the world's worst aviation disaster ... Queen Elizabeth II's Silver Jubilee tour moves onto Papua New Guinea, Bombay and Oman ... Back in England - sacked workers continue to picket the Grunwick photographic processing factory in Willesden. Flying pickets also target any chemist shops that use the services of Grunwick ... Car production at British Leyland grinds to a halt when three-thousand tool-makers walk out on strike ... 49-year-old Derek Robinson (aka Red Robbo) is union convener at the Longbridge factory ... 52-year-old US president Jimmy Carter pays a flying visit to Newcastle-upon-Tyne, and is given a warm welcome by the Geordie crowds ... The economy continues to falter under Jim Callaghan's Labour government ... Mrs. Thatcher's opposition Conservative party takes a significant lead in the opinion polls ... Political leaders from the richest seven countries in the world travel to London for the G7 summit. Helmut Schmidt represents West Germany, Valery Giscard d'Estaing represents France and Jimmy Carter represents the USA. The leaders discuss the global economy and also attend a state dinner with Queen Elizabeth II and the Duke of Edinburgh ... Life continues as normal for families around the country ... *Hawaii Five-O* is on ITV on Tuesday evenings - with 56-year-old Jack Lord as Steve McGarrett ... *It's A Knockout* is on BBC One on Friday evenings. A team from Beverley wins a closely fought contest against Wakefield and Calderdale, and will now compete in the Jeux Sans Frontieres competition later in the year ... The final episode of *Porridge* is shown on Friday the twenty-fifth of March - with young Lenny Godber leaving Slade Prison at the end of his sentence, and going on a romantic holiday with Fletch's daughter ... "Walking through an empty house, tears in my eyes. Here is where the story ends, this is goodbye..." ***Knowing Me Knowing You*** ("... Ah-haa") by Abba is number one in the pop chart for five weeks! ... 11-year-old schoolboy Stephen Coogan from Middleton in Manchester sits in his bedroom listening to records ... ***Pearl's A Singer*** ("... she stands up when she plays the piano") by Elkie Brooks reaches number eight ... 18-year-old Linda Lusardi (36C) from Wood Green is a popular new page three girl in *The Sun* ... 26-year-old cricketer Derek Randall scores 174 in England's second innings total of 417, but England lose the Centenary Test Match against Australia in Melbourne, after being bowled out for just 95 in the first innings ... 26-year-old Barry Sheene wins the 500cc motorcycle Grand Prix in Venezuela ... 22-year-old footballer Trevor Francis scores a goal for England (Clemence, Gidman, Cherry, Kennedy, Watson, Hughes, Keegan, Channon, Royle, T Francis, Hill and substitute Mariner) in a 5-0 victory over Luxembourg. Keegan, Kennedy and Channon (2) are also on the score-sheet. John Gidman and Paul Mariner make their international debuts. The victory gives England a feint hope of reaching next year's world cup finals ... 24-year-old Brian Little scores the winning goal as Ron Saunders' Aston Villa achieve a 3-2 victory (after extra-time) over Gordon Lee's Everton in the second replay of the League Cup final ... 20-year-old Alan Biley scores twice as Big Ron Atkinson's Cambridge Utd beat Aldershot 4-1 in Division Four ... 24-year-old Robin Friday scores twice as Cardiff City beat Luton Town 4-2 in Division Two - and the eccentric centre-forward celebrates by flicking a 'V' sign at Luton goalkeeper, Milija Aleksic ... "And I just got to be me-ee, free-ee, free-ee" - ***Free*** by Deniece Williams is the new number one pop single ... ***Whodunit*** ("... who killed my baby?") by Tavares is number five ... ***White Riot*** ("... I wanna riot. White riot, a riot of my own") by The Clash is number thirty-eight ... 41-year-old John Spencer collects £6,000 after winning the *Embassy* World Snooker Championship at the Crucible in Sheffield - by beating Cliff Thorburn from Canada in the final ... The domestic football season ends ... Bob Paisley's Liverpool are champions of Division One for the second year running. Ray Clemence, Phil Neal, Emlyn Hughes, Tommy Smith, Joey Jones, Phil Thompson, Ian Callaghan, Jimmy Case, Steve Heighway, Ray Kennedy, David Johnson, John Toshack, Terry McDermott and 26-year-old Kevin Keegan have all been outstanding ... Tony Book's Manchester City (with Joe Corrigan, Willie Donachie, Dave Watson, Mike Doyle, Asa Hartford, Peter Barnes, Gary Owen, Joe Royle, Brian Kidd and 27-year-old Dennis Tueart) are runners-up ... Keith Burkinshaw's Tottenham Hotspur are relegated along with Sunderland and Stoke City ... Andy Gray (of Aston Villa) and Malcolm 'Supermac' MacDonald (of Arsenal) share the accolade of top goal scorer - both men having scored twenty-five league goals for the season ... 42-year-old Brian Clough's Nottingham Forest gain promotion from Division Two ... "I would have given you all of my heart, but there's someone who's torn it apart" - Rod Stewart's double A-side single ***I Don't Want To Talk About It / First Cut Is The***

Deepest climbs to number one ... "Well good morning Judge, how are you today?" - ***Good Morning Judge*** by 10cc is number five ... 51-year-old Queen Elizabeth II visits Dundee, Aberdeen and Edinburgh as part of her Silver Jubilee tour ... 44-year-old Michael Caine and 41-year-old Donald Sutherland star in *The Eagle Has Landed* at cinemas ... 31-year-old Mary Millington features in *Come Play With Me* at 'special' cinemas ... "Only the crumbliest flakiest chocolate, tastes like chocolate never tasted before" - Cadbury's *Flake* adverts are on TV ... *Red Rum* wins the Grand National for a third time - 31-year-old Tommy Stack is the jockey and 46-year-old Ginger McCain is the trainer ... 43-year-old *Blue Peter* presenter John Noakes is filmed at the top of Nelson's Column, helping workman clean the 169 foot high monument in Trafalgar Square ... "Oh, what a…" ***Lonely Boy*** by Andrew Gold reaches number eleven in the pop chart ... ***Mah-Na, Mah-Ma*** ("... Doo-doo, doo-doo-doo") by Piero Umiliani reaches number eight ... Repairs are completed on Big Ben, and the historic Great Clock of Westminster is working again for the first time in nine months ... 30-year-old footballer Jimmy Greenhoff scores the winning goal in the FA Cup final as Tommy 'The Doc' Docherty's Manchester Utd defeat champions Liverpool 2-1. A ticket for the standing enclosure at the Empire Stadium in Wembley costs £2.50 ... Four days after the cup final - Terry McDermott, Tommy Smith and Phil Neal score the goals as Liverpool win the European Cup for the first time by beating Borussia Monchengladbach 3-1 in Rome ... "Welcome to the…" ***Hotel***

California ("... Such a lovely place. Such a lovely place. Such a lovely face") by The Eagles is number eight in the pop chart ... The ***Spot the Pigeon (E.P.)*** (with tracks: *Match Of The Day*, *Pigeons* and *Inside and Out*) by Genesis is number fourteen ... 19-year-old footballer Cyrille Regis transfers from non-league Hayes FC to West Bromwich Albion of Division One for a fee of £10,000 ... 38-year-old Terry Wogan presents the breakfast show on BBC Radio Two ... 51-year-old Pete Murray, 55-year-old Jimmy Young and 38-year-old 'Diddy' David Hamilton host programs during the day ... 43-year-old John Dunn presents the teatime show ... Housewives peg out the washing on 'new-fangled' (galvanised tubular steel framed) rotary clothes lines, before sitting down to read *Weekend* magazine ... A 4oz pack of *Co-op 99* tea costs 11½p ... An 8oz pack of *Co-op 99* coffee is 79p ... Adverts say, '*Twix* - the longer lasting snack'.

Summer 1977

God save the Queen

Street parties are held to celebrate Queen Elizabeth II's Silver Jubilee ... It rains ... Children eat cup cakes and jelly and ice-cream ... 'How's that for taste?" - Cans of *Top Deck* are available in 'Lemonade Shandy' and 'Limeade & Lager' flavours ... Discarded ring-pulls litter the country's parks and communal spaces ... "God save the queen. She ain't no human being. There is no future, in England's dreaming" - The Sex Pistols sing ***God Save The Queen*** ... The Ramones sing ***Sheena Is A Punk Rocker*** ... The Clash release their eponymous debut LP, which includes the tracks ***White Riot*** and ***London's Burning*** ... Punk bands play at music venues all around the country to crowds of pogo-ing youths ... 11-year-old schoolboy Nigel Blackwell from Birkenhead plays *Subbuteo* 'round his friend's house - and gets palmed off with a headless centre-forward ... 'Make Sun-Pat his daily spread. Smooth or crunchy, it tastes great!' - 10-year-old schoolboy Gordon Ramsey from Stratford-upon-Avon enjoys peanut butter sandwiches at teatime ... Families stay in and watch television at the weekend ... *Celebrity Squares* is on ITV on Saturday evenings ... The fifth series of *The Onedin Line* (with 45-year-old Peter Gilmore as James Onedin) is on BBC One on Sunday evenings ... 39-year-old

Australian businessman Kerry Packer causes a huge furore by signing thirty-five leading international cricketers to appear in an unofficial world series. 30-year-old England captain Tony Greig is one of the players choosing to join the 'Packer Circus' and, as a consequence, is sacked by the MCC ... 41-year-old jockey Lester Piggott rides *The Minstrel* to victory in the Epsom Derby ... The school holidays begin ... *Jackanory*, *Inch High Private Eye* and *Flash Gordon's Trip to Mars* are broadcast on BBC One during the day ... Children play-out, despite the inclement weather ... The Ford Way gang throw stones at the Handsacre estate gang in the field beside the brook in Old Road, Armitage near Rugeley ... "You've picked a fine time to leave me..." ***Lucille*** ("... with four hungry children and a crop in the field") by Kenny Rogers is number one in the pop chart ... "Oh, that's why I'm..." ***Easy*** ("... I'm easy like Sunday morning, yeah") by The Commodores is number nine ... Grown-ups buy tickets for the cinema ... *A Bridge Too Far* is now showing, with a multi-star cast which includes 46-year-old Sean Connery, 44-year-old Michael Caine, 40-year-old Edward Fox, 39-year-old Anthony Hopkins and 56-year-old Dirk Bogarde ... ***Show You The Way To Go*** by The Jacksons spends a week at number one in the pop chart ... ***Halfway Down The Stairs*** by The Muppets is number seven ... 51-year-old Queen Elizabeth II visits Lancaster, Preston, Manchester, Liverpool, Llandudno, Bangor, Hollyhead, Harlech, Milford Haven, Carmarthen, Llanelli, Swansea, Barry and Cardiff as part of her Silver Jubilee tour ... 32-year-old DJ Dave Lee Travis hosts the travelling Radio One Roadshow for five days in July. DLT's Roadshow week begins on the Marine Parade in Clacton-on-Sea and ends at Steyne Gardens in Worthing ... ***So You Win Again*** ("... You win again. Here I stand again, the loser") by Hot Chocolate is new at number one ... ***Fanfare For The Common Man*** by Emerson, Lake & Palmer is number two ... "Hey!" - 31-year-old Henry Winkler stars as The Fonz in *Happy Days* on ITV ... 47-year-old Brian Redhead and 33-year-old Nigel Rees present Radio Four's *Today* news program ... A mass-picket takes place outside the Grunwick photo processing plant in Willesden. Hundreds of representatives from various unions attend, including 39-year-old Arthur Scargill of the Yorkshire NUM ... *The Return of Reginald Perrin* - the fifth novel from 42-year-old writer David Nobbs is published ... A young woman is murdered in Leeds and it's feared that she's the fifth victim of the Yorkshire Ripper ... Police use riot-shields for the first time during a violent demonstration against members of the National Front in Lewisham. More than 200 people are arrested and 56 police officers injured ... "So pack your toys away, your pretty boys away. Your 45s away, your alibis away. Your Spanish flies away, your one more tries away. Your old tye-dyes away..." ***You're Moving Out Today*** by 30-year-old Carole Bayer Sager reaches number six in the pop chart at the end of June ... "Oh, Sam, Sam, you know where I am" - ***Sam*** by 28-year-old Olivia Newton-John reaches number six in early July ... 30-year-old popstar/ football chairman Elton John appoints 32-year-old Graham

Taylor as manager of Fourth Division Watford FC ... 29-year-old defender Trevor Cherry (of Leeds Utd) is sent off for England in a friendly against Argentina ... 21-year-old striker Andy Gray (of Aston Villa) is voted PFA 'Player of the Year' and PFA 'Young Player of the Year' ... Scottish fans invade the pitch, and break a crossbar, after Scotland have beaten England by two goals to one at Wembley - Gordon McQueen and Kenny Dalglish score for the Scots. Mick Channon scores a late penalty for England. ... *Lunn Poly* travel agents do a roaring trade on the high street ... Families enjoy a week at *Butlin's* or in a static caravan at the seaside ... 'Holiday campers exposed! The funniest take off of the season!' - 26-year-old Robin Askwith stars as Timmy Lea at cinemas in *Confessions from a Holiday Camp* ... Young men with hairy chests, gold medallions and shirts unbuttoned to the waist 'strut their stuff' on Saturday nights - hoping to impress the ladies ... ***Ain't Gonna Bump No More*** ("... with no big fat woman") by Joe Tex is number two in the pop chart ... "Burn baby, burn" - ***Disco Inferno*** by The Trammps is number sixteen ... There's a flurry of activity on football's transfer market ... Kevin Keegan leaves Liverpool and joins SV Hamburg for £500,000 ... 26-year-old Kenny Dalglish leaves Celtic and joins Liverpool as Keegan's replacement ... 28-year-old striker Mick Channon transfers from Southampton to Manchester City ... 23-year-old defender Kenny Burns transfers from Birmingham City to Brian Clough's newly promoted Nottingham Forest ... 29-year-old goalkeeper Jimmy Rimmer leaves Arsenal and joins Aston

Villa ... 32-year-old Pat Jennings leaves relegated Tottenham Hotspur to become Arsenal's new number one ... 49-year-old Tommy 'The Doc' Docherty is sensationally sacked by Manchester Utd after conducting an affair with the wife of the team's physiotherapist ... "Ooh, love. Ooh, lover boy. What're you doin' tonight, hey boy?" - ***Good Old Fashioned Lover Boy*** by Queen reaches number seventeen in the pop chart ... 47-year-old Dave Sexton succeeds 'The Doc' and is appointed manager of Manchester Utd ... 35-year-old Mike Brearley succeeds Tony Greig as England's cricket captain ... The first Test Match of the Ashes series, against Australia at Lord's, is drawn - with fast bowler Bob Willis taking 7 for 78. England then go on to win the next three matches (at Old Trafford, Trent Bridge and Headingley) and regain the Ashes. 21-year-old Ian Botham makes his Test debut at Trent Bridge and takes 5 wickets and scores 25 runs. 36-year-old Geoffrey Boycott scores 191 at Headingley. D L Amiss, J M Brearley (cpt), G Boycott, R A Woolmer, D W Randall, A W Greig, G D Barlow, G R J Roope, A P E Knott (wk), I T Botham, G Miller, C M Old, J K Lever, D L Underwood, M Hendrick and R G D Willis have all played a part in this fantastic Ashes victory ... Queen Elizabeth II's Silver Jubilee tour moves onto Ipswich, Norwich, Grimsby, Doncaster, Sheffield, Leeds, Wakefield, Harrogate, York, Hull, Middlesbrough, Sunderland and Newcastle-upon-Tyne ... Discotheques are all the rage ... Youngsters groove and girate on the dance floor at the local village hall, beneath flashing lights and a glittery disco ball ... "Oooh, I feel love, I feel love, I feel love, I feel love..." ***I Feel Love*** by Donna Summer climbs to number one in the pop chart - and stays there for four weeks ... "Baby, my love is on the line..." ***Baby Don't Change Your Mind*** ("... Don't change it") by Gladys Knight and the Pips reaches number four ... 26-year-old Barry Sheene is crowned 500cc motorcycle racing world champion for the second year running ... "Adrian! Adrian!" - *Rocky* with 30-year-old Sylvester Stalone is a huge hit at cinemas ... 49-year-old Roger Moore stars as James Bond (aka 007) in *The Spy Who Loved Me* - 29-year-old Barbara Bach is Anya Amasova and 37-year-old Richard Kiel is Jaws. Schoolboys watch, amazed, as Bond's white Lotus *Esprit S1* sports car (registration PPW 306R) turns into a submarine ... 45-year-old Brian Moore presents *On The Ball* on Saturday lunchtimes on ITV ... 50-year-old Don Revie resigns as England football manager to take up a coaching role in the United Arab Emirates on a salary of £60,000 a year - tax free! Revie is vilified by the press as he still had two years of his contract to run ... 55-year-old Ron Greenwood from West Ham Utd succeeds Revie as England manager ... 21-year-old tennis star Bjorn Borg beats 24-year-old Jimmy Conners in the men's singles final at Wimbledon ... 32-year-old Virginia Wade from Bournemouth wins the ladies' singles, beating Bette Stove from the Netherlands 4-6, 6-3, 6-1 in the final. (21-year-old Sue Barker was knocked-out in the semi-finals) ... "Hello, how are you? Have you been alright, through all these lonely, lonely, lonely, lonely, lonely nights? - ***Telephone Line*** by Electric Light Orchestra is number eight in the pop chart ... ***Give A Little Bit*** ("... Give a little bit of your love to me") by Supertramp is number twenty-nine ... Queen Elizabeth II's Silver Jubilee tour moves onto Wolverhampton, West Bromwich, Walsall, Birmingham, Coventry, Leicester, Chesterfield, Derby and Nottingham ... "Long ago, high on a mountain in Mexico, lived a young shepherd boy..." ***Angelo*** ("...Who met a young girl and he loved her so") by Brotherhood of Man is top of the pop chart ... ***Ma Baker*** ("... she taught her four sons. Ma-ma-ma-ma. Ma Baker, to handle their guns") by Boney M peaks at number two ... 'S' reg cars go on sale ... More and more foreign cars are being purchased ... The new Skoda *105* from Czechoslovakia has a top speed of 105 mph and can accelerate from 0-60 mph in 22 seconds ... The latest Volvo *244DL* from Sweden has a top speed of 95 mph and can reach 60 mph in 15 seconds ... Four star leaded petrol is 78p a gallon ... Queen Elizabeth II's Silver Jubilee tour moves onto Southampton, Torbay, Exeter, Plymouth, Falmouth, Truro, Bodmin, St. Austell, Bristol, Bath and Weston-super-Mare ... Families enjoy the late summer Bank Holiday - walking along the sea-front eating ice-creams ... Frozen ice-lollies now come with jokes and riddles printed on the sticks ... 12-year-old schoolboy Matthew Hall (aka Harry Hill) from Staplehurst in Kent enjoys a *Count Dracula.* His sister has a *Lemonade Fizz* ... 'Just one Cornetto, give it to me' - *Cornettos* are new ... "Aquarius, and my name is Ralph" - ***Float On*** by The Floaters reaches number one on the weekly hit parade ... "But baby (yeah, yeah)..." ***You Got What It Takes*** by Showaddywaddy is number two ... The new football season gets underway ... 28-year-old Lou Macari scores a hat-trick as Dave Sexton's Manchester Utd beat Willie Bell's Birmingham City 1-4 at St. Andrews ... Kenny Dalglish scores on his league debut for Liverpool in a 1-1 draw against Middlesbrough ... 'Diddy' David Hamilton presents the afternoon show on Radio One ... "There's no point in asking, you'll get no reply. Oh just remember, I don't decide. I got no reason, it's all too much. You'll always find us, out to lunch" - ***Pretty Vacant*** by The Sex Pistols is number six in the pop chart ... "Walking on the beaches, looking at the..." ***Peaches*** by The Stranglers is number eight ... Spiky haired adolescent kids sit in bus shelters, drinking *Olde English* cider and smoking *Silk Cut* cigarettes ... Graffiti on walls says, 'Oi! Punks Punks Punks rule OK' ... The availability of 'fast-food' has increased ... *McDonalds* now has ten restaurants in the UK ... Elvis Presley dies on the toilet in Memphis, aged 42.

Autumn 1977

Mister, your eyes are full of hesitation

The Silver Jubilee tour continues ... 51-year-old Queen Elizabeth II visits Northern Ireland before jetting off to Canada with her 56-year-old husband Prince Philip, Duke of Edinburgh ... 'Spearmint Flavoured Chewy Sweets' - *Pacers* go on sale ... 11-year-old Chris Evans from Warrington in Cheshire returns to school after the summer holiday ... Boys play conkers in the corner of the playground and exchange skateboarding stories ... A packet of Smiths *Football Crazy* smokey bacon crisps from the school tuck-shop costs 4½p ... 35-year-old Gordon Burns presents *The Krypton Factor* on television - a tough new game show where contestants are put through their paces in rounds of mental and physical agility ... Dads cut the grass on Sunday mornings ... The standard colour of *Flymo* 'hover' lawn-mowers has changed from blue and white, to bright orange ... "It's time to play the music, it's time to light the lights. It's time to meet the Muppets on the Muppet Show tonight" - Fozzie, Kermit, Animal, Miss Piggy and the Swedish Chef star in a new series of ITV's hugely popular *Muppet Show* ... "Meet the gang 'cause the boys are here, the boys to entertain you" - 47-year-old Windsor Davies, 44-year-old Don Estelle and 42-year-old Melvyn Hayes star in a new series of BBC

One's hugely popular situation comedy *It Ain't Half Hot Mum* ... 28-year-old Elizabeth Estensen, 35-year-old Nerys Hughes and 55-year-old Mollie Sugden star in a new series of *The Liver Birds* ... A Bill to make the wearing of seat-belts in cars compulsory fails to get through parliament ... Ford launches the all new *Granada* motorcar with prices from £5,913 - there's a choice of 2.3 litre and 2.8 litre petrol engines, and for the first time there's also a 2.1 litre diesel engine. The top-of-the-range *Ghia* model comes complete with headlamp washers as standard ... 'From Georgia to Texas ... and back, in 28 hours, with a truck-load of bootleg beer' - fathers and sons rush to the cinema to see *Smokey and the Bandit*, starring 41-year-old Burt Reynolds and a black Pontiac *Trans-Am* car ... "Way Down, where the music plays. Way down, like a tidal wave"- ***Way Down*** by the late Elvis Presley climbs to the top of the pop chart - and stays there for five weeks! ... "I remember Elvis Presley, Lord how I love to hear him sing. So, I'll adore him just forever, for he's the one and only king" - Danny Mirror sings ***I Remember Elvis Presley (The King Is Dead)*** ... The Adverts sing "Looking through..." ***Gary Gilmore's Eyes*** ... The dark nights draw in and families spend their evenings watching TV together ... The *Dutchess of Duke Street* (with 34-year-old Gemma Jones) is on BBC One on Saturday nights ... *Poldark* (with 35-year-old Robin Ellis) is broadcast on Sunday nights ... "I rented my apartment on a Monday at one, a-singin' doo-lolly-lolly, shicky-bum, shicky-bum" - ***Telephone Man*** by 28-year-old Meri Wilson climbs to number six on the weekly hit parade ... "From L.A. to New York..." ***From New York To L.A.*** by 29-year-old Patsy Gallant also reaches number six ... 28-year-old goalkeeper Peter Shilton leaves George Eastham's Stoke City and joins Brian Clough's newly promoted Nottingham Forest for £250,000 ... Liverpool sign 21-year-old defender Alan Hansen for £110,000 from Partick Thistle ... 19-year-old Cyrille Regis makes his debut for Ronnie Allen's West Bromwich Albion - and scores the winning goal in a 2-1 victory over Middlesbrough. (20-year-old Bryan Robson is also on the score-sheet for 'The Baggies') ... 49-year-old Tommy 'The Doc' Docherty is installed as the new manager of Derby County ... 57-year-old Sir Alf Ramsey takes over from Willie Bell as manager of Birmingham City ... "De, de-de, de-der" - ***Oxygene Part IX*** by Jean-Michel Jarre reaches number four in the pop chart ... ***Do Anything You Wanna Do*** by The Rods peaks at number nine ... Popstar Marc Bolan dies in a car crash at Barnes in London - just two weeks before his 30th birthday ... 44-year-old Frank Bough presents *Grandstand* on BBC One on Saturday afternoons ... 54-year-old Murray Walker commentates on motor racing events ... The six-wheeled Tyrrell Formula One racing car is used for the final time - Frenchman Patrick Depailler drives the experimental machine to a third placed finish in the Japanese Grand Prix. The race is won by Britain's James Hunt in a conventional four-wheeled McLaren ... Back in England - 6-year-old Helena Lovell from Armitage in Staffordshire receives a *Fisher Price* Kermit the Frog hand-puppet for her birthday ... 23-year-old footballer

Trevor Francis scores twice as Sir Alf Ramsey's Birmingham City beat John Neal's Middlesbrough 1-2 at Ayresome Park ... 23-year-old Mick Ferguson scores a hat-trick as Gordon Milne's Coventry City beat Tony Book's Manchester City 4-2 at Highfield Road ... 27-year-old Malcolm 'Supermac' MacDonald and 21-year-old Frank Stapleton score the goals as Terry Neill's Arsenal beat Dave Sexton's Manchester Utd 1-2 at Old Trafford ... 21-year-old Andy Gray scores twice as Ron Saunders' Aston Villa beat Bob Paisley's Liverpool 1-2 at Anfield ... "I-I-I don't wanna be like you" - ***Looking After Number One*** by The Boomtown Rats climbs to number eleven in the pop chart - 25-year-old Bob Geldof (the band's charismatic lead singer) has become one of the best known punk rockers in Britain ... The Sex Pistols' LP, *Never Mind The Bollocks Here's The Sex Pistols*, is number one in the album chart - 21-year-old Johnny Rotten and 20-year-old Sid Vicious are probably the two most infamous punk rockers in Britain ... 23-year-old Lucinda Prior-Palmer wins the three-day horse trial event at Burghley House on *George* ... "Woah-oh" ***Black Betty*** ("Bam-ba-lam!") by Ram Jam climbs to number seven in the pop chart ... "Ah, here we are, and here we are, and here we go. All aboard and we're hitting the road. Here we go-oh..." ***Rockin' All Over The World*** by Status Quo reaches number three ... The second series of *The New Avengers* begins on ITV, with Patrick Macnee as Steed, Gareth Hunt as Gambit and 31-year-old Joanna Lumley as Purdey ... The final series of *Dad's Army* begins on BBC - and sees Private Pike (played by 31-year-old Ian

Lavender) running out of petrol, as he drives his girlfriend home from the pictures ... "Don't you find shopping boring, though, Ange? Oh, I do. I hate it" - 31-year-old Alison Steadman stars in BBC One's Play For The Day *Abigail's Party* ... 44-year-old Barry Norman presents the late night movie review program *Film 77* on Sundays ... 24-year-old Jenny Agutter gets naked with 23-year-old Peter Firth in *Equus* at cinemas ... Dads suddenly become interested in Saturday morning television when 27-year-old Sally James joins *Tiswas* ... ***You're In My Heart*** ("... you're in my soul. You'll be my breath should I grow old. You are my lover, you're my best friend. You're in my soul") by 32-year-old Rod Stewart is number three in the pop chart ... "Come on Silver Lady take my word, I won't run out on you again, believe me. Oh, I've seen the light, it's just one more night without you" - ***Silver Lady*** by 34-year-old David Soul climbs to number one ... Pam Ayres, Little and Large and the Muppets appear in front of 51-year-old Queen Elizabeth II at the Silver Jubilee Royal Variety Performance ... 16-year-old William Hague makes a witty speech about old people at the Conservative party conference in Blackpool ... 13-year-old Alexander Boris de Pfeffel Johnson is a new border at Eton College ... "Whatever happened to dear old Lenin?" - ***No More Heroes*** ("...anymore") by The Stranglers enters the pop chart at number forty-nine ... "We like the music. We like that disco sound" - ***Black Is Black*** ("... I want my baby back) by La Belle Epoque climbs to number two ... 45-year-old Reginald Bosanquet and 50-year-old Sandy Gall present

ITN's *News at Ten* program ... Fire brigades all across the country go on strike for higher pay. Army operated 'Green Goddess' vehicles are used in place of fire-engines for the first time in nine years ... 47-year-old Michael Edwardes is the new chairman of car manufacturer British Leyland ... 50-year-old Derek Robinson (aka Red Robbo) addresses a mass meeting of workers at Longbridge ... An official enquiry into the strike at the Grunwick photographic processing factory in Willesden concludes that the sacked workers should now be re-instated. The bosses at Grunwick decide not to do so - and picketing continues ... "Yes sir, I can boogie, but I need a certain song. I can boogie. Boogie, boogie all night long" - ***Yes Sir I Can Boogie*** by Baccara is top of the hit parade ... ***We Are The Champions*** ("... my friend") by Queen is number two ... 11-year-old David Cameron from Marylebone in London watches television ... 'Power to the people!' - *Citizen Smith* with 27-year-old Robert Lindsay as Wolfie Smith (the leader of the Tooting Popular Front) is broadcast on BBC One on Thursday evenings ... Eamonn Andrews hosts *This is Your Life* on ITV on Wednesday evenings - 30-year-old Richard Beckinsale is one of the celebrities to be presented with the big red book ... Children rush home from school to watch *Secret Squirrel* and *Ivor the Engine* ... Home entertainment technology moves on apace ... Families have hours of fun playing Football, Tennis, Squash and Squash (Practice) on the Binatone *TV Master Mk IV* games console ... The new *Atari 2600* game system is launched - with the exciting *Combat* cartridge as part of the bundle ... Home communication technology moves on apace ... The iconic GPO trimphone now comes with state-of-the-art push-buttons and is available in green, ivory or two-tone blue ... *British Airways'* Concorde supersonic jet begins a new commercial route - flying direct to New York's John F. Kennedy Airport for the first time ... 55-year-old entrepreneur Freddie Laker launches his 'low price' *Skytrain* service - flying from Gatwick to New York for just £59 one-way ... "She is..." ***Watching The Detectives*** by 22-year-old Elvis Costello reaches number fifteen in the pop chart ... "Sitting in the front row..." ***Mary Of The 4th Form*** ("... turning all the boys on") by The Boomtown Rats (with 26-year-old punk rocker Bob Geldof) also peaks at number fifteen ... Siouxsie and the Banshees perform a night-time session for 38-year-old Radio One disc jockey John Peel ... 27-year-old Princess Anne gives birth to baby Peter - and Queen Elizabeth II becomes a grandmother in her Silver Jubilee year ... 10-year-old Andrew Lovell has his appendix removed at Stafford General Hospital ... Brian Clough's newly promoted Nottingham Forest are top of Football League Division One after thrashing Bobby Robson's Ipswich Town 4-0 at the City Ground, with all four goals scored by 26-year-old centre-forward Peter Withe ... Keith Burkinshaw's Tottenham Hotspur are second (behind Bolton Wanderers) in Division Two after thrashing Bristol Rovers 9-0 at White Hart Lane, with 21-year-old Colin Lee (a recent signing from Torquay Utd) scoring four goals, and 23-year-old Ian Moores bagging a hat-trick ... ***Calling Occupants Of Interplanetary***

Craft (The Recognised Anthem Of World Contact Day) by The Carpenters climbs to number nine in the pop chart ... "2-4-6-8 ain't never too late. Me and my radio truckin' on through the night. 3-5-7-9 on a double white line. Motorway sun coming up on the morning light" - ***2-4-6-8 Motorway*** by The Tom Robinson Band reaches number five ... "Twenty-two minutes late. Badger ate a junction box at New Malden" - 51-year-old Leonard Rossiter stars in the second series of *The Fall and Rise of Reginald Perrin* (a TV comedy based on a novel by 42-year-old David Nobbs from Orpington) ... 'Stop! You're Killing Me' - 48-year-old Ronnie Barker and 46-year-old Ronnie Corbett return as private detectives Piggy Malone and Charley Farley in a new series of *The Two Ronnies* ... "I was an impossible case, no-one ever could reach me. But I think I can see in your face, there's a lot you can teach me. So I wanna know, what's..." ***The Name Of The Game*** by Abba is number one in the pop chart ... There's been a slight improvement in the economy ... Unemployment has dipped to 1.3 million under Jim Callaghan's Labour government ... The annual rate of inflation is also down - to 10% (after reaching a record high of 26.9% two years ago) ... Young men, with long hair and leather-jackets, tear through housing estates on Yamaha *FS-1* (aka 'Fizzy') motorbikes ... Middle-aged men, with side-partings and polyester jackets, drive along 'B' roads in metallic green Austin *Allegro Special L.E.* motorcars ... Schoolboys look forward to Christmas ... The annual *Beezer Book* (with characters 'Pop, Dick and Harry' on the front cover) is now on sale.

Winter 1977 - 1978

Far have I travelled and much have I seen

The weather is cold and frosty in the North. It's mostly mild in the South ... Parents take their children to matinee films at the local cinema during the school holiday ... Walt Disney's *Herbie Goes to Monte Carlo* is now showing ... Families get ready for Christmas ... Housewives serve food on heated *Hostess* trollies ... 'Get busy with the fizzy - Sodastream' - *Sodastreams* make refreshing fizzy drinks ... *Superglue* is now available in shops ... Firemen continue their industrial action. Army operated 'Green Goddess' vehicles attend emergency 999 call-outs ... The Yorkshire Ripper strikes again - attacking a 25-year-old woman in Leeds ... Chrysler launches the *Horizon* motorcar. Showroom price for the entry level *LS* model is £3,320, and top speed is 95 mph. Fuel consumption can be as high as 50 mpg - when driven sensibly ... Husbands buy their wives a bottle of new *Opium* perfume (by Yves Saint Laurent) for Christmas ... "Let's have a ball at the hall tonight. Boogie girl till the early bright. Make a scene with the record machine..." ***Dancin' Party*** ("... tonight") by Showaddywaddy is number four in the pop chart ... "And it's me you need to show..." ***How Deep Is Your Love*** by The Bee Gees is number three ... Steven Spielberg's *Close Encounters of a Third Kind* (with Richard

Dreyfuss and Melinda Dillon) is on general release at picture houses ... "Magic, our Morris!" - series three of *Oh No, It's Selwyn Frogitt* (with 49-year-old Bill Maynard in the title role) is on TV ... 32-year-old Wimbledon tennis champion Virginia Wade is voted BBC's 'Sports Personality of the Year' ... 30-year-old DJ Simon Bates is the new presenter of Radio One's mid morning show ... "Far have I travelled and much have I seen. Dark distant mountains with valleys of green" - ***Mull Of Kintyre*** by 36-year-old Paul McCartney and his band Wings is number one ... The ***Floral Dance*** by The Brighouse and Rastrick Brass Band is number two ... Hallmark Records release *The Best of Top of the Pops '77* - a budget priced cover-version pop compilation LP with blonde Jilly Johnson pictured on a sheep-skin rug on the sleeve ... Hi-fi technology moves on apace ... A Ferguson *Music Centre* (comprising of LW/MW/VHF decoder, multi-speed record deck and cassette player/recorder) costs £129.95 at *Argos* ... A pair of Alba stereo headphones are £5.95 ... 'Is it live, or is it Memorex?' - *Memorex* recordable tapes offer high quality music reproduction ... England's footballers play a crucial match against Italy at Wembley. 26-year-old Kevin Keegan and 29-year-old Trevor Brooking score the goals as Ron Greenwood's team achieves a 2-0 victory - but still fails to qualify for next year's world cup finals. Keegan and Brooking, along with Ray Clemence, Phil Neal, Trevor Cherry, Emlyn Hughes (captain), Dave Watson, Ray 'Butch' Wilkins, Steve Coppell, Bob Latchford and Peter Barnes, will all miss out on the finals in Argentina ... 22-year-old Tony Woodcock scores twice as Brian Clough's newly promoted Nottingham Forest beat Dave Sexton's Manchester Utd 0-4 at Old Trafford. Forest follow this win with a 1-1 draw against Liverpool and then a 0-2 victory over Newcastle Utd - to stay top of Division One ... 30-year-old convicted murderer Leslie Grantham is out of prison, after serving ten years, and is now forging a career as an actor ... ***White Christmas*** by the late Bing Crosby reaches number five in the pop chart ... ***Mull Of Kintyre*** by Wings stays at number one for the Christmas period ... Excited schoolboys make a wish for a skateboard or *Tin Can Alley* or *Flight-Deck* ... The new *Sportel* TV games console (with simulated tennis, squash and football) is also popular ... A *Hornby* train set (with a high-speed 125 British Rail engine) costs £19.50 ... A *Kodak EK4* instant camera is £29.95 ... *Ker-Plunk* is £2.45 ... Families settle down in front on the telly ... "Follow the yellow brick road" - *The Wizard of Oz* is on BBC One on Christmas Day ... 30-year-old Elton John and 37-year-old Penelope Keith are special guests on the *Morecambe and Wise Christmas Show* in the evening ... On Boxing Day - millions enjoy *It's a Christmas Knockout* (presented by 67-year-old Eddie Waring and 48-year-old Stuart Hall) and *The Two Ronnies* (with 48-year-old Ronnie Barker and 47-year-old Ronnie Corbett) ... Over on ITV, Eamonn Andrews presents his big red book to 77-year-old Earl Mountbatten of Burma (a cousin of Queen Elizabeth II, and great grandson to Queen Victoria) on *This Is Your Life* ... Groups of young men attend football matches, standing together on packed terraces and taunting supporters of the opposing team ... Sammy Chung's Wolverhampton Wanderers gain a 3-1 victory over Jimmy Armfield's Leeds Utd at the Molineux, and fans clash in the subway behind the South Bank ... Tony Book's Manchester City beat Bill McGarry's Newcastle Utd 4-0 at Maine Road, with 28-year-old Dennis Tueart scoring a hat-trick ... "You can try. (You can try). You can try. (You can try). You can try, to tell the world the reason why..." ***Belfast*** by Boney M climbs to number eight on the hit parade ... ***It's A Heartache*** ("... nothing but a heartache. Hits you when it's too late. Hits you when you're down") by Bonnie Tyler is number four ... "Didn't he do well?" - 49-year-old Bruce Forsyth bows out of the *Generation Game* ... 30-year-old Farrah Fawcett-Majors leaves *Charlie's Angels* and is replaced by 26-year-old Cheryl Ladd ... 51-year-old Jimmy Savile OBE presents *Jimmy Savile's Old Record Club* on Sunday afternoons on Radio One ... 63-year-old Charlie Chester presents *Your Sunday Soapbox* on Radio Two ... The Phantom Flan Flinger appears on children's TV show *Tiswas* ... 28-year-old Patrick Duffy is *The Man from Atlantis* - a person with super-human strength and the ability to breath underwater ... "Oh yeah? Shoo-ey, magoo-ey!" is a common phrase used by disbelieving kids - as they rub their chins in an exaggerated style ... Movie star Charlie Chaplin dies in Switzerland aged 88 ... Back in England - men go to the pub ... A pint of lager in the Red Lion is 50p ... Richard Baker reads the news on BBC One ... An 18-year-old woman is murdered in Huddersfield ... A

21-year-old woman goes missing in Leeds ... The firemen's strike comes to an end - with a negotiated pay increase of ten percent. Red fire-engines are operational once again and the army's 'green goddess' emergency vehicles are returned to storage ... The opinion polls show that 65-year-old prime-minister, Jim Callaghan, and his Labour government are closing the gap on Margaret Thatcher's Conservative opposition ... ***Mull Of Kintyre*** by Paul McCartney and Wings remains at number one in the pop chart until late January ... "Don't know when I've been so blue. Don't know what's come over you" - ***Don't It Make My Brown Eyes Blue*** by 27-year-old Crystal Gayle is number five ... 30-year-old Elton John is the guest star on ITV's hugely popular program *The Muppet Show*, where he performs *Don't Go Breaking My Heart* as a duet with Miss Piggy ... Children devour *Old English Flavours* of *Spangles* ... Bill Giles presents the weather forecast on BBC One ... Heavy snowstorms hit the UK and some schools and factories are forced to close. The East of the country is worst hit - and the seaside piers at Herne Bay, Margate and Skegness are battered by a raging North Sea ... "Well Daddy who? Daddy Cool. Daddy who..?" ***Daddy Cool*** ("... Daddy Cool, Daddy Cool. Cool, Daddy Cool") by Darts climbs to number six in the pop chart ... ***Love's Unkind*** by 29-year-old Donna Summer is number three ... *The Professionals* is new on ITV, with 53-year-old Gordon Jackson as Cowley, 32-year-old Martin Shaw as Doyle and 31-year-old Lewis Collins as Bodie - all three men, part of a national security agency called CI5 ... *All Creatures Great and Small* is new on BBC, with 52-year-old Robert Hardy as Siegfried Farnon, 37-year-old Christopher Timothy as James Herriot and 26-year-old Peter Davison as Tristan Farnon - all three men, part of a 1930s veterinary practice in the Yorkshire Dales ... "May the force be with you" - Queues form outside cinemas as *Star Wars* arrives in Britain. 25-year-old Mark Hamill is Luke Skywalker, 34-year-old Harrison Ford is Han Solo and 20-year-old Carrie Fisher is Princess Leia ... *Blake's 7* is on TV with 32-year-old Gareth Thomas as Roj Blake ... "I thought I could hear the curious tone of the cornet, clarinet and big trombone" - 39-year-old Terry Wogan performs his own version of the ***Floral Dance*** on *Top of the Pops*, and the song climbs to number twenty-one in the pop chart ... "We're..." ***Jamming*** ("... jamming, and I hope you like jamming, too") by 32-year-old Bob Marley & The Wailers reaches number nine ... There's a major shock in the world of boxing: 24-year-old underdog Leon Spinks defeats favourite Muhammad Ali by a split-decision, after fifteen rounds in Las Vegas - Spinks becomes the new, undisputed heavyweight champion ... Back in England - Brian Clough's newly promoted Nottingham Forest are six points clear at the top of Football League Division One. 35,743 people are at the City Ground to see Archie Gemmill score in Forest's 2-0 victory over Terry Neill's Arsenal ... West Bromwich Albion appoint 38-year-old Big Ron Atkinson as manager ... 38-year-old Leighton Rees is the first ever World Darts Champion ... A new smaller £1 note is issued with Isaac Newton on the front ... "Nah pop no style. A strictly roots" - ***Uptown Top Ranking*** by Althia and Donna is new at number one in the pop chart ... "Well you can tell by the way I use my walk I'm a woman's man, no time to talk" - ***Stayin' Alive*** by The Bee Gees (a group comprising of the three brothers Gibb: 31-year-old Barry and 28-year-old twins Robin and Maurice) is number four ... Millions of people enjoy an evening in front of the telly ... Ernest Bishop (played by 52-year-old Stephen Hancock) is shot and killed at Mike Baldwin's factory in *Coronation Street* on ITV ... "Flippin' 'eck, Tucker!" - school kids rush home to watch *Grange Hill* on BBC One, starring 14-year-old Todd Carty as Tucker Jenkins, 13-year-old Terry Sue-Patt as Benny Green, 15-year-old George Armstrong as Alan Hargreaves and 12-year-old Michelle Herbert as Trisha Yates ... Fletch and Godber are out of Slade prison as a new TV sit-com called *Going Straight* begins on Friday nights at 8.30 p.m. ... "He's out to make a killing girl, he's out to make a score. And maybe if you're willing girl, he's gonna ask for more. Oh-oh Figaro, he's got magic, oh-oh!" - ***Figaro*** by The Brotherhood of Man spends a week at number one in the pop chart ... "Ooooh, here comes that man again. Something in the way he moves makes me..." ***Sorry I'm A Lady*** by Baccara is number eight ... BBC One programs on a Saturday night include: *Jim'll Fix It* - with 51-year-old Jimmy Savile OBE; *Dr. Who* - with 44-year-old Tom Baker as the Doctor, 26-year-old Louise Jameson as his assistant Leela and K9 as the dog shaped robot K9; *Saturday Night at the Movies*; *Mike Yarwood in Persons* - with 36-year-old impersonator Mike

Yarwood; *Starsky and Hutch* - starring 34-year-old Paul Michael Glaser as Starsky, and 34-year-old David Soul as Hutch; *News* - read by 53-year-old Kenneth Kendall; and *Match of the Day* - introduced by 49-year-old Jimmy Hill ... "If you change your mind, I'm the first in line. Honey I'm still free..." ***Take A Chance On Me*** by Abba is number one for three weeks ... ***Hotlegs*** ("... I love ya honey!") by 33-year-old Rod Stewart is number five ... 34-year-old Anna Ford is ITN's first female news reader ... 56-year-old Jimmy Young from Cinderford presents the mid morning show on Radio Two, before *Waggoners' Walk* comes on at 12.15 ... Prosperous people keep a cactus in a pot on the kitchen windowsill ... Primary school children are forced to learn 'country dancing' in time for the school Spring Fayre ... 29-year-old Noel Edmonds presents *Multi-Coloured Swap Shop* on BBC One on Saturday mornings - assisted by 37-year-old John Craven and 21-year-old Keith Chegwin ... 45-year-old Frank Bough introduces *Grandstand* straight afterwards ... 36-year-old Bob Wilson presents *Football Focus* ... 25-year-old defender Gordon McQueen transfers from Jimmy Armfield's Leeds Utd to Dave Sexton's Manchester Utd for £500,000 ... 24-year-old midfielder Graeme Souness transfers from John Neal's Middlesbrough to Bob Paisley's Liverpool for £350,000 ... 17-year-old striker Craig Johnston makes his debut for Middlesbrough in a 1-2 away win against Sir Alf Ramsey's Birmingham City ... Ken Shellito's Chelsea beat Bobby Robson's Ipswich Town 5-3 at Stamford Bridge and move up to thirteenth in Division One ... Tottenham Hotspur remain top of Division Two after a 1-1 draw against Orient in front of 32,869 spectators at White Hart Lane. (21-year-old striker Colin Lee is on the score-sheet for Spurs) ... "I'm..." ***Wishing On A Star*** ("... to follow where you are") by Rose Royce is number three in the pop chart ... ***Mr. Blue Sky*** ("... please tell us why you had to hide away for so long (so long)? Where did we go wrong?" by Electric Light Orchestra is number six ... People enjoy a night out on the town ... Courting couples make the most of dimly lit back row seats at their local cinema ... 24-year-old John Travolta stars in *Saturday Night Fever* ... 'Cool' young men blow-dry their hair and 'style-in' a centre parting ... 'Cool' young women have bubble perms ... Tear-away teenagers sniff glue near the garages behind the shopping precinct ... "Denis, Denis, oh with your eyes so blue. Denis, Denis, I got a crush on you. Denis, Denis, I'm so in love with you, oh-ohh" - ***Denis*** by Blondie (featuring 32-year-old Debbie Harry) climbs from number eleven to number five in the pop chart ... ***Come Back My Love*** by Darts moves down from number two to number three ... Schoolboys begin saving up for a skateboard. A plywood *Flyer De Lux* (with double ball bearing rubber wheels) costs £7.40 at toy-shops ... A tub of *Slime* by Matel is £1.25 ... Adverts say, 'Wrigley's Spearmint Gum - carry the big fresh flavour!'

Spring 1978

'Cause the wicked carried us away in captivity

"Ten-four good buddy" - the cult of CB radio sweeps the country - even though it's illegal ... Ford introduces a new version of the *Transit* van - this latest model has a redesigned radiator grill and stylish new indicator lights at the front ... Talbot introduces the *Rancho* - a rugged and capacious 'off-road' motorcar ... "Out on the wiley, windy moors we'd roll and fall in green. You had a temper like my jealousy, too hot, too greedy" - ***Wuthering Heights*** by 19-year-old Kate Bush moves to the top of the hit parade - and stays there for four weeks ... ***(I Don't Wanna Go To) Chelsea*** by 23-year-old Elvis Costello and the Attractions is number sixteen ... The opinion polls put Margaret Thatcher's opposition Conservative party slightly ahead of Jim Callaghan's governing Labour party ... 60-year-old Chancellor of Exchequer Denis Healey cuts income tax rates for the lowest paid workers ... 36-year-old Fred West and his 24-year-old wife, Rosemary, murder 18-year-old Shirley Robinson and bury her body beneath their house at 25 Cromwell Street in Gloucester ... 33-year-old bent copper DS Derek Ridgewell is arrested and charged with conspiring to steal mailbags from the Royal Mail ... The *Amoco Cadiz* oil tanker sinks and spills its cargo into the sea ... Ford launches the *MkIII Capri* motorcar with four round headlights replacing the two rectangular ones. The *3.0S* model costs £4,593, has a top speed of 122 mph and accelerates from 0-60 mph in 8 seconds ... ***I Love The Sound Of Breaking Glass*** by 29-year-old Nick Lowe is number seven in the pop chart ... "Winding your way down on..." ***Baker Street*** by Gerry Rafferty (with its catchy and infectious saxophone break) is number three ... 49-year-old Bob Holness presents the breakfast show on LBC Radio ... ITV axes *Opportunity Knocks* (presented by 58-year-old Hughie Green) and replaces it with *The Kenny Everett Video Show* - Cupid Stunt declares, "It's all done in the best possss-ible taste!" ... Alf Roberts (played by 46-year-old Bryan Mosley) marries Renee Bradshaw (played by 40-year-old Madge Hindle) in *Coronation Street* ... A new comedy series called *Mixed Blessings*, starring Christopher Blake and Muriel Odunton (as a newly wed mixed race couple), begins on ITV ... 27-year-old Simon Groom replaces 39-year-old Peter Purves as a presenter on BBC One's children show *Blue Peter* ... Oxford win the Boat Race after the Cambridge boat sinks in the River Thames ... "And he painted..." ***Matchstalk Men And Matchstalk Cats And Dogs*** by Brian and Michael is number one in the pop chart ... ***I Can't Stand The Rain*** ("... 'gainst my window, bringing back sweet memories") by Eruption is number five ... 58-year-old football manager Sir Alf Ramsey is sacked by Birmingham City after his team is defeated 4-0 by Coventry City ... 37-year-old Jim Smith is installed as the new boss at St. Andrews ... Football referee

Pat Partridge makes a mistake in the League Cup final by awarding a (incorrect) penalty, which 25-year-old John Robertson scores to give Nottingham Forest a 1-0 victory over Bob Paisley's Liverpool ... Football hooligans invade the pitch and fighting breaks out at an FA Cup quarter-final match between Millwall and Ipswich Town ... 28-year-old striker Malcolm 'Supermac' MacDonald scores twice as Arsenal beat Manchester Utd 3-1 in front of 40,739 spectators at Highbury ... 29-year-old striker Alan Gowling transfers from First Division Newcastle Utd to Second Division Bolton Wanderers for £120,000 ... 20-year-old Sian Adey-Jones (36C) from Denbighshire is a popular new page three girl in *The Sun* ... 'Is she or isn't she?' - adverts for *Harmony Hairspray* are on TV ... "Cause she's good for me, and it would really make me happy to..." ***Never Let Her Slip Away*** by Andrew Gold is number five on the hit parade ... ***I Wonder Why*** ("... you love me like you do") by Showaddywaddy is number two ... The eastern side of the UK lies under thick snow ... 'Forty-two!' - *The Hitch-Hiker's Guide to the Galaxy*, a fantastic new sci-fi comedy written by 26-year-old Douglas Adams, is on Radio Four ... *The Little and Large Show*, featuring 36-year-old Eddie Large and 35-year-old 'Supersonic' Syd Little, airs for the first time on BBC One ... 19-year-old footballer Gordon Cowans scores a goal for Aston Villa in a 2-0 victory over Newcastle Utd. 22-year-old Andy Gray is also on the score-sheet for Villa, after returning from a recent injury ... 19-year-old Terry Butcher makes his debut for Ipswich Town in a match against Everton at Goodison

Park ... ***If You Can't Give Me Love*** ("... honey they ain't enough") by 27-year-old Suzi Quatro is number four in the pop chart ... ***Too Much Too Little Too Late*** ("... to lie again with you") by Johnny Mathis & Deniece Williams climbs to number three ... 43-year-old Brian Clough leads Nottingham Forest to the Division One football title - just twelve months after gaining promotion from Division Two. Peter Shilton, Viv Anderson, Colin Barrett, Kenny Burns, Larry Lloyd, Ian Bowyer, Archie Gemmill, John McGovern, Martin O'Neill, John Robertson, Peter Withe and 22-year-old Tony Woodcock have all been outstanding ... Bob Paisley's Liverpool are runners-up ... Youngsters queue outside *Tiffany's* nightclub in Exeter on Thursday and Saturday evenings - hoping to gain access past the thick-set bouncers ... "Then I get..." ***Night Fever*** ("... night fever. We know how to do it") by The Bee Gees is number one in the pop chart ... ***Everybody Dance*** ("... der-der-doo-doo, clap your hands, clap your hands") by Chic is number twelve ... 33-year-old Graham Taylor leads Watford to the Division Four football title - just twelve months after becoming manager of Elton John's team ... The St. Joseph's junior school under-11 football team (from Rugeley) defeats local rivals Pear Tree 7-3 in a top-of-the-table clash - Gary Till, Peter Deeley, Nick Bates and twins, Robert and Donald Harvey, all get their names on the score-sheet ... 45-year-old Ray 'Dracula' Reardon wins the *Embassy* World Snooker Championship at the Crucible in Sheffield - beating Perrie Mans from South Africa in the final ... Approximately 100,000 people march from Trafalgar

Square to Victoria Park to watch an Anti Nazi League / Rock Against Racism concert featuring X-Ray Spex, Steel Pulse, The Clash and the Tom Robinson Band ... 24-year-old Altab Ali is stabbed to death on Alder Street in Whitechapel ... Men flock to the cinema to see 44-year-old Joan Collins (36-24-37) performing on a swing in a raunchy new film called *The Stud* ... "She's so, twentieth century. She's so, nineteen-seventies. She's a modern girl. (Oh yeah!)" - ***She's So Modern*** by the Boomtown Rats is number twelve in the pop chart ... ***News Of The World*** by The Jam is number twenty-seven ... 31-year-old Dave Lee Travis (aka The Hairy Cornflake) takes over from Noel Edmonds as host of Radio One's breakfast show ... "By the rivers of Babylon, there we sat down. Ye-eah we wept, when we remembered Zion" / "Brown girl in the ring, tra-la-la-la-la" - the double A-sided pop single ***Rivers Of Babylon* and *Brown Girl In The Ring*** by Boney M is number one for five weeks! ... 28-year-old footballer Roger Osborne scores the only goal of the game as Bobby Robson's Ipswich Town beat Terry Neill's Arsenal 1-0 in the FA Cup final. 47-year-old referee Derek Nippard and his two linesmen make the most of the occasion by conducting a lap of honour at the end of the match. A ticket for the standing enclosure at the Empire Stadium in Wembley costs £2.50 ... 27-year-old Kenny Dalglish scores the only goal of the game as Liverpool win the European cup for the second year running by beating Club Brugge 1-0 at Wembley. 30-year-old left-back (and captain) Emlyn Hughes lifts the gleaming silver trophy ... 11-year-old Andrew Lovell and 11-year-old Teresa Hurley perform a dos-a-dos in the country dancing display at the St. Joseph's junior school Spring Fayre in Rugeley ... 30-year-old Steve Heathcote runs the weekly Youth Club at Armitage village hall on Wednesday evenings ... "Ooh-wah, ooh-wah, cool cool kitty, tell us about..." ***The Boy From New York City*** by Darts is number two on the weekly hit parade ... ***What A Waste*** ("What a waste, but I don't mind") by 36-year-old Ian Dury reaches number nine ... The Yorkshire Ripper strikes twice - murdering women in Leeds and Manchester ... Footballers, Bob Latchford, Tony Currie and 20-year-old Peter Barnes score the goals as Ron Greenwood's England team (Shilton, Mills, Cherry, B Greenhoff, Watson, Wilkins, Coppell, T Francis, Latchford, Brooking, Barnes and substitutes Currie and Mariner) beats Wales 1-3 at Ninian Park ... "Miss Jones! Miss Jones!" - the final episode of *Rising Damp* airs on ITV, with Frances de la Tour, Richard Beckinsdale, Don Warrington and starring 52-year-old Leonard Rossiter as Rigsby ... ***Because The Night*** ("... belongs to lovers. Because the night belongs to lust") by the Patti Smith Group is number five in the pop chart ... ***Do It, Do It Again*** ("... Do it, do again with love") by 35-year-old Raffaella Carra is number nine ... Middle-aged men mow the lawn on Sunday mornings ... Adverts say, 'Qualcast Concorde - It's a lot less bother than a hover!' ... Keep-fit fanatics go jogging in the park, wearing iridescent lycra tracksuits and headbands ... Trendy kids in Brutus stretch jeans, Adidas *Mamba* trainers and (red, white and blue) sweatbands on their wrists, hang about in bus-shelters ... "We're the people you don't wanna know, we come from places you don't wanna go" - ***Angels With Dirty Faces*** by Sham 69 is number nineteen in the pop chart ... ***Nice 'n' Sleazy*** by The Stranglers is number twenty-one ... "Bingo Master's Breakout!" - The Fall perform a night-time session for Radio One disc jockey John Peel ... A pint of lager in the Red Lion is 58p.

Summer 1978

Grease is the word

The sun shines ... *Grease* mania sweeps the nation ... "I got chills, they're multiplying, and I'm losing control, 'cause the power you're supplying, it's electrifying!" - ***You're The One That I Want*** by 29-year-old Olivia Newton-John and 24-year-old John Travolta is number one in the pop chart ... ***Love Is In the Air*** ("... everywhere I look around") by John Paul Young is number five ... Matt (played by Frederick Pyne) marries Dolly (played by Katherine Barker) in popular TV soap-opera *Emmerdale Farm* ... 45-year-old Ishaque Ali dies of heart failure after being attacked by a gang of racists in Hackney ... 52-year-old Warren Mitchell stars in *The Saga of Alf Garnett* on ITV ... 15-year-old Georgios Kyriacos Panayiotou from Hertfordshire and his best friend, Andrew Ridgeley, write pop songs together in Georgios' bedroom ... 10-year-old schoolboy Tim Partington meets 10-year-old Selena Alexander under bridge number 59 on the Trent & Mersey canal ... Children rush to the sweet-shop for a Sherbet *Dip Dab* ... 11-year-old Paul 'Gazza' Gascoigne from Gateshead pulls a daft face and makes his friends laugh ... BBC One broadcasts *Jackanory*, *Help! It's the Hair Bear Bunch* and *Belle and Sebastian* during the school summer holiday ... 44-year-old John Noakes leaves children's TV show *Blue Peter* - after serving as a presenter for twelve and a half years ... "Where are you all coming from? / From Smurfland where we belong / Are you talking just like us? / No, we Smurf, it's much less fuss" - ***The Smurf Song*** by Father Abraham and the Smurfs shoots up the pop chart to number two ... ***Annie's Song*** by 38-year-old flautist James Galway is number three ... 38-year-old jockey Greville Starkey rides *Shirley Heights* to victory in the Epsom Derby ... The last remaining pickets at the Grunwick photographic processing factory in Willesden call off their dispute - the workers have lost ... Mike Baldwin sacks Hilda Ogden from his factory on ITV's *Coronation Street* - Hilda's co-workers show their support by going on strike ... 48-year-old Stuart Hall presents *It's A Knockout* on BBC One. A team from Cleethorpes comes out on top after a closely fought contest with Gainsborough and Lincoln. Cleethorpes will now compete in the Jeux Sans Frontieres competition later in the year ... The Lib-Lab pact (a political arrangement between David Steel's Liberals and the Labour government) comes to an end, and Jim Callaghan's position as prime-minister is now vulnerable ... 52-year-old leader of the Conservative opposition Margaret Thatcher pushes for a general election but Mr. Callaghan resists ... 52-year-old Queen Elizabeth II welcomes 60-year-old Romanian President Nicolae Ceausescu and his wife First Lady Elena on an official state visit to Britain ... "Oooh, he's here again. The..." ***Man With The Child In His Eyes*** by 19-year-old Kate Bush is number six in the pop chart ... ***(Don't Fear) The Reaper*** by Blue

Oyster Cult is number sixteen ... The sixth series of BBC One's popular historical drama *The Onedin Line* (with 46-year-old Peter Gilmore and 41-year-old Jill Gascoine) begins on Sunday evenings ... The twelfth series of *Z Cars* (with 32-year-old Douglas Fielding as PC Alec Quilley and 47-year-old Jimmy Ellis as Inspector Bert Lynch) is transmitted on Wednesday evenings, after *The Big Time* (presented by 38-year-old Esther Rantzen) ... Teenagers attend discos at Youth Club halls and Play-Scheme centres ... A carton of orange squash (with a straw) costs 3½p ... A packet of KP *Outer-Spacer*s is 5p ... ***Ca Plane Pour Moi*** ("... moi, moi, moi, moi. Ca plane pour moi") by Plastic Bertrand climbs to number five on the hit parade ... ***Pump It Up*** ("... when you don't really need it") by 23-year-old Elvis Costello and the Attractions is number twenty-four ... 18-year-old Joanne Latham (36DD) from Wolverhampton is a popular new page three girl in *The Sun* ... Trendy young girls wear long 'gypsy' style skirts, with bold floral prints and a decorative white frill showing at the hem ... Trendy young boys wear 'capped sleeve' T-shirts and dark blue jeans ... Assorted *Toffos* are now available - with regular, chocolate, strawberry and banana flavours all in one packet ... Old hippies wear denim jeans and sandals, and smoke spliffs round their mate's flat ... ***Davy's On The Road Again*** ("... wearin' different clothes again") by Manfred Mann's Earth Band is number six in the pop chart ... ***Run For Home*** by Lindisfarne reaches number ten ... 22-year-old tennis star Bjorn Borg wins the Wimbledon men's championship for the third consecutive year, beating 25-year-old Jimmy Conners 6-2, 6-2, 6-3 in the final ... 21-year-old Martina Navratilova wins the women's title for the first time, defeating 23-year-old Chris Evert 2-6, 6-4, 7-5 in the final ... 31-year-old DJ Simon Bates presents the *Top 20* chart show on Radio One on Sunday evenings ... Teenagers wait for their favourite songs, then press 'play' and 'record' on their radio/cassettes ... "Don't you know I'll be your..." ***Substitute*** ("... whenever you want me, ooh, a-ooh") by Clout is number two in the chart ... ***Identity*** ("... is the crisis, can't you see?") by X-Ray Spex (with 21-year-old Poly Styrene) is number twenty-four ... Schoolboy John 'Fuzz' Townshend celebrates his fourteenth birthday with a hamburger, and a side order of French fried potatoes, at the *Wimpy* bar in Wolverhampton ... Teenage boys sneak into their local picture house to see *The Playbirds* - a raunchy new film starring 32-year-old Mary Millington ... England's footballers take no part in the Argentinian world cup ... Ally MacLeod's Scotland team beats the Netherlands 3-2 with goals from Archie Gemmill and Kenny Dalglish ... A pair of black and white Adidas *World Cup 78* football boots (with six red screw-in studs) costs £19.75 ... A pack of World Cup '78 *Top Trumps* costs 50p ... "Ride the range all the day, till the first fading light. Be with my western girl, around the fire, oh so bright" - ***Wild West Hero*** by Electric Light Orchestra is number six on the hit parade ... ***A Little Bit Of Soap*** ("... will wash away your lipstick on my face") by Showaddywaddy reaches number five ... 'T' reg cars go on sale ... British Leyland launches its range of *Princess Series*

2 motorcars priced from £4,232. All models come with *Triplex 10/20* laminated windscreens. The 4-cylinder *1700 L* also has a clock, a heated rear window and a top speed of 99 mph. The 6-cylinder *2200 HLS* has front headrests, a push-button radio and a top speed of 104 mph ... *Top Gear* is on BBC Two with 39-year-old William Woollard and 33-year-old Angela Rippon ... 13-year-old schoolgirl Genette Tate goes missing as she's delivering newspapers near her home in Devon ... 28-year-old DJ Kid Jensen hosts the travelling Radio One Roadshow for five days in August. The Kid's Roadshow week begins at the Glebe in Bowness and ends at Eirias Park in Colwyn Bay ... ***Airport*** ("... you've got a smiling face") by The Motors is number four in the pop chart ... "Tick-tock, tick-tock, tick-tock" - ***Like Clockwork*** by The Boomtown Rats is number six ... 35-year-old Mike Brearley is England's cricket captain for the summer series against Pakistan and New Zealand. 21-year-old batsman David Gower makes his Test debut at Edgbaston and hits a boundary off his first ball. 22-year-old 'all-rounder' Ian Botham scores a century and takes eight wickets in one innings at Lord's ... 27-year-old Barry Sheene finishes third in a rain affected 500cc motorcycle Grand Prix at Silverstone. Kenny Roberts wins to become the new world champion ... Pope Paul VI dies in Rome at the age of 80. He's succeeded by 65-year-old Pope John Paul ... Back in England - people enjoy a night out at the cinema ... *Revenge of the Pink Panther*, with 52-year-old Peter Sellers as Inspector Clouseau and 60-year-old Herbert Lom as Chief Inspector Dreyfus, is now showing ... 'The First

Time was Only a Warning' - *Damien: Omen II* is also on general release ... *Evita* by Andrew Lloyd Webber opens in the West End ... Children go round to their (well-off) mate's house and have hours of fun playing on the electronic *Atari 2600* games console ... Teenagers 'hang-out' in amusement arcades ... The *Pong* video game is hugely popular ... "She is cruel and heartless to pack me for Gordon. Just 'cause he's better looking than me, just 'cause he's cool and trendy. But I know he's a moron. GORDON IS A MORON!' - ***Jilted John*** by Jilted John is number four on the hit parade ... ***If The Kids Are United*** ("... they will never be divided") by Sham 69 is number nine ... ***You're The One That I Want*** by Olivia Newton-John and John Travolta is still number one - and remains at the top of the chart for nine weeks! ... BBC One TV programs on a Saturday night include: *Emu's Broadcasting Company* - with 43-year-old Rod Hull and Emu; *News* - read by 44-year-old Richard Whitmore; *Wonder Woman* - starring 27-year-old Lynda Carter (37-25-35) as Diana Prince; *Saturday Night at the Movies*; *Seaside Special* - with various star acts including Jim 'Nick Nick' Davidson, Roger de Courcey with Nookie Bear, Bernie Clifton, The Black Abbotts, Stu Francis and The Krankies; *Kojak* - with 56-year-old Telly Savalas; and *Sailor* - a documentary about life in the Royal Navy ... "Loose fallen leaves lie undisturbed now, 'cause you're not here" - ***Forever Autumn*** by 31-year-old Justin Hayward is number five in the pop chart ... ***5.7.0.5.*** ("... but there's no reply") by City Boy climbs to number eight ... ITV programs on a Saturday night include: *Celebrity*

Squares - hosted by 50-year-old Bob Monkhouse; *Happy Days* - featuring 32-year-old Henry Winkler as the Fonz and 24-year-old Ron Howard as Richie Cunningham; *Gambit* - with Fred Dinenage and Michelle Lambourne; *The Life and Times of Grizzly Adams*; a feature film at 8 p.m; *ITN News* at 10 p.m; and *The South Bank Show* - introduced by 38-year-old Melvyn Bragg ... 57-year-old Humphrey Lyttelton is chairman for a new series of *I'm Sorry I Haven't A Clue* on BBC Radio Four. Panelists Graeme Garden, Barry Cryer, Willie Rushton and Tim Brooke-Taylor partake in a new game called 'Mornington Crescent' ... Middle aged men with 'twin-deck' record turntables, large speakers and transit vans advertise their services in local newspapers as Mobile Disco operators ... "If you're thinkin' you're too cool to boogie; boy oh boy, have I got news for you" - ***Boogie Oogie Oogie*** by A Taste of Honey is number three in the pop chart ... ***It's Raining*** ("... raining down on me, yeah") by Darts is number two ... Argentinian World Cup footballers Ossie Ardiles (aged 25) and Ricardo Villa (aged 26) sign for newly promoted Tottenham Hotspur ... 23-year-old left-back Alan Kennedy transfers from Newcastle Utd to Liverpool for £330,000 ... 29-year-old midfielder Colin Suggett moves from Norwich City to Newcastle Utd on a free transfer ... 26-year-old centre-forward Peter Withe transfers from Nottingham Forest to Newcastle Utd for £225,000 ... Trendy boys (in suede 'brothel creeper' shoes) pluck up the courage to ask girls (in knee-high 'crazy boots') for the last dance at the mobile disco in the village hall ... "And now that we've come to the end of our rainbow, there's something I must say out loud. You're once, twice..." ***Three Times A Lady*** ("... and I love you") by The Commodores is new at number one in the pop chart ... *Monster Munch* crisps go on sale.

Autumn 1978

Let's all Smurf together

The weather is inclement ... Children return to school after the summer holidays ... Boys play *Top Trumps* in the corner of the playground ... "I say, I don't like cricket. Oh no. I love it" - ***Dreadlock Holiday*** by 10cc spends a week at number one ... "Space travel's in my blood. There ain't nothin' I can do about it" - ***Another Girl, Another Planet*** by The Only Ones is a minor hit - the record fails to make the Top 75 ... The film *Grease* goes on general release at cinemas across the country ... 45-year-old Barry Norman interviews John Travolta on the late night movie review program, *Film 78*, on BBC One ... Teenage boys chalk 'T-birds' on the back of their black PVC ('leather-look') zip-up jackets ... "Well-a-well-a-well-a-huh. Tell me more, tell me more. Did you get very far? Tell me more, tell me more. Like, does he have a car?" - ***Summer Nights*** by John Travolta and Olivia Newton-John reaches number one in the pop chart - and stays there for seven weeks! ... ***Grease*** ("... is the word") by 44-year-old Frankie Valli is number three ... The new football season is underway ... Bob Paisley's Liverpool thrash Keith Burkinshaw's Tottenham Hotspur (with Argentinian World Cup stars Ossie Ardiles and Ricardo Villa in the Spurs' team) by seven goals to nil at Anfield. 26-year-old Liverpool midfielder Terry McDermott heads home the seventh goal, after running the length of the pitch to get on the end of a Steve Heighway cross ... "Do me a favour, Guv!" - 36-year-old John Thaw and 30-year-old Dennis Waterman star as Reagan and Carter in a new series of ITV's popular, hard-hitting cop drama *The Sweeney* ... The last ever episode of BBC's *Z Cars* is broadcast on Wednesday the twentieth of September ... ***Oh What A Circus*** ("... Oh, what a show. Argentina has gone to town over the death of an actress called Eva Peron") by 31-year-old David Essex is number three in the pop chart ... "You abandoned me..." ***Love Don't Live Here Anymore*** by Rose Royce is number two ... Bread is in short supply after industrial action by bakers. Queues form outside shops as panic buying breaks out ... Fifty Vietnamese boat people are given sanctuary in England after being rescued by a British ship in the South China Sea ... Bulgarian defector Georgi Markov is murdered at a bus stop in London after being injected with poison from the point of an umbrella ... "Waiting for the sunrise, soul dancin' in the dark..." ***Summer Night City*** by Abba climbs to number five in the pop chart ... "Ra-ra..." ***Rasputin*** ("... Russia's greatest love machine") by Boney M reaches number three ... *The Better World of Reginald Perrin* - the sixth novel from 43-year-old writer David Nobbs is published ... 22-year-old Argentinian footballer Alberto Tarantini signs for Birmingham City and scores in a 1-1 home draw against Bristol City ... 19-year-old Kevin Mabbutt scores a hat-trick as Alan Dicks' Bristol City beat Manchester Utd 1-3 at Old

Trafford ... Brian Clough's Nottingham Forest win 0-1 against Ian Greaves' Bolton Wanderers - and Forest remain unbeaten after sixteen league games ... 28-year-old striker Malcolm 'Supermac' MacDonald of Arsenal is out, injured - awaiting an operation on his knee ... Brendan Batson plays alongside Cyril Regis and Laurie Cunningham in Big Ron Atkinson's West Bromwich Albion team ... The Three Degrees perform their new song ***Givin' Up Givin' In*** on *Top of the Pops* ... Queen release the single ***Bicycle Race*** - a 'limited edition' disc comes with a free poster showing a group of naked women on bikes ... ***Picture This*** ("... a sky full of thunder. Picture this, my telephone number") by Blondie (featuring 33-year-old Debbie Harry) is number twelve in the pop chart ... "Where did you go? I was searchin' (searchin') on a one-way street. I was hopin' (hopin') for a chance to meet. I was waitin' for the operator on the line" - ***Sweet Talkin' Woman*** by Electric Light Orchestra is number six ... A light-blue, three-wheeled *Invacar* is parked at the side of the football pitch at St. Andrews as Birmingham City lose 0-1 to rivals Aston Villa, with a goal from 22-year-old Andy Gray ... 36-year-old Muhammad Ali regains the WBA heavy-weight world boxing title by beating 25-year-old Leon Spinks in New Orleans ... Back in England - 66-year-old Labour prime-minister Jim Callaghan decides not to call a general election just yet, even though some opinion polls now put his party ahead of the Tories. 52-year-old Leader of the Opposition Margaret Thatcher accuses Callaghan of running scared ... 13-year-old paper boy Carl Bridgewater is murdered at a farmhouse near Stourbridge and a wide-scale search begins to find his killer ... In a separate incident - a crazed gunman kills three people in West Bromwich before driving off in a car and murdering a fourth person at a petrol station in Nuneaton. Police chase the killer to Buxton where he's eventually caught and arrested ... ***Summer Nights*** by John Travolta and Olivia Newton-John remains at number one in the pop chart ... ***Who Are You*** by The Who slides down the chart to number twenty-two. The group's drummer, Keith Moon, dies aged 32 at his flat in Mayfair ... Pope John Paul dies just thirty-three days after becoming leader of the Catholic church. 58-year-old Karol Wojtyla from Poland succeeds the late pontiff - and takes the name John Paul II ... "Seems like a nice boy" - 55-year-old Larry Grayson is the new host of *The Generation Game* on BBC One. 26-year-old Isla St. Clair is his assistant ... 51-year-old Terry Scott goes searching up the loft, hoping to find an old '78' recording of *The Hut-Sut Song* by The Melba Trio in BBC sit-com *Happy Ever After* ... "Harmful elements in the air, symbols clashing everywhere" - ***Hong Kong Garden*** by Siouxsie and the Banshees is number seven in the pop chart ... ***Supernature*** by Cerrone is number eight ...Sid Vicious' girlfriend Nancy Spungen is found stabbed to death in a hotel room in New York ... Back in England - Trendy kids spend evenings at roller-discos ... ***You Make Me Feel (Mighty Real)*** by Sylvester is number eight in the pop chart ... "I wanna..." ***Kiss You All Over*** ("... and over again") by Exile is number six ... Footballers, Garry Birtles and Colin Barrett, score the goals as Brian Clough's Nottingham Forest knock Bob Paisley's Liverpool out of the European Cup in the first round. (Forest will now face AEK Athens in round two) ... 20-year-old David O'Leary is on the score-sheet for Terry Neill's Arsenal in a 2-3 victory over John Neal's Middlesbrough at Ayresome Park in Division One ... "Well how am I supposed to feel with all the things you don't reveal, and you can thank your lucky stars that we're not as smart as we'd like to think we are" - ***Lucky Stars*** by 23-year-old Dean Friedman reaches number three in the pop chart ... "Let's all smurf together. It's smurfing kind of weather and it's very easy if you try" - ***Dippety Day*** by 43-year-old Father Abraham and The Smurfs reaches number two ... Miss Piggy performs a duet with 38-year-old Raquel Welch on *The Muppet Show*. Fozzie the bear tries to be more assertive. Animal the drummer is wild and crazy. Kermit the frog holds things together ... VHS and Betamax video recorders are now available ... "Confused? You Will Be" - the American sit-com *Soap* is on late night ITV ... "Magic, our Morris!" - series four of *Oh No, It's Selwyn Frogitt* (starring 49-year-old Bill Maynard) is on evening-time ITV ... Almost twenty-million people watch as Ray Langton (played by 35-year-old Neville Buswell) walks out on his wife Deidre and baby Tracy in *Coronation Street* - and goes off to build a new life in Holland ... 35-year-old Ian Ogilvy drives a white Jaguar *XJ-S* and stars as Simon Templar in *The Return of the Saint* ... A sport hatch version of the Vauxhall *Cavalier* motorcar goes on sale ... Car theft is increasing ... Ford make 'central-locking' a standard feature on the *Granada GL* and *Granada Ghia* models ... Suburban housewives take turns to host tea and coffee mornings ... 'A drink's too wet without one' - *Rich Tea* biscuits are advertised on telly ... 'When it comes to Foreign Affairs' - 21-year-old Suzanne Danielle, 60-year-old Kenneth Connor and 52-year-old Kenneth Williams star in *Carry On Emmanuelle* at cinemas ... "Bright eyes, burning like fire" - *Watership Down* is also now showing ... "Oooh, Betty" - 36-year-old Michael Crawford plays Frank Spencer in a new series of *Some Mothers Do 'Ave 'Em* ... 'Reach for the Star, it's Britain's Best Buy' - the brand new *Daily Star* newspaper costs 6p ... 'Free. The Boomtown Rats Pull-Out Poster' - the brand new *Smash Hits* magazine (aimed at teenagers) costs 25p ... "The pulse of the corner boys just sprang into action, and young Billy watched it under the yellow street light, and said, tonight, of all nights, there's gonna be a fight" - ***Rat Trap*** by The Boomtown Rats reaches number one in the pop chart, replacing *Summer Nights* which had held top spot for seven weeks. To mark the occasion, 27-year-old Bob Geldof rips up a photograph of John Travolta and Olivia Newton-John on *Top of the Pops* ... Trendy families enjoy chilli con carne for dinner with a glass of Liebfraumilch wine ... Grease mania continues ... "Stranded at the drive-in, branded a fool. What will they say Monday at school?" - ***Sandy*** by 24-year-old John Travolta is number two in the pop chart in early November ... "But now there's nowhere to hide since you pushed my love aside. I'm out of my head..." ***Hopelessly Devoted To You*** by 30-year-old Olivia Newton John is number two in mid November ... 33-year-old Dennis Nilsen strangles 14-year-old Stephen Holmes at Melrose Avenue in Cricklewood and hides his body beneath the floor-boards ... 12-year-old Mark Gatiss from Sedgefield scares his friends by telling chilling ghost stories ... 11-year-old Steve Pemberton from Blackburn visits the local shop with his mum ... A loaf of bread costs 27p ... A pint of milk is 13p ... "Everyone's a fruit and nut case" - 58-year-old Frank Muir advertises Cadbury's *Fruit & Nut* on TV.

Winter 1978 - 1979

In the dock of Tiger Bay. On the road to Mandalay

"Solid Gold. Ray-dee-oh One" - Radio One's frequency moves from 247m to 275m and 285m on medium wave transmission ... "But what was the year?" - 32-year-old disc jockey Simon Bates presents the *Golden Hour* during his mid morning show ... "Ahhh, freak out! Le Freak c'est Chic" - ***Le Freak*** by Chic climbs to number seven in the pop chart ... "Well, this car could be systematic, hydromatic, ultramatic. Why, it could be..." ***Greased Lightnin'*** by John Travolta is number eleven ... Hallmark Records release *The Best of Top of the Pops '78* - a budget priced cover-version pop compilation LP with a hot disco babe pictured on the sleeve ... KP *Discos* - a new type of crisps are now on sale in shops ... Families enjoy an evening in, playing *Connect Four* and *Hungry Hippos* ... The IRA resumes its bombing campaign on mainland Britain. Devices are activated in Manchester, Liverpool, Coventry, Bristol and Southampton - thankfully there are no fatalities ... "There's nothin' for us in Belfast, the Pound's old and that's a pity" - Stiff Little Fingers perform ***Alternative Ulster*** ... "He's a germ free adolescent. Cleanliness is her obsession. Cleans her teeth ten times a day. Scrub away, scrub away, scrub away, the SR way" - ***Germ Free Adolescents*** by X-Ray Spex (with 21-year-old

Poly Styrene) reaches number nineteen in the weekly pop chart ... Concrete cows stand proudly in a field near the ultra-modern town of Milton Keynes ... The final episode of series two of *The Professionals* (with Doyle driving a 'Diamond White' Ford *Escort RS2000* and Bodie driving a 'Strato Silver' Ford *Capri 3.0S*) grips late night TV viewers on Saturday the ninth of December ... Workers at the BBC organise a 24-hour strike on Thursday the twenty-first of December, and nineteen million people tune in to watch a repeat of *The Sweeney* over on ITV ... The final section of M180 motorway opens near Scunthorpe and motorists can now speed between Doncaster and Grimsby in under an hour ... 124 million tonnes of coal have been mined in the UK this year - roughly the same amount as last year - but the number of miners has decreased to just 240,000 ... The total number of unemployed people has risen to 1.5 million ... Bill-board posters say, 'Labour Isn't Working' ... Jim Callaghan's minority Labour government survives a vote of confidence in the House of Commons - but there's a growing consensus that the 66-year-old prime-minister's time at Number 10 could be nearing the end ... Industrial action forces *The Times* newspaper to close down ... Ron Greenwood's England football team beats Czechoslovakia 1-0 at Wembley with a goal from 23-year-old Steve Coppell of Manchester Utd. 22-year-old Nottingham Forest full-back Viv Anderson makes his international debut, and becomes England's first black player. The full line-up for the match is: Shilton, Anderson, Cherry, Thompson, Watson, Wilkins, Keegan,

Coppell, Woodcock, Currie, P Barnes and substitute Latchford ... ***Tommy Gun*** ("... you ain't happy 'less you got one") by The Clash reaches number nineteen in the pop chart ... "Oh, how can you ever let me down? (Down)" - ***Promises*** by The Buzzcocks peaks at number twenty ... Nottingham Forest's long unbeaten run comes to an end when Liverpool win a top-of-the-table clash by two goals to nil at Anfield - with both goals scored by 27-year-old Terry McDermott ... Big Ron Atkinson's West Bromwich Albion achieve a 3-5 victory over Dave Sexton's Manchester Utd at Old Trafford - with goals from Tony 'bomber' Brown (2), Len Cantello, Laurie Cunningham and 20-year-old Cyril Regis ... Terry Neill's Arsenal thrash Tottenham Hotspur 0-5 at White Hart Lane - with 22-year-old Liam Brady scoring a sublime chip shot, and 25-year-old Alan Sunderland bagging a hat-trick ... "It's behind you!" - Middle-class families enjoy an evening at the Pantomime ... 63-year-old Peter Butterworth appears as Widow Twankey in *Aladdin* at the Coventry Theatre ... 13-year-old Brooke Shields plays a child prostitute in the film *Pretty Baby* at cinemas ... "If you want my body and you think I'm sexy, come on sugar tell me so" - ***Da Ya Think I'm Sexy?*** by Rod Stewart is number one in the pop chart ... "Where are you all coming from? / We're from Dartmoor on the run / How did you work out your route? / We followed the arrows on our suit" - ***A Taste Of Aggro*** by The Barron Knights is number three ... Parents take their young children to department stores to visit Father Christmas' grotto. Reluctant girls and boys sit on the knee of an elderly stranger (dressed in a red coat and wearing a false white beard) and claim to have "been good" - in the hope of getting the Christmas present they most desire ... A 'figure-of-eight' *Scalextric* race set costs £23.95 from *Argos* ... A *Hornby* British Rail High Speed Passenger (oval shaped) train set is £19.75 ... A *Palitoy* Family Tree House is £7.95 ... A *Palitoy* 'Girl's World' head with growing hair is £8.45 ... An *Action Man* soldier with 'Eagle-Eyes' is £3.60 ... *Lego* sets now contain realistic mini figures of people ... 43-year-old Ted Rogers stars with Dusty Bin on television in the Christmas special of popular game show *3-2-1* ... Frank Spencer learns to fly in the Christmas special of *Some Mothers Do 'Ave 'Em* ... BBC One broadcasts the network premiere of *The Sound of Music* ... ITV transmits the James Bond film *Diamonds Are Forever* ... "Hark now hear the angels sing, a King was born today. And man will live for evermore, because of Christmas Day" - ***Mary's Boy Child - Oh My Lord*** by Boney M climbs to number one in the singles chart ... 36-year-old Mike Brearley leads England's cricketers on an Ashes tour of Australia. England win the opening Test in Brisbane by seven wickets. In the second Test (at Perth), England win again with 21-year-old batsman David Gower scoring a century, and 29-year-old fast bowler Bob Willis taking 5 wickets for 44 runs. Graham Yallop's Aussies gain a victory in the third Test at Melbourne, and England take a 2-1 lead into the new year ... Back in Britain - the weather turns cold and snow begins to fall ... 'Make someone happy with a phone-call' - cartoon bird 'Buzby' advertises the services of the Post Office's telecommunications department on TV ... "I'm in the phone booth, it's the one across the hall. If you don't answer, I'll just ring it off the wall" - ***Hanging On The Telephone*** by Blondie (featuring 33-year-old Debbie Harry) climbs to number five in the pop chart ... "Hello, this is Joanie, I'm sorry but I'm not home" - ***Hello This Is Joanie (The Telephone Answering Machine Song)*** by 40-year-old Paul Evans is number six ... "Leave it alone!'" - the fourth (and final) series of ITV's popular, hard-hitting cop drama *The Sweeney* (starring 36-year-old John Thaw as Jack Reagan and 30-year-old Dennis Waterman as George Carter) comes to an end ... Young men pop into the newsagent on their way to work ... 'Meet her on Page Seven' - a photograph of a topless 'Starbird' is a popular feature in the new *Daily Star* newspaper ... A copy of the latest *Mayfair* magazine is 60p ... Miniature models of *Coca-Cola* cans on silver chain necklaces are popular Christmas gifts for girls ... *Stretch Armstrong* is popular for boys ... The new year brings freezing weather and drifting snow ... Public sector workers go on strike ... Lorry drivers go on strike ... Disgruntled workers stand on picket lines outside factory gates - warming themselves next to fires in rusty oil drums ... Rubbish piles up on the streets ... There are food shortages in shops and frequent power cuts throughout the country ... 66-year-old prime-minister Jim Callaghan leaves the UK to attend a conference in the Caribbean ... *The Sun* newspaper uses the headline, 'Crisis? What Crisis?' ... "Young man, there's no need to feel down. I said, young man, pick yourself off the ground" - ***YMCA*** by The Village People is number one in the pop chart ... "They got me on..." ***Milk And Alcohol*** by Dr. Feelgood is number nine ... England's cricketers are successful down-under. 27-year-old Derek Randall scores 150 runs in Sydney. 23-year-old 'all-rounder' Ian Botham scores 74 runs and takes 4 wickets for 42 at Adelaide - and Brearley's team wins the Ashes by five Test Matches to one. G Boycott, G A Gooch, D W Randall, J M Brearley (cpt), D I Gower, I T Botham, G Miller, R W Taylor (wk), P H Edmonds, J E Emburey, C M Old, R G D Willis, J K Lever and M Hendrick have all played a part in England's resounding victory ... Back in England - power cuts continue and shops and businesses are forced to close early ... There's no heating in schools ... Grave diggers go on strike ... For most people, it truly is a winter of discontent ... "Life, isn't everything. Isn't everything" - ***Song For Guy*** by 31-year-old Elton John climbs to number four in the pop chart ... "Ooh, baby..." ***Lay Your Love On Me*** by Racey is number three ... Football matches go ahead in freezing conditions ... Bob Paisley's Liverpool (top of Division One) play against Dave Smith's Southend Utd (eighth in Division Three) in an FA Cup tie on a snow covered pitch with an orange ball - the game ends in a 0-0 draw, with Liverpool going on to win the replay ... 31-year-old Keith Weller wears white tights for Leicester City and scores a brilliant goal in a 3-0 victory over Norwich City ... 40-year-old Terry Wogan hosts the first edition of *Blankety Blank* on BBC One ... 63-year-old actor Peter Butterworth dies of a heart attack in Coventry ... The film

Halloween, with 20-year-old Jamie Lee Curtis, is now showing at cinemas ... "A finger of Fudge is just enough to give your kids a treat. A finger of Fudge is just enough until it's time to eat" - Cadbury's *Fudge* bars are advertised on telly ... Sixteen-hundred car workers are laid-off at British Leyland's Cowley factory because of a shortage of components ... 51-year-old Derek Robinson (aka Red Robbo) leads a mass walk-out of thousands of workers at Longbridge ... "Control this is six-seven here, I can hear you loud and I can hear you clear" - ***Car 67*** by Driver 67 is on *Top of the Pops* ... "In the deserts of Sudan and the gardens of Japan. From Milan to Yucatan, every woman, every man" - ***Hit Me With Your Rhythm Stick*** by Ian and the Blockheads is number one ... ***Don't Cry For Me Argentina*** by The Shadows is number nine ... Radio One's weekday schedule of disc jockeys is: 33-year-old Dave Lee Travis - aka 'The Hairy Cornflake' (7 a.m. to 9 a.m.), 32-year-old Simon Bates (9 a.m. to 11.30 a.m.), 35-year-old Paul Burnett (11.30 p.m. to 2 p.m.), 36-year-old Tony Blackburn (2 p.m. to 4 p.m.) and 30-year-old Andy Peebles (4 p.m. to 5.30 p.m.) ... "Walk, in silence" - Joy Division perform a night-time session for 39-year-old John Peel ... "Do you remember, twenty-first night of..." ***September*** by Earth Wind and Fire is number three in the pop chart ... Mobile discos at village halls play hit tunes such as ***Contact*** by Edwin Starr and ***I Was Made For Dancin'*** by Leif Garrett ... Teenagers dance, snog and choke on smokey dry-ice ... 21-year-old punk-rocker Sid Vicious suffocates on his own vomit and dies in his sleep after a party in New York ... Back in England - kids rush home from school to watch the second series of *Grange Hill* on BBC One - Mr. 'Bullet' Baxter is the new PE teacher. Cathy Hargreaves is a new friend for Trisha Yates ... 35-year-old Richard O'Sullivan stars as *Dick Turpin* on ITV - 22-year-old Michael Deeks is Swift Nick, Turpin's trusty sidekick ... ***Chiquitita*** ("... tell me what's wrong. You're enchained by your own sorrow") by Abba is number two in the pop chart ... "I am a..." ***Woman In Love*** by The Three Degrees is number three ... 33-year-old John Lowe is the World Darts Champion after beating Leighton Rees in the final at *Jollees* nightclub in Stoke-on-Trent ... 24-year-old footballer Trevor Francis leaves Birmingham City and joins high-flying Nottingham Forest for a new record transfer fee of £1,180,000 ... 23-year-old Steve Coppell scores twice as Dave Sexton's Manchester Utd beat Tony Book's Manchester City 0-3 at Maine Road - Utd move up to ninth in Division One ... 30-year-old Neil Warnock scores the winning goal for Crewe Alexandra in a 1-0 victory over Halifax Town - a bottom-of-the-table clash in Division Four ... Schoolboys hang posters of 33-year-old Debbie Harry on their bedroom walls ... *Parallel Lines* by Blondie is number one in the LP chart ... "Once I had a love and it was a gas, soon turned out, had a..." ***Heart Of Glass*** by Blondie is number one in the singles chart ... ***King Rocker*** by Generation X climbs to number eleven ... "A cup o' tea an' a slice o' cake" - *Worzel Gummidge*, starring 59-year-old Jon Pertwee and with 41-year-old Una Stubbs as Aunt Sally, is on ITV ... BBC One TV programs on a Saturday night include:

The Pink Panther Show; *News* - read by Peter Woods; *Jim'll Fix It* - presented by Jimmy Savile OBE; *Dr. Who* - starring Tom Baker; *Saturday Night at the Movies*; *The Two Ronnies* - with 49-year-old Ronnie Barker and 48-year-old Ronnie Corbett; *Starsky and Hutch* - starring Paul Michael Glaser and David Soul; and *Match of the Day* - introduced by 50-year-old Jimmy Hill ... ***Oliver's Army*** ("... is here to stay. Oliver's Army are on their way. And I would rather be anywhere else but here today") by 24-year-old Elvis Costello and the Attractions is number two in the pop chart ... "This is..." ***The Sound Of The Suburbs*** by The Members is number twelve ... Punk poet, 30-year-old John Cooper Clarke, performs to crowds of 'new-wave' kids at rock venues all around the country ... Striking workers at British Leyland's Longbridge factory vote to return to work - just as a new strike begins at Leyland's Rover plant in Solihull ... A London based pop group called Gentry changes its name to Spandau Ballet - at the suggestion of 19-year-old journalist Robert Elms ... Trendy young things in garish costumes gather once a week at *Billy's* nightclub in Soho ... *Boots* sell out of Max Factor make-up ... Moulinex curling tongs cost £3.29 at *Argos* ... A Braun *SDE850* hairstyling set with a 850-watt, 2-speed hair-dryer is £18.99.

Spring 1979

When the feeling's gone and you can't go on

There's more heavy snow ... 63-year-old MP Airey Neave is killed by a car bomb at Westminster - the Irish National Liberation Army claims responsibility ... The country remains in crisis ... 66-year-old prime-minister Jim Callaghan is under severe pressure ... "At first I was afraid, I was petrified. Kept thinking I could never live without you by my side" - ***I Will Survive*** by 29-year-old Gloria Gaynor spends four weeks at number one in the pop chart ... "I'm having so much fun. My lucky number's one. Ah! Ooh! Ah! Ooh!" - ***Lucky Number*** by 29-year-old Lene Lovich reaches number three ... 11-year-old schoolboy Paul Merson from Harlesden plays football with his friends in the park ... 21-year-old midfielder Graham Rix and 22-year-old striker Frank Stapleton score the goals as Arsenal beat Bristol City 2-0 in League Division One at Highbury ... "Wow! Wow! Wow! Wow! Unbelievable" - ***Wow*** by 20-year-old Kate Bush is number fourteen on the weekly hit parade ... TV viewers are gripped by exciting storylines in soap-operas: In *Coronation Street* - Deidre Langton fears her young daughter is trapped beneath rubble after a lorry crashes into 'The Rovers Return' pub. Thankfully, 2-year-old Tracy is unhurt ... In *Crossroads* - Jill Harvey has a scatterbrained idea and

Adam Chance tries to talk her out of it ... In *Emmerdale Farm* - Joe Sugden deals with the death of a ewe ... ***In The Navy*** ("... yes you can sail the seven seas") by The Village People is number two in the pop chart ... ***Can You Feel The Force?*** by The Real Thing is number five ... The football season is drawing to a close ... 26-year-old Ossie Ardiles scores twice as Keith Burkinshaw's Tottenham Hotspur beat Tommy Docherty's Derby County 2-0 at White Hart Lane ... 23-year-old Aston Villa striker Andy Gray returns after a four month injury lay-off and scores in a 3-0 victory over Ian Greaves' Bolton Wanderers at Villa Park ... 17 million people stay in to watch *Top of the Pops* on Thursday evenings ... 7-inch pop singles have risen in price - they now cost 85p ... "The Sweeney's doin' ninety 'cause they've got the word to go. They get a gang of villains in a shed up at Heathrow" - ***Cool For Cats*** by Squeeze is number two in the pop chart ... ***Something Else / Friggin' In The Riggin'*** by The Sex Pistols moves down to number eleven after peaking at number three ... ***Pop Muzik*** by M is a new entry at number twenty-eight ... 31-year-old actor Richard Beckinsale dies of a heart attack at his home in Sunningdale ... 'A Tennis Love Match' - 24-year-old tennis player John Lloyd marries 24-year-old tennis player Chris Evert in Florida ... Back in England - public sector workers continue to strike ... Skilled workers at British Leyland factories threaten to 'down-tools' unless a pay demand of £90 a week is met ... Jim Callaghan's Labour government loses a motion of confidence in the House of Commons and a general election is called ... The

Conservatives are triumphant and 53-year-old Margaret Thatcher becomes prime-minister. (Conservatives: 339 seats, Labour: 269 seats, Liberals: 11 seats). Britain's first ever female prime-minister enters 10 Downing Street saying, "Where there is despair, may we bring hope" ... ***Tragedy*** by The Bee Gees slides down the pop chart after peaking at number one ... "Try some, buy some, fe-fi-fo-fum. Talk about..." ***Pop Muzik*** by M moves up to number two ... 52-year-old Geoffrey Howe is the new Chancellor of the Exchequer ... 60-year-old Willie Whitelaw is Home Secretary and 59-year-old Lord (Peter) Carrington is Foreign Secretary ... 36-year-old John Major is the new MP for Huntingdonshire ... 'You'll Believe A Man Can Fly' - 26-year-old Christopher Reeve is *Superman* at cinemas ... 44-year-old (over-worked) writer David Nobbs collapses in Manchester and spends a few days in hospital ... "How can the light that burned so brightly, suddenly burn so pale..." ***Bright Eyes*** by Art Garfunkle climbs to number one in the pop chart - and stays there for six weeks! ... ***Some Girls*** ("... will. Some girls won't. Some girls need a lot of lovin', and-a, some girls don't") by Racey reaches number two ... 28-year-old Barry Sheene rides his Suzuki to victory in the opening Grand Prix of the 500cc motorcycle racing season ... 22-year-old footballer Garry Birtles scores twice, and 23-year-old Tony Woodcock scores once, as Brian Clough's high-flying Nottingham Forest achieve a 3-2 victory over Lawrie McMenemy's Southampton in the League Cup final at Wembley ... "Choo-choo train, truckin' down the track" - ***One Way Ticket*** by Eruption reaches number five in the pop chart ... ***Hooray Hooray It's A Holi-Holiday*** by Boney M is number three ... Fifteen million TV viewers watch teams compete in a new series of BBC One's ever popular outdoor show, *It's a Knockout*. 49-year-old Stuart Hall is presenter of the program. 64-year-old Arthur Ellis is referee - ensuring fair use of 'the joker' ... 31-year-old Bob Carolgees, and his puppet 'Spit the Dog', are new on ITV's children's show *Tiswas* ... The word 'bagsy' is new in the dictionary ... 'Soft, Juicy, Delicious. Big Bubbles, No Troubles' - *Hubba Bubba* bubble gum goes on sale ... The evil Yorkshire Ripper strikes again - a 19-year-old female is murdered in Halifax ... A fire in a crowded *Woolworths* store in the centre of Manchester claims the lives of ten people ... 46-year-old Frank Bough presents *Grandstand* on BBC One on Saturday afternoons ... 46-year-old Dickie Davies presents *World Of Sport* on ITV ... 18-year-old footballer Gary Lineker scores the winning goal for Second Division Leicester City in a match against Notts County ... 17-year-old Ian Rush makes his debut for Third Division Chester City in a match against Sheffield Wednesday ... 18-year-old Mark Falco scores on his debut for First Division Tottenham Hotspur in a 1-3 win against Bolton Wanderers ... 29-year-old Malcolm 'Supermac' MacDonald returns from a long term injury and scores for Arsenal in a 1-1 draw against Chelsea at Stamford Bridge. (37-year-old goalkeeper Peter 'the cat' Bonetti makes his 600th and final appearance for Chelsea in the same match) ... ***Dance Away*** ("... the heartache") by Roxy Music is new at number two in the pop chart ... "Dance! ..." ***Boogie***

Wonderland by Earth Wind and Fire is number eight ... 28-year-old Kenny Dalglish, 24-year-old Alan Kennedy and 27-year-old Terry McDermott score the goals as Bob Paisley's Liverpool beat Aston Villa 3-0 (in front of 50,570 spectators at Anfield) to become the new champions of Division One - with two games of the season still remaining. Liverpool players - Ray Clemence, Phil Neal, Phil Thompson, Alan Hansen, Emlyn Hughes, Alan Kennedy, Ray Kennedy, Terry McDermott, Steve Heighway, David Johnson, Kenny Dalglish, Jimmy Case and 25-year-old Graeme Souness have all been in fine form ... Cloughie's Forest are runners-up ... Big Ron Atkinson's West Bromwich Albion (with Tony Godden, Brendan Batson, Derek Statham, John Wile, Ally Robertson, Len Cantello, Ally Brown, Tony 'bomber' Brown, Cyrille Regis, Laurie Cunningham and 22-year-old Bryan Robson) are third ... ***Boys Keep Swinging*** by 32-year-old David Bowie climbs to number seven in the pop chart ... "Breaking rocks in the hot sun. I fought the law, and the law won" - ***The Cost Of Living E.P*** (with tracks: *I Fought The Law, Groovy Times, Gates Of The West* and *Capital Radio*) by The Clash is number twenty-two ... 51,482 spectators turn out at Selhurst Park to see 36-year-old Terry Venables' Crystal Palace team record a 2-0 victory over 58-year-old Harry Potts' Burnley 2-0 and become champions of Division Two ... 34-year-old Graham Taylor leads Watford to runners-up position in Division Three - and Elton John's football club gains promotion to Division Two ... Great excitement builds for the FA Cup final between Terry Neill's Arsenal and Dave

Sexton's Manchester Utd on Saturday the twelfth of May. With just five minutes of the game remaining, Arsenal are 2-0 in front, with goals from Brian Talbot and Frank Stapleton. Gordon McQueen and Sammy McIlroy then grab two quick goals to bring Utd level, before the match turns on its head again, when 25-year-old Alan Sunderland scores a dramatic (last minute) winner for Arsenal. The thrilling cup final ends in a 3-2 victory for 'The Gunners'. A ticket for the standing enclosure at the Empire Stadium in Wembley costs £2.50 ... "It's like thunder, lightning. The way you love me is frightening. You better knock, knock..." ***Knock On Wood*** ("... baby") by 23-year-old Amii Stewart is number six in the pop chart ... "It's number one all over heaven" - ***The Number One Song In Heaven*** by Sparks is number fourteen ... *Danger UXB* is a popular new drama on ITV ... 50-year-old politician Jeremy Thorpe stands trial at the Old Bailey - accused of conspiring to commit murder ... 20-year-old Crystal Palace footballer Kenny Sansom (a left-back) makes his debut for Ron Greenwood's England team (Corrigan, Cherry, Sansom, Wilkins, Watson, Hughes, Keegan, Currie, Latchford, McDermott, Cunningham and substitutes Brooking and Coppell) in a 0-0 draw against Wales at Wembley ... 25-year-old striker Trevor Francis scores a diving header as Brian Clough's high-flying Nottingham Forest defeat Malmo 1-0 to win the European Cup. 29-year-old captain John McGovern lifts the silver trophy in front of Forest's jubilant fans at the Olympic Stadium in Munich - Forest are champions of Europe! ... 32-year-old DJ Simon

Bates presents the *Top 40* chart rundown on Radio One on Sunday evenings ... "I know a girl from a lonely street. Cold as ice cream but still as sweet. Dry your eyes..." ***Sunday Girl*** by Blondie (featuring 33-year-old Debbie Harry) is number one ... ***Reunited*** ("... and it feels so good") by Peaches and Herb is number four ... 31-year-old snooker player Terry Griffiths wins the *Embassy* World Championship - beating 29-year-old Dennis Taylor in the final at the Crucible in Sheffield ... 32-year-old Elton John performs a pop concert in the USSR - becoming the first Western popstar to play behind the iron curtain ... Back in England - property prices continue to rise at a rapid rate. The average cost of a house now stands at £19,000 ... 17-year-old Joanne Latham (36-23-36) from Wolverhampton appears topless on page three of *The Sun* ... "You're so hot, teasing me, so you're blue but I can't take a chance on a chick like you, that's something I couldn't do" - ***Does Your Mother Know*** by Abba is number four in the pop chart ... "When I saw her there, she was a real disgrace. I thought..." ***Nice Legs Shame About Her Face*** by The Monks is number nineteen ... 'Beep! Beep!' - *Space Invaders* arcade game is exciting and new ... Progressive middle-class families enjoy the convenience of small, hatch-back motorcars ... 'Ah, bravo Figaro. Bravo, bravissimo. Sono il factotum. Della citt-ah. Della citt-ah. Della citt-ah. DELLA CITT-AH! La la la la la la la la la! - The ultra-modern Fiat *Strada* is 'Handbuilt by Robots' ... British Leyland introduces a new *Maxi 1750 HLS* with twin carburettor and walnut dash.

Summer 1979

There's a knock at the door, and just for a second
I thought I remembered you

The summer is mostly dull with thundery showers ... 11-year-old Chris Boardman from Hoylake in Merseyside plays out with his friends ... Schoolboys do 'no-handed' on Raleigh *Europa* racer bicycles ... 10-year-old Peter Lovell and 9-year-old Darren Rock race around 'the block' on their bikes at Ford Way in Armitage ... 37-year-old Gordon Burns presents a new series of *The Krypton Factor* on ITV ... *Seaside Special* is on BBC One on Saturday evenings - Ken Dodd, Cilla Black and Rod Hull with Emu take turns presenting the show ... Skinny kids in drainpipe jeans listen to portable radio/cassette machines in bus-shelters, while smoking Player's *No. 6* cigarettes ... "Roxanne, you don't have to put on the red light. Those days are over. You don't have to sell your body to the night" - ***Roxanne*** by The Police (with 27-year-old lead singer, Sting) is number twelve in the pop chart ... "Little mummy's boy, he wasn't very old. Though he was very small, he did what he was told" - ***Jimmy Jimmy*** by The Undertones (with 20-year-old lead singer, Feargal Sharkey) is number sixteen ... 48-year-old Michael Edwardes is knighted in the Queen's Birthday Honours list ... 52-year-old union leader Derek Robinson (aka Red Robbo) addresses a mass meeting of workers at Longbridge ... *The Comedy*

Store opens in Soho - a new venue for 'alternative' comedians, with 27-year-old anarchist Alexei Sayle introducing the acts ... Teenage boys sneak into their local picture house to see *Lemon Popsicle* (an 'X' rated film with some nudity) ... "You can..." ***Ring My Bell*** by 22-year-old Anita Ward moves to the top of the pop chart ... "Something happened along the way, and yesterday was all we has" - ***After The Love Has Gone*** by Earth Wind and Fire reaches number four ... 38-year-old DJ Ed 'stewpot' Stewart hosts the travelling Radio One Roadshow for five days in August. Stewpot's Roadshow week begins at Torre Abbey Meadows in Torquay and ends on The Island in St. Ives, Cornwall ... 36-year-old jockey Willie Carson rides *Troy* to victory in the Epsom Derby ... Prime-minister Mrs. Thatcher announces that gas and electricity prices will be increased next year ... Chancellor of the Exchequer Geoffrey Howe slashes the top rate of income tax from 83% to 60% and introduces 15% VAT ... MPs vote against the reintroduction of capital punishment ... 'The antidote to panel games' - 58-year-old Humphrey Lyttelton is chairman for a new series of *I'm Sorry I Haven't A Clue* on BBC Radio Four. 36-year-old Graeme Garden, 44-year-old Barry Cryer, 41-year-old Willie Rushton and 39-year-old Tim Brooke-Taylor are panelists on the popular comedy show ... "I never thought it would happen, with me and the girl from Clapham" - ***Up The Junction*** by Squeeze is number two in the pop chart ... ***Gertcha*** by Chas & Dave is number twenty ... 23-year-old tennis star Bjorn Borg defeats 27-year-old Roscoe Tanner 6-7, 6-1, 3-6, 6-3, 6-4 at Wimbledon in the men's singles final - to make it three consecutive championship victories in last three years ... 22-year-old Martina Navratilova beats 24-year-old Chris Evert-Lloyd 6-4, 6-4 in the women's final. It's Navratilova's second Wimbledon singles' title ... Cricketers Mike Brearley and Geoffrey Boycott stride out together to open the batting for England against India at Edgbaston. 37-year-old Brearley makes 24 runs. 38-year-old Boycott hits 155. 22-year-old David Gower (batting at number five) scores 200 not out and England win by 83 runs ... 23-year-old 'all-rounder' Ian Botham takes 5 wickets for 35 runs in the second Test at Lord's ... England's cricketers progress to the final of the (one-day, sixty-over) Prudential Cup tournament, but lose to the West Indies after a dramatic batting collapse ... *CHiPs* is on ITV on Saturday evenings with Erik Estrada as Ponch - a Californian motorcycle highway patrol cop ... *Police Woman* is on ITV on Saturday nights with Angie Dickinson (38-23-36) as Pepper - an under-cover police officer in L.A ... 28-year-old DJ Peter Powell presents the lunchtime show on weekdays on Radio One ... 29-year-old Kid Jenson presents the teatime show ... ***We Are Family*** ("... I got all my sisters with me") by Sister Sledge is number eight ... "Looking for some..." ***Hot Stuff*** ("... baby, this evening") by 30-year-old Donna Summer is number twelve ... 'Nude at Last' - 18-year-old Joanne Latham (36-23-36) from Wolverhampton bares all in *Penthouse* magazine ... "Rock on Tommy!" - 41-year-old Tommy Cannon and 35-year-old Bobby Ball are on TV ... 51-year-old Roger Moore stars as James Bond (aka 007) in

Moonraker at cinemas. 71-year-old Bernard Lee is M. 64-year-old Desmond Llewelyn is Q. 52-year-old Lois Maxwell is Miss Moneypenny ... 33-year-old Sylvester Stallone stars as Rocky Balboa in *Rocky II* ... A seventh series of *The Onedin Line* (with 47-year-old Peter Gilmore and 42-year-old Jill Gascoine) begins on BBC One on Sunday evenings ... *Ask The Family* with 51-year-old Robert Robinson is broadcast at teatime on Mondays ... *Petrocelli*, with 40-year-old Barry Newman, is broadcast on Friday nights ... "It's cold outside, and the paint's peeling off of my walls. There's a man outside, in a long coat, grey hat, smoking a cigarette" - ***Are 'Friends' Electric?*** by Tubeway Army climbs to number one in the pop chart - and stays there for four weeks ... "No, I've got no time to play your silly games..." ***Silly Games*** by Janet Kay is number two ... Movie star John Wayne dies aged 72 in California ... Back in England - prominent politician Jeremy Thorpe is cleared of attempted murder. As Thorpe leaves court, he tells reporters the verdict was, "totally fair, just and a complete vindication." ... The nation watches on television as 22-year-old athlete Sebastian Coe sets a new world record by running 800 metres in just 42.33 seconds at a meeting in Oslo. Twelve days later, Coe sets another world record - running the mile in just 3 minutes 48.95 seconds ... 31-year-old Camille Keaton stars in *I Spit On Your Grave* at 'special' cinemas ... 68-year-old Thora Hird stars in *In Loving Memory* on ITV ... "I can't, I can't, I can't stand losin'. I..." ***Can't Stand Losing You*** by The Police peaks at number two in the pop chart ... The double A-sided single ***Angel Eyes / Voulez-Vous*** by Abba reaches number three ... ***My Sharona*** by The Knack reaches number six ... 'V' reg cars go on sale ... The Ford *Cortina MkIV* now has wrap-around bumpers, redesigned indicator lights and a new front grill. The top-of-the-range 2.3 litre *Ghia* has a top speed of 108 mph and accelerates from 0-60 mph in 10.5 seconds ... Four star leaded petrol has risen to an all time high price of 98p a gallon ... People enjoy a day out at the seaside ... 'The Revolution' is a new ride at Blackpool Pleasure Beach ... A nudist beach opens in Brighton ... Rock band Led Zeppelin play in front of 200,000 people at Knebworth ... Crowds flock to watch summer motorcycling events ... At White City, 26-year-old Dave Jessup takes part in the finals of the International Speedway championship ... At Silverstone, 27-year-old Kenny Roberts (on a Yamaha) pips 28-year-old Barry Sheene (on a Suzuki) by the narrowest of margins to win the 500cc Grand Prix ... "Wanted, boy you're everything I ever..." ***Wanted*** by The Dooleys is number three in the pop chart ... "Horace Wimp, this is your life, go out and find yourself a wife" - ***The Diary Of Horace Wimp*** by Electric Light Orchestra is number eight ... There's a flurry of activity on football's transfer market ... 23-year-old Laurie Cunningham leaves West Bromwich Albion and joins Real Madrid for £995,000 ... 23-year-old Tony Woodcock leaves Nottingham Forest and joins Cologne for £600,000 ... 31-year-old Emlyn Hughes leaves Liverpool (after twelve years) and joins Wolverhampton Wanderers for £90,000 ... 29-year-old Malcolm 'Supermac' MacDonald of Arsenal is forced into early retirement after failing to recover from a knee injury ... The new season begins ... Terry McDermott scores twice as Bob Paisley's Liverpool beat Terry Neill's Arsenal 3-1 in the FA Charity Shield at Wembley ... 22-year-old Ray 'Butch' Wilkins makes his debut for Manchester Utd in a 1-1 draw against Lawrie McMenemy's Southampton in Division One ... "And daddy doesn't understand it, he always said she was good as gold. And he can see no reason, 'cause there are no reasons. What reason do you need to be shown? Tell me why..." ***I Don't Like Mondays*** by The Boomtown Rats spends four weeks at number one in the pop chart ... ***Hersham Boys*** ("... Hersham boys! Laced up boots and corduroys!") by Sham 69 enters the chart at number twenty-three, and climbs to number six two weeks later ... 37-year-old Fred West and his 25-year-old wife Rosemary murder 16-year-old Alison Chambers and bury her body beneath their house at 25 Cromwell Street in Gloucester ... 'We did it, say Provos' - the headline in *The Sun* newspaper tells the bloody story from Ireland: 79-year-old Earl Mountbatten of Burma (a cousin of Queen Elizabeth II, and great grandson to Queen Victoria) and three other people are killed by an IRA bomb at County Sligo. A few hours later - eighteen British soldiers are killed when booby-trap bombs explode at Warrenpoint in Northern Ireland ... Back in England - people settle down for a night in front of the telly ... 'We are sorry that programmes have been interrupted. There is an industrial dispute. Transmissions will start again as soon as possible' - ITV technicians go on strike for eleven weeks -

and soap-opera fans are deprived of *Crossroads*, *Emmerdale Farm* and *Coronation Street* ... 22-year-old athlete Sebastian Coe sets a third world record of the summer - running 1,500 metres in 3 minutes 32.1 seconds ... 33-year-old glamour model Mary Millington commits suicide at her home in Surrey ... "It's so funny, how..." ***We Don't Talk Anymore*** by 38-year-old Cliff Richard climbs to number one in the pop chart - and stays there for four weeks ... "Why must you record my phone calls? Are you planning a bootleg LP?" - ***Gangsters*** by The Special AKA is number six ... "Life is timeless, days are long when..." ***When You're Young*** by The Jam is new in at number twenty-five ... Trendy kids buy black *Harrington* jackets. Really trendy kids buy red *Harrington* jackets ... The art of 'consumer marketing' is conveyed by smart young businessmen wearing open-neck shirts and *Farah* trousers ... Adverts for chocolate bars pose the question, 'Would you risk it for a *Swisskit*?' ... Adverts for lager beer pose the question, 'Wouldn't you rather be *Hemeling*?' ... Adverts for instant coffee claim that, '*Mellow Birds* will make you smile'.

Autumn 1979

I'll send an S.O.S. to the world

"Bankety-blank. Blankety-blank. Blankety Blank!" - 41-year-old Terry Wogan hosts a new series of *Blankety Blank* on BBC One ... 32-year-old Simon Bates presents Radio One's *Top 40* show for the final time before handing over to 36-year-old Tony Blackburn ... ***We Don't Talk Anymore*** by Cliff Richard remains at number one ... ***Bang Bang*** ("... the mighty fall") by 23-year-old B.A. Robertson is number two ... "Oh..." ***Angel Eyes*** by Roxy Music is number four ... 53-year-old Conservative prime-minster Margaret Thatcher and 52-year-old Chancellor of the Exchequer Geoffrey Howe are under pressure ... Inflation is running high - at over 11% ... The Minimum Lending Rate is raised to 17% ... Britain's economy has moved into recession ... NHS prescription charges are increased from 20p to 45p ... A loaf of bread goes up from 28p to 30p ... 'Don't Panic' - *The Hitch-Hiker's Guide to the Galaxy*, a novel by 27-year-old Douglas Adams, is published ... 'It'll never take off' - 35-year-old Michael Rodd presents a feature on a new-fangled concept called the 'mobile telephone' on BBC's science program *Tomorrow's World* ... ITV is back on air after three months of industrial action by technicians ... "I could be so good for you. Love you like you want me to" - a brand new program called *Minder* begins on Monday nights at 9.00 p.m. - starring 31-year-old Dennis Waterman as Terry, and 54-year-old George Cole as Arthur ... Series three of *The Professionals* is on Saturday nights at 9.00 p.m. - with Bodie in a Ford *Capri 3.0S*, Doyle in a Ford *Escort RS2000* and Cowley in a Ford *Granada 2.8 Ghia* ... Vauxhall replaces the ageing *Viva* motorcar with the all new, front-wheel drive *Astra.* The 1200cc model has a top speed of 88 mph and prices start from just £3,404 ... "Here in my car I feel safest of all. I can lock all my doors, it's the only way to live in..." ***Cars*** by 21-year-old Gary Numan spends a week at number one in the pop chart ... ***Don't Bring Me Down*** ("... Grooss!!") by Electric Light Orchestra is number three ... "Rolling the ball. Rolling the ball. Rolling the ball. Rolling the ball to me" - The ***On Stage E.P.*** (which includes the tracks *Them Heavy People* and *James And The Cold Gun*) by 21-year-old Kate Bush is number ten ... 53-year-old prime-minister Mrs. Thatcher opens the Central Milton Keynes Shopping Centre - where there are more than 130 shops including *John Lewis*, *C&A*, *Boots*, *Woolworths*, *Our Price*, *British Home Stores* and *Waitrose* ... "Just a castaway, on an island lost at sea-oh. Another lonely day, with no one here but me-oh" - ***Message In A Bottle*** by The Police climbs to number one - and stays there for three weeks ... "When, I met you in the restaurant, you could tell I was no debutante. You asked me what's my pleasure, 'a movie or a measure?' I'll have a cup of tea, and tell you of my..." ***Dreaming*** by Blondie (featuring 34-year-old Debbie Harry) is number two ... 49-year-old business leader Sir

Michael Edwardes proposes a major restructuring of British Leyland - which involves factory closures and thousands of job losses. 52-year-old union leader Derek Robinson (aka Red Robbo) is sacked ... 'In space no one can hear you scream' - *Alien* (a terrifying new film) is now showing at the pictures - starring 29-year-old Sigourney Weaver and 39-year-old John Hurt ... *Not The Nine O'Clock News* (a new topical comedy program) debuts on television - with 24-year-old Rowan Atkinson, 26-year-old Mel Smith, 29-year-old Pamela Stephenson and 30-year-old Chris Langham ... A mod revival is underway, with youngsters wearing fishtail parka coats and loafer shoes ... "I got ya number, written on the..." ***Back Of My Hand*** by The Jags climbs to number seventeen in the pop chart ... "This is the time, the..." ***Time For Action*** by Secret Affair is number thirteen ... Millions listen in to Radio One's *Top 40* show on Sunday evenings ... "Oh-a-ho, you were the first one. Oh-a-ho, you were the last one..." ***Video Killed The Radio Star*** by Buggles is new at number one ... "We're only..." ***Making Plans For Nigel*** ("... We only want what's best for him") by XTC is number seventeen ... At lunchtimes, schoolboys come rushing out of double Maths to play Humbug on the playground ... 12-year-old Michael Bayliss from Burntwood dislocates a finger ... 23-year-old footballer Andy Gray has a fall-out with his manager, Ron Saunders, at Aston Villa, and transfers to John Barnwell's Wolverhampton Wanderers for a new record fee of £1.47 million. (Gray scores his first goal for Wolves in a 2-3 away win against Everton) ... 25-year-old Trevor Francis and

23-year-old Tony Woodcock each score twice as Ron Greenwood's England team (Shilton, Neal, Mills, Thompson, Watson, Wilkins, Keegan, Coppell, T Francis, Brooking, Woodcock and substitute McDermott) defeats Northern Ireland 1-5 in Belfast ... "This thing called love, I just can't handle it. This thing called love, I must get round to it. I ain't ready..." ***Crazy Little Thing Called Love*** by Queen peaks at number two in the pop chart ... ***Gimme Gimme Gimme (A Man After Midnight)*** ("... won't somebody help me chase the shadows away?") by Abba is number three ... 50-year-old Leonard Parkin presents ITN's *News at 5.45* ... A female student is murdered in Bradford and it's feared she's the twelfth victim of the evil Yorkshire Ripper ... 15-year-old schoolboy Martin Allen goes missing as he's travelling on the underground in London ... *Shoestring* is an exciting new TV drama on BBC One - starring 28-year-old Trevor Eve as private detective Eddie Shoestring ... *Cloppa Castle* is popular with children ... "Who's the daddy?" - 22-year-old Ray Winstone stars in *Scum* at cinemas ... *Pot Noodle* is launched - it's the latest concept in 'quick and easy' hot food ... "Hey you! Don't watch that! Watch this! This is the heavy, heavy monster sound..." ***One Step Beyond*** by Madness (with 18-year-old lead singer, Suggs) is number seven in the pop chart ... "I bought my baby, a red radio. He played it all, a go-go, a go-go" - ***On My Radio*** by The Selecter (with 26-year-old singer Pauline Black) is number eight ... "Rudy..." ***A Message To You Rudy*** by The Specials (with 20-year-old singer Terry Hall and 24-year-old keyboard player Jerry Dammers) is number ten ... Kids gather together at *Tiffany's* club in Coventry to enjoy a night of Ska and 2-Tone music. Rude Boys wear tight-fitting 'tunic' suits, shirts with cutaway collars and narrow ties. Rude Girls wear black and white checkered dresses ... Northern Soul enthusiasts head for the *Wigan Casino* and attend 'all-nighters' - spinning and dropping to the sounds of Jimmy Radcliffe, Edwin Starr and Dean Parrish. Trendy young men wear black *Solatio* basket-weave shoes with metal segs in the soles ... Heavy-metal rockers douse themselves in patchouli oil (aka hippy juice) and head for the *Bandwagon* in North-West London ... ***Bomber*** by Motorhead enters the hit-parade at number sixty-seven ... ***Since You've Been Gone*** ("I'm outta my head, can't take it") by Rainbow is number six ... ***Whatever You Want*** by Status Quo is number four ... Flashy London teenagers swirl and flounce on the dancefloor at *The Blitz* nightclub in Covent Garden - 20-year-old Steve Strange decides who will (and who won't) be admitted to hear the 'futuristic' electronic music played inside ... "Please, keep them away. Don't let them touch me" - ***Complex*** by Gary Numan enters the pop chart at number fifteen ... The Human League's debut LP, *Reproduction*, is number thirty-four in the album chart ... The weather turns cold ... People stay in, watching television ... ITV programmes on a Saturday night include: *Magpie* - presented by 26-year-old Tommy Boyd, 33-year-old Mick Robertson and 32-year-old Jenny Hanley; *Mr. and Mrs.* - hosted by 51-year-old Derek Batey; *The Muppet Show*; *3-2-1* - featuring Ted Rogers and Dusty Bin; *The Comedians* - with Lee Wilson, Mick Miller, Stan Boardman and 39-year-old Roy Walker; *Hawaii Five-O* - starring 58-year-old Jack Lord as Steve McGarrett; and *News at Ten* - read by 51-year-old Alastair Burnet ... A scandal is reported at Buckingham Palace - 72-year-old Anthony Blunt (Queen Elizabeth II's former art advisor) is exposed as a Soviet spy ... ***One Day At A Time*** ("... sweet Jesus, that's all I'm asking from you") by 39-year-old Lena Martell climbs to number one on the hit parade - and stays there for three weeks ... "Every day that I'm without you hurts, just, a little bit more than I've ever been hurt before" - ***Every Day Hurts*** by Sad Café is number three ... Poorly children stay home from school ... 'Sore throat need soothing?' - Gargling with *TCP Antiseptic* relieves irritation'.

Christmas 1979

Hey! Teachers! Leave them kids alone!

The weather is wet and windy ... Schoolboys go out in rain-proof kagools ... 11-year-old schoolboy Matt Le Tissier from Saint Peter Port in Guernsey plays out with his friends ... Footballers Mick Channon and Phil Boyer are on the score-sheet as Lawrie McMenemy's Southampton defeat Alan Durban's Stoke City 3-1 at The Dell ... 24-year-old Andy Gray scores twice as John Barnwell's Wolverhampton Wanderers beat Bolton Wanderers 3-1 at the Molineux ... Grown-ups stay indoors watching television ... 46-year-old Barry Norman presents the late night film review program, *Film 79*, on BBC One ... *Meteor* (a disaster movie, starring 41-year-old Natalie Wood, 49-year-old Sean Connery and 67-year-old Karl Malden) is now showing at cinemas ... Gail Potter (played by 28-year-old Helen Worth) marries Brian Tilsley (played by 22-year-old Christopher Quinten) in ITV's ever popular soap-opera *Coronation Street* ... ***When You're In Love With A Beautiful Woman*** ("... it's hard") by Dr. Hook spends three weeks at number one in the pop chart ... ***Nights In White Satin*** ("... never reaching the end. Letters I've written, never meaning to send") by The Moody Blues is number nine ... 55-year-old Kenneth Kendall reads the news on BBC One ... Inflation rises to 13.4% ... A loaf of bread goes up from 30p to 32p ... Road tax is set to rise from £50 a year to £60 ... Prime-minister Mrs. Thatcher demands a multi-million pound rebate from the European Union ... The Conservative government introduces a new Housing Bill giving council house tenants the right to buy their homes ... A Welsh nationalist group called Meibion Glyndwr sets fire to English-owned cottages in Wales ... 24-year-old Tim Martin opens *Martin's Free House* in Muswell Hill - the first *JD Wetherspoon's* pub ... "I didn't get where I am today by being nice" - 58-year-old John Barron is C. J. and 53-year-old Leonard Rossiter is Reginald Perrin in the third series of *The Fall and Rise of Reginald Perrin* (a TV comedy based on a novel by 44-year-old David Nobbs from Orpington) ... "It's behind you!" - Middle-class families enjoy an evening at the Pantomime ... 36-year-old singer Cilla Black appears in *Aladdin* at the Wimbledon Theatre ... 26-year-old comedian Jim 'Nick Nick' Davidson stars alongside The Krankies in *Babes in the Wood* at the Bristol Hippodrome ... "I hope my leg don't break..." ***Walking On The Moon*** by The Police is new at number one in the pop chart - glossy posters of band members: Sting, Andy and Stewart, adorn the bedroom walls of trendy teenagers ... "Live your life off the wall. Live it..." ***Off The Wall*** by 21-year-old Michael Jackson is number seven ... "He's a spacer, a star chaser" - ***Spacer*** by Sheila B Devotion is number eighteen ... Hallmark Records release *The Best of Top of the Pops '79* - a budget priced cover-version pop compilation LP with blonde Carolyn Evans in a see-through body stocking on the sleeve ... 23-year-old record breaking athlete Sebastian Coe is BBC's 'Sports Personality of the Year' ... "London calling to the underworld. Come out of the cupboard, you boys and girls" - ***London Calling*** by The Clash is number eleven in the singles chart ... "Ace, a journey on a train. Always been the same. Lookin' out windows" - *Word Salad* by Fischer Z is number sixty-six in the album chart ... 18-year-old Boy George is the new cloakroom attendant at *The Blitz* nightclub in Covent Garden ... "He's not the Messiah, he's a very naughty boy!" - *The Life of Brian* (a film from Monty Python) is now showing at cinemas ... BBC One TV programs on a Saturday night include: *The Basil Brush Show* - with Billy Boyle and Basil Brush; *Dr. Who* - with 45-year-old Tom Baker as the Doctor, 28-year-old Laila Ward as his assistant Romana and K9 as the dog shaped robot K9; *Larry Grayson's Generation Game* - starring 56-year-old Larry Grayson and 27-year-old Isla St Clair; *Secret Army* - featuring Clifford Road as Kessler and Angela Richards as Monique; *Shirley Bassey* - with the popular 42-year-old singer from Cardiff; *Dallas* - with Larry Hagman as JR and Linda Gray as Sue Ellen; *News* - read by 49-year-old Peter Woods; *Match of the Day* - introduced by 51-year-old Jimmy Hill; and *Parkinson* - a chat-show hosted by 44-year-old Michael Parkinson ... *The Times* newspaper is back on sale after almost a year away ... 22-year-old footballer Glenn Hoddle scores on his debut for Ron Greenwood's England in a 2-0 victory over Bulgaria. (32-year-old defender Dave Watson is also on the score-sheet). England's full line-up for the match is: Shilton, Neal, Mills,

Thompson, Watson, Wilkins, Keegan, Coppell, T Francis, Brooking, Woodcock and substitute McDermott ... "Sup up your beer and collect your fags. There's a row going on down near Slough" - ***Eton Rifles*** by The Jam is number three in the pop chart ... "Rudy!..." ***A Message To You Rudy*** by The Specials is number ten ... Young mods sew beer towels onto their fishtail parka coats ... 'A Way of Life' - 21-year-old Phil Daniels and 19-year-old Leslie Ash star in *Quadrophenia* at cinemas ... 23-year-old Bo Derek (36-24-34) stars in the movie *"10"* - alongside 44-year-old Dudley Moore ... Bob Paisley's Liverpool and Dave Sexton's Manchester Utd are neck and neck at the top of Division One. The two teams meet at Anfield on Boxing Day where 24-year-old Alan Hansen and 29-year-old David Johnson score the goals in a 2-0 victory for Liverpool ... Terry Neill's Arsenal beat Keith Burkinshaw's Tottenham Hotspur 1-0 on the same day with a goal from Alan Sunderland ... Bill McGarry's Newcastle Utd beat Tommy 'The Doc' Docherty's Queens Park Rangers 4-2 in Division Two, with goals from Tommy Cassidy, Alan Shoulder and Peter Withe (2) ... 37-year-old Mike Brearley leads England's cricketers on a three-match tour against Greg Chappell's Australians down-under. 24-year-old all-rounder Ian Botham takes 11 wickets, and 39-year-old batsman Geoff Boycott scores 99 not out in the opening Test Match at Perth, but England lose by 138 runs ... Back in Britain - 34-year-old Dennis Nilsen strangles 23-year-old Kenneth Ockenden at Melrose Avenue in Cricklewood and hides his body beneath the floorboards ... An estimated 25 million viewers watch *Larry Grayson's Generation Game* on Christmas night on BBC One. Larry's Christmas conveyor belt contains a tumbler dryer, a food hamper, an oven/toaster/grill, a 'cuddly' Rudolph the Red Nosed Reindeer, an automatic tea maker, three bottles of Champagne and a bucket, TV game, Christmas cake and a box of chocolates, a slow cooker, silver plated goblets and a tray, food mixer, 'cuddly' type-writer, a hair dryer and a stand, bottle of port/stilton cheese and biscuits, sherry decanter and six glasses, two baby Orvilles, electric car racing set and a silver plated candelabra ... "Oh, I wish I'd looked after me teeth" - 32-year-old Pam Ayres' *Christmas Special* is on ITV ... "We don't need no education. We don't need no thought control. No dark sarcasm in the classroom, teachers leave those kids alone" - ***Another Brick In The Wall (Part 2)*** by Pink Floyd is number one at Christmas ... ***Living On An Island*** ("... looking at another line. Waiting for my friend to come and we'll get high") by Status Quo is number sixteen ... 'The Total Control Slotless Racing System' - schoolboys make a wish at Christmas for a *TCR* racing set - with cars that really overtake ... The ultra-modern electronic game *Simon* (from MB Electronics) costs £21.95 ... The *Big Trak* remote control vehicle (also from MB Electronics) is £39.95 ... An Atari video computer system (with two 'joy-stick' remote controllers) is £155.00 ... On Christmas Day, housewives cook turkey, boil sprouts and take a drink in the kitchen ... Adverts say, '*Harvey's Bristol Cream* - the best sherry in the world' ... 35-year-old Michael Fish presents the weather on BBC One

... Temperatures plummet ... Heavy frost and thick fog covers the country ... "The moon is right. The spirit's up. We're here tonight and that's enough. Simply having a..." ***Wonderful Christmas Time*** by 38-year-old Paul McCartney is number six in the pop chart ... "I believe in angels, something good in everything I see" - ***I Have A Dream*** by Abba peaks at number two ... "Now, what you hear is not a test, I'm rappin' to the beat" - ***Rapper's Delight*** by The Sugar Hill Gang reaches number three ... "We wish you a merry Christmas and a happy New Year" - ***A Merry Jingle*** by The Greedies is number twenty-eight ... *Smash Hits* magazine costs 30p and is available fortnightly ... Prime-minister Mrs. Thatcher travels to Washington for talks with 55-year-old US president Jimmy Carter ... 122 million tonnes of coal have been mined in Britain this year - roughly the same amount for each of the past five years ... The average price of a house has almost doubled in three years - it now stands at £22,000 ... The average weekly wage is £110.70 ... Families all across the country enjoy *Vesta* curry with rice for tea. Some indulge in Birds Eye *Arctic Roll* for pudding ... People enjoy a night out at their local pub on New Year's Eve, and raise a glass to toast in the 1980s ... A pint of *Carling Black Label* in the Red Lion costs 64p.

Printed in Great Britain
by Amazon

76654666R00196